Deb Christian Religious Epistemology

C000161579

ALSO AVAILABLE FROM BLOOMSBURY

A Radical Pluralist Philosophy of Religion, by Mikel Burley
Beyond the Control of God?, edited by Paul M. Gould
Explaining Evil, edited by W. Paul Franks
Human Dignity in the Judaeo-Christian Tradition, edited by John Loughlin
Intellectual, Humanist and Religious Commitment, by Peter Forrest
Progressive Atheism, by J. L. Schellenberg
Religious Language, Meaning and Use, by Robert K. Bolger
and Robert C. Coburn

Debating Christian Religious Epistemology

An Introduction to Five Views on the Knowledge of God

Edited by
**John M. DePoe and
Tyler Dalton McNabb**

BLOOMSBURY ACADEMIC
LONDON • NEW YORK • OXFORD • NEW DELHI • SYDNEY

BLOOMSBURY ACADEMIC
Bloomsbury Publishing Plc
50 Bedford Square, London, WC1B 3DP, UK
1385 Broadway, New York, NY 10018, USA

BLOOMSBURY, BLOOMSBURY ACADEMIC and the Diana logo are trademarks of
Bloomsbury Publishing Plc

First published in Great Britain 2020

Copyright © John M. DePoe, Tyler Dalton McNabb and Contributors, 2020

John M. DePoe and Tyler Dalton McNabb have asserted their right under the Copyright,
Designs and Patents Act, 1988, to be identified as Editors of this work.

Cover image: *The Mystic Marriage of Saint Catherine of Siena*, Giovanni di Paolo
© Artokoloro Quint Lox Limited / Alamy Stock Photo

All rights reserved. No part of this publication may be reproduced or
transmitted in any form or by any means, electronic or mechanical,
including photocopying, recording, or any information storage or retrieval
system, without prior permission in writing from the publishers.

Bloomsbury Publishing Plc does not have any control over, or responsibility for, any
third-party websites referred to or in this book. All internet addresses given in this
book were correct at the time of going to press. The author and publisher regret any
inconvenience caused if addresses have changed or sites have ceased to exist, but can
accept no responsibility for any such changes.

A catalogue record for this book is available from the British Library.

A catalog record for this book is available from the Library of Congress.

ISBN: HB: 978-1-3500-6274-0
PB: 978-1-3500-6273-3
ePDF: 978-1-3500-6272-6
eBook: 978-1-3500-6276-4

Typeset by Newgen KnowledgeWorks Pvt. Ltd., Chennai, India
Printed and bound in Great Britain

To find out more about our authors and books visit www.bloomsbury.com
and sign up for our newsletters.

This book is dedicated to our teachers who have instructed and inspired us to think maturely about religious epistemology, Timothy McGrew (for John) and Victoria Harrison (for Tyler). Additionally, we dedicate this book to our families who have patiently endured our absences while we have worked to bring it to fruition. Thank you for your love and support!

Contents

Preface

The genesis of this book can be traced to many stimulating debates that we (Tyler and John) have had in recent years as our paths crossed at academic conferences. Both of us passionately advocate for our distinctive approaches, especially lobbying our views before up-and-coming graduate students. In these exchanges, we discovered that much was misunderstood about our positions—commonly repeated inaccuracies about our positions or ignorance of answers given to standard objections. Furthermore, we both expressed frustrations in finding a suitable text for a course on religious epistemology. It seemed that virtually every available text was either too specialized or failed to represent multiple views (especially our own) in a fair or teachably accessible way. Moreover, through these exchanges we developed a strong friendship and admiration for one another. In a short time, it occurred to us to rectify this situation by producing our own volume that would serve the purposes that we perceived were currently absent.

Rather than attempting to write a standard introductory textbook coauthored by the two of us, we believe that a text authored by representatives from multiple views on religious epistemology gives readers a fairer representation of each view and creates a format that is more engaging for readers. In addition to ourselves, we rounded up the other contributors to help us bring this vision to life. The primary criteria in selecting these contributors were that each one represents an important approach to religious epistemology, has a history of talented and spirited philosophical writing, and is someone we respect as philosopher, especially in the realm of religious epistemology. We believe we have succeeded in meeting contributors who meet these guidelines.

However, we are aware that some readers may be concerned that our book fails to include some perspective or represent a particular tradition. All we wish to say to concerns of this sort is that no conscious effort was made to exclude any points of view, and it is inherent to making any selections that regrettably others must be excluded. This collection is not intended, for instance, to be a comprehensive survey of Christian religious epistemologies.

It is our hope to illuminate and inspire our readers to think more carefully and deeply about religious epistemology through this book. Indeed, we hope that this book will make its way into many classrooms at the undergraduate, seminary, and possibly even graduate level as a first or second pass at some of the core issues of religious epistemology. For those who want to go deeper than this introductory text, we invite them to check out the academic works from our contributors as well as the articles and books cited throughout these debates as natural next steps in their discovery of religious epistemology. In other words, this text has been designed to be only the first word on religious epistemology, not the last.

John M. DePoe and Tyler Dalton McNabb

Introduction to Religious Epistemology

John M. DePoe and Tyler Dalton McNabb

A religious epistemology is a set of standards used to evaluate the standing of a person's religious belief at a given time. While taking into consideration many of the traditional topics found in religious studies and the philosophy of religion (e.g., natural theology, the problem of evil, and the coherence of religious doctrine), religious epistemology itself typically stands independently of these topics as a measuring stick to determine the epistemic value of religious beliefs related to them. In other words, religious epistemology is the study of the standards and practices concerning beliefs pertaining to religion. We shall introduce religious epistemology by reviewing some relevant portions of epistemology and particular topics from the philosophy of religion that pertain to the debates that make up the principal focus of this book.

Topics from Epistemology

The work of the past century in epistemology has largely focused on issues like the concept of justification, the standards for knowledge, and the significance of evidence for the rationality of religious beliefs. More recently, there have been signs of burgeoning trends in virtue religious epistemology and developing analyses of social epistemological phenomena related to religious beliefs. In what follows, readers will be introduced to many of these epistemic concepts and some of their applications to religious belief.

Belief

Perhaps the first concept to discuss in epistemology is belief. Belief is a propositional attitude that asserts or affirms the truth of the belief's propositional content. What philosophers typically have in mind when they talk about the propositional content of a belief is what the belief means. Two token beliefs may be different (perhaps expressed in different words or languages), but they could express the same proposition and have the same meaning (such as "Snow is white" and "La nieve es blanca"). Often in classic works of philosophy, bare belief is referred to as opinion. Some recent work on the concept of belief has developed some important aspects to the nature of belief. For instance, much ink has been spilt explicating the differences between narrow content and wide content in intentional mental states. The narrow content view restricts the contents of belief to what's "inside the head,"[1] whereas advocates of the wide content view allow the contents of belief to extend beyond the boundaries of one's skull and into the broader environment.[2] When Socrates of classical Athens believed that he was drinking water, was the propositional content of that belief restricted to descriptions in his head (e.g., clear, odorless, refreshing liquid) or did it include the physical structure of the water in his environment (e.g., H_2O)? One recent development on belief worth highlighting is the distinction drawn between alief and belief.[3] Alief picks out a kind of mental state with associatively linked content that is representational, affective, and behavioral and that is activated by features of the subject's internal or ambient environment. Someone may believe that it is safe to skydive after responsibly studying the recreational hobby, but that same person may still refuse to participate in skydiving out of a visceral fear of death that occurs whenever they are faced with the reality of jumping out of an airplane in flight. The person's belief that skydiving is safe is contrasted with their alief that affects them with paralyzing fear.

The nature of belief itself is not hotly debated in this volume. However, many of these controversies about belief could prove to make a significant difference in one's religious epistemology. For instance, if one accepts a wide theory of meaning about belief, it is possible that two apparently different beliefs (when looked at narrowly) appear to be incompatible while they are in fact complementary or equivalent in meaning.[4] Perhaps the apparent differences within the doctrinal beliefs from one religious tradition viewed across time could be reconciled and unified by a wide content view of belief. Moving to the next aspect of belief, possibly the distinction between alief and belief could be employed to adjudicate questions about how people's affective and behavioral dispositions often contradict their stated religious beliefs. Rather than always thinking it must be a case of gross hypocrisy, perhaps there are situations that are better explained by drawing upon the concept of alief. In any case, there are many untapped possibilities for epistemologists to revisit what it means to be a religious believer (and nonbeliever) in light of these new avenues for understanding belief itself.

Justification

Justification is the characteristic that a person's belief is held appropriately. Sometimes the notion of epistemic justification is meant to indicate that a belief is likely to be true.[5] Typically, justification is a feature of beliefs that can come in degrees (being more or less justified). Also, it is standardly accepted that a person can be justified in believing a false proposition. While there is a commonsensical ring to the implied differences between having a justified belief and an unjustified belief, philosophers have expressed numerous accounts as to what constitutes these differences. Two camps emerged at the end of the twentieth century that still largely define the landscape of justification today, internalism and externalism.[6] Internalism is an umbrella term for theories of justification that maintain a belief is justified for a person at a time if and only if that person is aware of some significant feature (to be defined by a particular theory) that contributes to the belief's justification. Externalism, on the other hand, is a term for theories of justification that deny that a belief is justified for a person at a time if and only if the person is aware of some significant feature that contributes to the belief's justification. Externalists tend to emphasize that justification denotes that a belief has been produced in the right way (to be defined by a particular theory), such as being highly reliable.[7] These externalist standards can be met without the subject being aware that his belief meets whatever criterion is taken as the externalist standard. To put the matter simply, internalists claim justification consists of a person's being aware of good reasons for holding the belief, whereas externalists claim that justification consists in nothing more than the belief being produced in the right way. Some philosophers have attempted to bridge these different accounts of justification by insisting on pluralist views of justification whereby there are a variety of different means for a person to have justified beliefs.[8]

In the context of religious beliefs, different theories of epistemic justification present different standards for determining when religious beliefs are held appropriately or inappropriately. Often, internalists present high standards for a person's belief to be justified, while externalists generally uphold conditions that are easily attained. The different standards create juxtaposing benefits and criticisms for each view. Internalism might uphold the rigorous standards for judging when a person holds a belief appropriately, but these standards may be too high for people to attain them under normal circumstances. Externalism may employ standards that are easily attained, but it might be too liberal in conferring justification to beliefs. Traditionally, internalists have maintained that religious beliefs are justified when a person is aware of good reasons that support one's religious beliefs, such as a convincing proof from natural theology, a sound argument from the problem of evil, or a powerful religious experience. Externalists often cash out justification in terms of whether one's cognitive faculties are producing religious beliefs reliably or appropriately. Perhaps they might argue that God designed human cognitive systems to possess religious beliefs of a certain nature and therefore these beliefs (when produced by God's design plan) are justified, or others might argue that the human brain has been molded by evolutionary processes in such a way that it is utterly unreliable and unfit to deliver religious beliefs. Clearly, different theories of justification entail important differences in how to evaluate the appropriateness of holding particular religious beliefs.

Structure of Beliefs

Another important issue epistemologists debate relates to the proper way to structure a set of beliefs, or a person's noetic structure. The two most prominent views are called foundationalism and coherentism. Foundationalists distinguish between basic and nonbasic beliefs. Basic beliefs are those that are not based on argument or inference from other beliefs, which comprise the foundation of a person's noetic structure from which other beliefs can be based. Properly basic beliefs have the requirement that they must meet the appropriate standards for justification or knowledge without argument or inference from other beliefs. At least three different standards for properly basic beliefs are debated by contributors in this volume: incorrigibility (DePoe), seemings (Gage and McAllister), and produced in accordance with proper function (McNabb). Nonbasic beliefs are those beliefs that are inferred from other beliefs. While foundationalism has been the dominant view among epistemologists, the support for coherentism has remained steady (if not growing) in recent years. Coherentism describes a structure of justification or knowledge where beliefs provide mutual support for one another. Typically, coherentists stress that what they mean by coherence is something stronger than mere coherence, but coherence in this more robust sense is more akin to the beliefs offering meaningful explanatory relations to one another. Another way to look at the difference in these two approaches to the structure of justification or knowledge is that foundationalists believe that justification or knowledge justifies in a "one-way direction," whereas coherentists accept that justification or knowledge justifies in multiple "directions" simultaneously.

In religious epistemology, one intense debate that relates to the structure of justification or knowledge concerns the status of belief in God: Is it properly basic? Alvin Plantinga has famously argued that belief in God can be held in a properly basic way.[9] The traditional approach has maintained that appropriately affirming or denying belief in God should be inferred from other justified beliefs. Much of this debate has focused on the standards for properly basic beliefs and how to apply them to religious beliefs, like the existence of God.

Evidence

Evidence is often thought to be closely related to the concept of justification. The more evidence one has for a belief, typically the more justification one has for that belief. Epistemologists have put forward many different accounts of what constitutes evidence for a belief. Some think that evidence must be propositional,[10] others say that evidence can be nonpropositional.[11] For those who hold a propositional view of evidence, they insist that evidence must play a role in logical inference, which they argue can only occur if it is propositional. Advocates for the nonpropositional view of evidence may point out how sensory experiences or even physical objects are commonly recognized as evidence in everyday discourse.

One of the great debates in religious epistemology concerns whether it is a requirement for a person to have evidence in order for his religious beliefs to be justified. Evidentialism is the name given to the position that a religious belief needs evidence in order to count as justified or knowledge. One of its contraries, fideism, is the view that it is inappropriate for religious beliefs to be held on the basis of evidence. Proper religious belief, on the fideist view, is antithetical to evidence as it may depreciate the nature of faith. Other views, such as reformed epistemology, believe that evidence could shore up the justificatory status of religious beliefs, while not requiring that all religious beliefs need evidence. In short, virtually all perspectives on religious epistemology will take a stand on what counts as evidence for religious beliefs and whether evidence is required for religious beliefs to meet the canons of justification and knowledge.

Related to the controversies of the role of evidence in religious epistemology is deciding where the burden of proof lies in religious epistemology. Some approaches advocate that nonbelief is the proper starting point for religious belief,[12] which entails that there must be sufficient evidence in order to sway a person to accept religious belief in an epistemically appropriate way. Others maintain that religious belief is the epistemically appropriate starting point, and therefore the onus rests on nonbelievers to present sufficient evidence to justify nonbelief.[13] Those that place the onus on religious belief may point out that the burden of proof often rests on those who positively assert a belief in a debate or that religious belief appears to be more complex than nonbelief. A prominent reason some religious believers give for placing the burden of proof on nonbelief include that the risks of falsely believing in God are not nearly as significant as falsely believing that there is no God. At the heart of this debate are important claims about the nature of evidence and its proper role in the place of religious epistemology.

Defeaters

Epistemologists commonly employ the concept of defeasibility to refer to the susceptibility of a belief to lose its status as justified or knowledge. Defeaters, then, are those conditions that demote a person's belief that once enjoyed the status of justification or knowledge. Much work has been published in the attempt to define, classify, and list exhaustively defeaters.[14] Two of the most commonly discussed defeaters are undercutting defeaters and rebutting defeaters. Undercutting defeaters describe conditions that take away the justification for a belief without providing any reason to believe the negation of the belief. For instance, suppose a person under normal circumstances sees a blue widget and forms the belief that there is a blue widget before him. Then, someone points out that there is a blue light overhead the widget. Consequently, the person will no longer be justified in believing that the widget is blue, but this situation does not justify that the widget is not blue. A rebutting defeater, by contrast, is a condition whereby a belief's justification or knowledge is revoked due to acquiring good reason for another belief that is incompatible with it. An example of this could occur when someone is justified in believing that a second person is 29 years old on the basis of the second person's generally reliable testimony. However, the first person discovers the birth certificate of the second person, which shows she is really 32 years old. In this case, the first person acquires a rebutting defeater for the initially justified belief that the second person is 29 years old because he has good reason to believe the second person is actually 32 years old.

In religious epistemology, putative defeaters are regularly debated. For instance, an atheist may attempt to point out an undercutting defeater for someone's belief in God based on religious experience by pointing out that the same experience can be replicated naturally by psychologists using a "Persinger helmet."[15] Or perhaps one's confidence in the principle of sufficient reason touted in the cosmological argument can be defeated in light of discovering that virtual particles fluctuate in and out of existence without any apparent cause or reason.

Someone could respond to a defeater by marshaling a defeater for the defeater. These are referred to as defeater-defeaters.[16] It may turn out that the defeater itself is liable to losing its credibility, which in turn can relinquish the demotion in epistemic status that the defeater originally imposed on the otherwise justified belief. For instance, in response to the "Persinger helmet" defeater for religious belief based on religious experience, someone could point out that having a natural cause for an artificially concocted religious experience does not imply that genuine religious experiences lack a supernatural basis.[17] Indeed, posing a natural explanation for religious belief does not seem to eliminate God's agency in the process, but only pushes it back one step (perhaps God brought about the religious experience through the natural causes).[18] A defender of the cosmological argument might issue a defeater-defeater to the defeater for the principle of sufficient reason based on virtual particles by coming to believe that virtual particles do not literally pop in and out of existence without any cause or reason but that these particles' behavior takes place in a fluctuating vacuum of energy, which may explain their existence and behavior.[19] If successful, these defeater-defeaters reinstate the initial justification these beliefs possessed before they were impugned by their defeaters. To deal with some issues that are commonly raised regarding the standards of knowledge, many epistemologists have added to their other conditions for knowledge that there are no undefeated defeaters for the belief in question.

Knowledge

Knowledge is standardly held to be the highest epistemic good. The standards for possessing knowledge, however, have been a matter of great controversy throughout recorded philosophy. Virtually everyone accepts that knowledge is necessarily factive, that is, that a necessary condition for knowledge is true belief. Of course, knowledge is usually thought to be something more than mere true belief, but what more is needed? For many, the additional requirement is certainty.[20] While the criterion of certainty captures many commonplace insights about knowledge, it also clearly entails a vast amount of skepticism since the overwhelming majority of our beliefs (religious or otherwise) lack the absolute certainty demanded by this standard.[21] Often thought to be a more attainable standard, Plato introduced the idea that knowledge consists of justified true belief.[22] The justified true belief account of knowledge has garnered a significant following throughout the history of philosophy and is often called the standard view of knowledge. While not demanding absolute certainty, the justified true belief account of knowledge (or tripartite theory of knowledge) requires that true beliefs possess a sufficient degree of justification in order to count as knowledge. It is widely believed, however, that Edmund Gettier's paper "Is Justified True Belief Knowledge?" signaled the demise of the tripartite theory of knowledge.[23] Gettier famously demonstrates how it is possible for a belief that is clearly not an instance of knowledge to meet the standards of the justified true belief theory of knowledge, thereby debunking the theory by way of counterexample.[24]

In many ways the Gettier problem also served as an impetus for the development of externalist theories of justification since some had initially thought the examples produced by Gettier were a product of deficient account of justification. (As it turned out, these alternative accounts of justification failed to yield theories of justification that were "Gettier-proof."[25]) Others thought the traditional analysis of knowledge could be amended by adding that no defeaters exist for the belief.[26] To avoid these and other related problems with the traditional analysis of knowledge, some have even suggested that knowledge is a primary mental state incapable of being analyzed into component parts.[27]

Another influential approach to the concept of knowledge is called contextualism.[28] Contextualism is the view that the standards for knowledge vary depending on the context. When there is a low-stakes context (such as when a friend asks if the bank is open Monday at 5:30 p.m.), the standards for knowledge can be easily attained. But once the context includes higher stakes (such as when a friend asks if the bank is open Monday at 5:30 p.m. so he can make a payment or else he will lose his house), the standards for knowledge are raised. Those who oppose contextualism are called invariantists because they argue that the standards for knowledge do not vary according to the circumstances in which the belief is asserted.

While there is much more that can be said about current state of the debate over the concept of knowledge, it is sufficient to note here that there are many differing views. With these different standards of knowledge come different results as to what one can know about religion, and it is often fruitful to examine these standards as champions and critics of religious beliefs declare what can and cannot be known about religion.

Topics from Philosophy of Religion

Having reviewed some epistemic concepts related to religious epistemology, next we shall review some important topics from philosophy of religion that intersect with religious epistemology. A religious epistemology typically offers a framework for thinking about these topics, although some approaches to religious epistemology may necessitate taking a side on one or more of these topics.

Natural Theology

Roughly put, natural theology is the study of God, apart from revelation. More specifically, the idea of natural theology is that we can come to know that God exists and what He is like without making use of divine revelation. Historically, arguments from fine-tuning, cosmology, morality, and miracles have been put forth in order to show that God exists. The contributors of this volume all have different views on the role these arguments should play in one's overall epistemology.

For example, as a classical evidentialist, DePoe sees the success of these arguments as vital to the justification status of a religious belief. However, on the opposite side of the spectrum, Scott Oliphint is theologically opposed to the project of natural theology. Dalton McNabb, Baldwin, and Gage and McAllister have various views in between. Closer to DePoe's view, Gage and McAllister argue that it isn't necessary for a subject to utilize natural theology in order for her belief to be justified; however, when a subject encounters a potential defeater, she will likely need to utilize resources from natural theology in order to prevent epistemic defeat. And closer to Oliphint's view, while McNabb isn't theologically or philosophically opposed to natural theology, he doesn't think that natural theology needs to play a role in one's doxastic process, even when reflecting on potential defeaters. For important contributions to the literature on natural theology, we recommend that our readers see William Lane Craig and J. P. Moreland's *The Blackwell Companion to Natural Theology*[29] and Richard Swinburne's *The Existence of God*.[30]

Divine Hiddenness

In addition to touching on the role of natural theology, we have asked each contributor to discuss how their epistemology would handle a potential defeater. Specifically, we asked each contributor to engage the problem of divine hiddenness and the problem of epistemic peer disagreement.

The problem of divine hiddenness can be summarized in the following question: Why isn't the existence of God more obvious? If God is all-loving, all-powerful, and all-present, then wouldn't God want to (1) make His existence more obvious, and (2) wouldn't He possess the power to do so? Perhaps God would come down from heaven on clouds and let everyone know that He is there, or perhaps He would write in the sky that He is watching. God would make it such that there wouldn't be any nonresistant nonbelievers. All who would believe if they just had sufficiently good evidence would indeed believe. But, so the objection goes, there are nonresistant nonbelievers, so God doesn't exist. Again, you can find the contributors responding to this objection in various ways. However, interestingly enough, several of the contributors seem to come to the same conclusion that God's existence actually is obvious and there isn't such thing as reasonable nonbelief. One clear exception to this can be found in Baldwin's essay where Baldwin argues that while there is reasonable nonbelief for those in a nonbelieving tradition of inquiry, the existence of reasonable nonbelief needn't threaten theists with respect to the rationality of their belief. For a primer on the problem of divine hiddenness, our readers should see J. L. Schellenberg's *The Hiddenness Argument*.[31]

Epistemic Peer Disagreement

What should a subject do if she believes that p, but her friend, who she judges to be just as smart and knowledgeable as she is, believes $\neg p$? Is she rational to continue to believe that *p* with the same level of credence that she does now? Or should she give equal weight to her epistemic peer and significantly decrease her credence in her belief that *p*, perhaps to the point of suspending her belief altogether? Those who think that there are at least some cases where a subject can continue to believe with the same degree of credence are known as steadfast advocates, as a subject can remain steadfast in her belief despite peer disagreement. Those who think that a subject, when confronted with genuine epistemic peer disagreement, should decrease her credence and/or perhaps suspend belief altogether advocate for what is known as a conciliatory view. For a good introduction on epistemic peer disagreement, we encourage our readers to see David Christensen and Jennifer Lacky's *The Epistemology of Disagreement*.[32] Having surveyed various issues related to both epistemology and the philosophy of religion, we now move to summarize the various epistemologies that will be put forward and defended.

Religious Epistemologies and a Battle Royale

First up is DePoe's Classical Evidentialism. In his chapter, DePoe argues that in order for *S*'s belief that *p* to be considered properly basic, *S*'s belief that *p* needs to be incorrigible. All other beliefs require arguments in order for the beliefs to be properly situated in a subject's noetic structure. In attempting to make his view plausible, DePoe argues that any good epistemology needs to capture how beliefs have the right sort of connection to truth, and how a subject is internally rational. DePoe argues that Classical Evidentialism best explains how these requirements can be met. DePoe then goes on to flesh out the religious implications of his epistemic theory.

Our second chapter is written by Gage and McAllister. Gage and McAllister endorse what is known as Phenomenal Conservatism. Roughly, the idea is that *S*'s belief that *p* is justified if *S* has a seeming that *p*, and *S* lacks a defeater for her belief that *p*. In this volume, Gage and McAllister argue that Phenomenal Conservatism avoids the problem of skepticism that plagues Classical Evidentialism and it avoids certain counterexamples to externalist accounts. Gage and McAllister argue that while theistic belief can be justified by strong seemings, ultimately, in order to deflect potential defeaters, a theist will need to make use of resources from natural theology.

In our third chapter, McNabb advances the thesis of Proper Functionalism. Roughly the thesis of Proper Functionalism is that a belief is warranted if and only if the belief is produced from properly functioning faculties that are successfully aimed at truth. McNabb then uses Proper Functionalism to argue for the plausibility of reformed epistemology. In defending the thesis that religious belief can be held rationally apart from argument, McNabb discusses the possibility of the existence of a cognitive faculty that has a design plan that is aimed toward producing theistic belief. Following Plantinga, McNabb calls this faculty the *sensus divinitatis*. McNabb then defends the possibility of warranted theistic belief from this perspective.

Our fourth chapter is a defense of a Covenantal Epistemology by Oliphint. Covenantal Epistemology is a strictly Christian epistemology. It utilizes the creation, fall, redemption narrative to describe how theists are rational in their belief and why atheism is irrational. Oliphint defends his epistemology primarily by way of exegesis of Christian Scripture.

Finally, our last contributor Baldwin argues for Alasdair MacIntyre's tradition-based account of rationality by suggesting that (1) it is impossible to escape tradition, (2) liberalism is self-defeating, and (3) encyclopedia and genealogy epistemological views are flawed. Baldwin then argues that theistic belief is a rational belief insofar as the epistemic evaluation is made from within one's own theistic tradition. Having surveyed the various religious epistemologies in this volume, we now turn to DePoe's defense of Classical Evidentialism.

Notes

1. Two prominent accounts of the narrow content view include Jerry A. Fodor, *Psychosemantics: The Problem of Meaning in the Philosophy of Mind* (Cambridge, MA: MIT Press, 1987), and Richard A. Fumerton, "What and about What Is Internalism?," in *Internalism and Externalism in Semantics and Epistemology*, ed. Sanford C. Goldberg (Oxford: Oxford University Press, 2007), 35–50.
2. Two influential papers on the wide content view include Hilary Putnam, "The Meaning of 'Meaning,'" in *Philosophical Papers: Mind, Language and Reality* (Cambridge: Cambridge University Press, 1975), 215–71, and Tyler Burge, "Individualism and the Mental," *Midwest Studies in Philosophy* 4, no. 1 (1979): 73–121.
3. Tamar Szabó Gendler, "Alief and Belief," *The Journal of Philosophy* 105, no. 10 (2008): 634–63.
4. For some early works in this vein, see Richard B. Miller, "The Reference of 'God,'" *Faith and Philosophy* 3, no. 1 (1986): 3–15, and William P. Alston,

"Referring to God," *International Journal for Philosophy of Religion* 24, no. 3 (1988): 113–28.

5. See Stewart Cohen, "Justification and Truth," *Philosophical Studies* 46, no. 3 (1984): 279–95.

6. One influential demarcation of this position is Richard A. Fumerton, "The Internalism/Externalism Controversy," *Philosophical Perspectives* 2 (1988): 443–59.

7. Such as Alvin I. Goldman, "What Is Justified Belief?," in *Justification and Knowledge*, ed. G. S. Pappas (Dordrecht: D. Reidel, 1979), 1–23.

8. For example, Ernest Sosa, *A Virtue Epistemology: Apt Belief and Reflective Knowledge* (Oxford: Oxford University Press, 2009).

9. Alvin Plantinga, *Warranted Christian Belief* (Oxford: Oxford University Press, 2000).

10. Such as Donald Davidson, "A Coherence Theory of Truth and Knowledge," in *Truth and Interpretation: Perspectives on the Philosophy of Donald Davidson* (Malden, MA: Blackwell, 1986), 423–38, and Timothy Williamson, *Knowledge and Its Limits* (Oxford: Oxford University Press, 2000).

11. Robert Audi, "Contemporary Modest Foundationalism," in *The Theory of Knowledge: Classical and Contemporary Readings*, ed. Louis Pojman, 3rd ed. (Belmont, CA: Wadsworth, 2003), 174–82, and James Pryor, "The Skeptic and the Dogmatist," *Noûs* 34, no. 4 (2000): 517–49.

12. Antony Flew, "The Presumption of Atheism," *Canadian Journal of Philosophy* 2, no. 1 (1972): 29–46.

13. William Wainwright, "The Burden of Proof and the Presumption of Theism," in *Does God Exist?: The Craig-Flew Debate*, ed. Stan W. Wallace (New York: Routledge, 2003), 75–84.

14. Two examples include John L. Pollock and Joseph Cruz, *Contemporary Theories of Knowledge*, 2nd ed. (Lanham, MD: Rowman & Littlefield, 1999), and Michael Bergmann, "Defeaters and Higher-Level Requirements," *The Philosophical Quarterly* 55, no. 220 (2005): 419–36.

15. Michael A. Persinger, "Religious and Mystical Experiences as Artifacts of Temporal Lobe Function: A General Hypothesis," *Perceptual and Motor Skills* 57, no. 3 (suppl.) (1983): 1255–62, and Michael A. Persinger, "Are Our Brains Structured to Avoid Refutations of Belief in God? An Experimental Study," *Religion* 39, no. 1 (2009): 34–42.

16. For more, see John L. Pollock, "Defeasible Reasoning," *Cognitive Science* 11, no. 4 (1987): 481–518.

17. John Hick, *The New Frontier of Religion and Science: Religious Experience, Neuroscience, and the Transcendent* (New York: Palgrave Macmillan, 2006), 79.

18. Richard Swinburne, *Is There a God?*, 2nd ed. (Oxford: Oxford University Press, 2010), 113–21.

19. William Lane Craig and James D. Sinclair, "The Kalam Cosmological Argument," in *The Blackwell Companion to Natural Theology*, ed. William Lane Craig and J. P. Moreland (Malden, MA: Blackwell, 2009), 182–3.

20. One adherent to this view is Panayot Butchvarov, *The Concept of Knowledge* (Evanston, IL: Northwest University Press, 1970).

21. One influential critique of the standard of certainty is John Locke, *An Essay Concerning Human Understanding*, ed. Kenneth Winkler, reprint ed. (Indianapolis, IN: Hackett, 1996), bk. IV, especially chapter 9.

22. Plato, *Theaetetus*, ed. Bernard Williams, trans. M. J. Levett (Indianapolis, IN: Hackett, 1992). Those who study Plato will stress that Plato does not appear to endorse this view of knowledge.

23. Edmund L. Gettier, "Is Justified True Belief Knowledge?," *Analysis* 23, no. 6 (1963): 121–3.

24. For a brief aid in understanding Gettier's arguments, see John M. DePoe, "Gettier's Argument against the Traditional Account of Knowledge," in *Just the Arguments: 100 of the Most Important Arguments in Western Philosophy*, ed. Michael Bruce and Steven Barbone (Malden, MA: Wiley-Blackwell, 2011), 156–8.

25. For an account and evaluation of many of these amendments for the standards of knowledge, see Robert Shope, *The Analysis of Knowledge: A Decade of Research* (Princeton, NJ: Princeton University Press, 1983).

26. Thomas Paxson and Keith Lehrer, "Knowledge: Undefeated Justified True Belief," *The Journal of Philosophy* 66, no. 8 (1969): 225–37.

27. Williamson, *Knowledge and Its Limits*.

28. For an influential account of contextualism, see Keith DeRose, "Contextualism and Knowledge Attributions," *Philosophy and Phenomenological Research* 52, no. 4 (1992): 913–29.

29. William Lane Craig and James Porter Moreland, eds., *The Blackwell Companion to Natural Theology* (Malden, MA: Blackwell, 2009).

30. Richard Swinburne, *The Existence of God*, 2nd ed. (Oxford: Oxford University Press, 2004).

31. J. L. Schellenberg, *The Hiddenness Argument: Philosophy's New Challenge to Belief in God* (Oxford: Oxford University Press, 2015).

32. David Christensen and Jennifer Lackey, *The Epistemology of Disagreement: New Essays* (Oxford: Oxford University Press, 2013).

1

Classical Evidentialism

John M. DePoe

Is it ever reasonable to hold religious beliefs without evidence? The purpose of this essay is to spell out a reasonable way to answer this question negatively. Because my position maintains that evidence is required for holding reasonable or justified beliefs, it is called "evidentialism." There are, of course, some very implausible accounts of religious epistemology that have been labeled "evidentialism" (that no reflective person has ever held), which are set up as straw men and refuted without any consideration for more reasonable versions of this position. For example, one popular philosophy of religion textbook actually describes evidentialists as endorsing that most people hold their religious beliefs in an irrational way, while affirming that only an elite few are capable of having justified beliefs about religion.[1] Needless to say, the evidentialist position is highly unpopular among philosophers today. (I sometimes wonder if evidentialism's disfavor in contemporary philosophy is due primarily to poor public relations.) Fortunately, truth is not determined by counting noses, and I intend to make a compelling case for evidentialism in what follows.

Since there are many variations on, not to mention misconceptions of, the evidentialist position, I will begin by defining my account of evidentialism. After this brief description, I will present the main reasons for accepting evidentialism. Then, some applications of this epistemology to topics in philosophy of religion will be explored. Finally, the essay will close by considering an objection to my position.

Defining Classical Evidentialism

Evidentialism, boiled down to its basics, is the position that affirms that beliefs require sufficient evidence in order to be justified. The "classical" descriptor to this view denotes that my version of evidentialism is wedded to a version of classical foundationalism. My exposition of the definition of Classical Evidentialism will revolve around unpacking these two notions.

So, what does it mean to hold that beliefs require sufficient evidence in order to be justified? Let's start with the concept of evidence.[2] Evidence consists of a person's awareness of good reasons or grounds that imply that the propositional content of the belief is true (or likely to be true).[3] It is important to notice that this technical definition of evidence is different from some colloquial and loose ways of talking about evidence. Sometimes people talk about evidence as though it is nothing more than a physical object. Unfortunately, this loose way of talking about evidence conceals a number of significant features of evidence. For instance, a prosecutor might argue in a courtroom that the defendant's fingerprints on the murder weapon are evidence of the defendant's guilt. But the physical object alone does not point to the defendant's guilt. After all, one needs to be aware that fingerprints are unique to each person, and that the probability of the defendant's innocence dramatically diminishes in light of his fingerprints' presence on the murder weapon. Additionally, the physical object alone can't justify the guilt of the defendant without somebody being aware of it. For these reasons, evidence requires that a subject is aware of it and that it indicates the truth of the proposition for which it is evidence.[4] In sum, this account of evidence entails that for a belief to be justified, a person must be aware of good reasons or grounds that support the truth of the belief.

Classical foundationalism is the second component of Classical Evidentialism.[5] Foundationalism is the position that a properly ordered noetic structure, or system of beliefs, consists of beliefs inferentially supporting other beliefs in a single direction (i.e., no circular justification), which ultimately are based on beliefs that are noninferentially justified. Or, to describe it starting from the "bottom," classical foundationalism's noetic structure "begins" with noninferentially justified beliefs that provide inferential support for other beliefs "above" them, which in turn may inferentially support other beliefs "higher" up.[6] Noninferentially justified beliefs are commonly called "basic beliefs," and when these beliefs are justified they are called "properly basic beliefs." Although it is unfashionable in the current philosophical climate,[7] historically classical foundationalism has been the favored approach to epistemology for thinkers as diverse as St. Augustine of Hippo, John Locke, Bertrand Russell, C. J. Lewis, and Roderick Chisholm.[8]

Since noninferentially justified beliefs provide the foundation for the whole system of beliefs to possess justification and knowledge, it is important that these basic beliefs are nonarbitrarily tethered to truth. For this reason, classical foundationalists depart from other varieties of foundationalism by maintaining that basic beliefs must be incorrigible. To say that a belief is incorrigible means that the subject stands in an uncorrectable position with respect to the truth of that belief. For instance, if someone is having an excruciating headache, nobody (not even a neuroscientist who has run a series of diagnostic tests on this person) is in a better epistemic position to correct this person and inform him that he is not experiencing a headache. Perhaps the simplest and most readily available form of incorrigible belief takes place when the subject is pointing to the qualities of his own experience in believing, "I am being appeared to *thusly*."[9] Incorrigible beliefs are impervious to falsehood, which guarantees a connection to truth at the most basic level of belief in classical foundationalism.

How should we think about justification on Classical Evidentialism? The key to understanding the classical foundationalist account of justification is to see how this account of justification maintains the subject's awareness of his evidence and how the connection to truth is guaranteed throughout inferential links in a properly arranged noetic structure. Both of these elements are secured through direct acquaintance. Direct acquaintance, according to Bertrand Russell, occurs when a person stands in a "direct cognitive relation to the object, i.e. when [the subject is] directly aware of the object itself."[10] Elsewhere, he writes, "we have *acquaintance* with anything of which we are directly aware, without the intermediary of any process of inference or any knowledge of truths."[11] Thus, I am directly acquainted with the auditory sensations of footsteps echoing from the hallway, whereas I am indirectly acquainted with the person's presence in the hallway (by way of inference from the sounds of his footsteps).

While direct acquaintance itself is not a kind of knowledge or justified belief, it can serve as the basis for knowledge or justified belief. Loosely following Richard Fumerton's analysis,[12] I take epistemic justification for any belief, *p*, to consist of a person having three direct acquaintances: (i) direct acquaintance with his grounds for believing that *p* is the case, (ii) direct acquaintance with the thought that *p* is the case, and (iii) direct acquaintance with the truth-bearing relationship that holds between a person's grounds for believing that *p* is the case and the person's thought that *p* is the case. The truth-bearing relationship in the third acquaintance can refer to a number of different relations such as correspondence or entailment among the strongest connections to truth, and making probable or being the best explanation to denote a belief's probabilistic connection to truth. Importantly, the person who has these three direct acquaintances is holding a belief that is a nonarbitrarily connected to truth, and he is aware of why his belief is true.

In sum, Classical Evidentialism is an account of religious epistemology that adopts evidentialism and classical foundationalism. Evidentialism affirms that beliefs are justified when they are adequately supported by evidence and evidence consists of a subject's awareness of good reasons that support a belief's truth. Foundationalism maintains that some beliefs are basic (justified noninferentially), and classical foundationalism holds that properly basic beliefs must be incorrigible. Direct acquaintance provides the means by which subjects can be aware of the nonarbitrary connection to truth that is necessary for a belief to be justified.

The Case for Classical Evidentialism

Having defined Classical Evidentialism, the next task is to provide reasons to believe it is the correct account of religious epistemology. Any plausible account of epistemic justification must satisfy two important desiderata, an objective requirement and a subjective requirement. My primary argument for Classical Evidentialism is that it best satisfies both of these conditions.

Objectively, epistemic justification requires a connection to truth.[13] This means that justification necessarily indicates that a belief enjoys some intrinsic and nonarbitrary link to truth. Believing that the butler's fingerprints are on the murder weapon (in conjunction with a set of background beliefs), for example, indicates the truth that the butler committed the murder *because* the butler's fingerprints are unlikely to be on the murder weapon if he is innocent and they are very likely to be on the weapon if he is guilty. Alternatively, thinking that the butler committed a crime on nothing more than the evidence one gleans in a response from a "magic eight ball" (a gag toy that reveals random answers to yes/no questions) is exceptionally dubious because the random answers of the magic eight ball are in no way connected to the truth of the matter. Clearly, one feature that distinguishes justified beliefs from unjustified beliefs is that they possess an objective connection to truth.

The subjective requirement for epistemic justification is that it must provide assurance of the belief's truth to those who possess it. Epistemology is performed from the first-person perspective, and any realistic approach to epistemology will describe epistemic justification from that perspective. Epistemologists who have traditionally attempted to provide an analysis of epistemic justification in terms that are manifest from the first-person perspective are called internalists, and those who believe that justification includes factors beyond the purview of first-person awareness are called externalists. I find externalist accounts of justification unsatisfying and practically useless because they describe epistemology from a perspective that in practice no one possesses. "Solving" epistemic questions outside of the first-person perspective presents "solutions" from a perspective alien to the actual practices of epistemology.[14] At best, they offer conditional or hypothetical "solutions" without any guidance as to how an individual can have assurance that he meets those conditions. Thus, the strongest objective connection to truth is worthless without providing the believer any subjective assurance or awareness of the belief's connection to truth.

Laurence BonJour has illustrated the importance of the subjective condition for epistemic justification with his well-known example of Norman, the clairvoyant:

> Norman, under certain conditions which usually obtain, is a completely reliable clairvoyant with respect to certain kinds of subject matter. He possesses no evidence or reasons of any kind for or against the general possibility of such a cognitive power or for or against the thesis that he possesses it. One day Norman comes to believe that the President is in New York City, though he has no evidence either for or against this belief. In fact, the belief is true and results from his clairvoyant power under circumstances in which it is completely reliable.[15]

Is Norman justified in believing that the president is in New York City? If the objective connection to truth is all that matters, then the answer should be "yes." However, we are reluctant to judge that Norman's belief is justified. The thought experiment elicits the insight that Norman's belief, despite its strong objective connection to truth, fails to include everything that appropriately belongs to a justified belief. According to BonJour, the point of his example is to highlight that epistemic justification should give the believing subject some perspective on the reasonableness of his belief.

"From [Norman's] perspective," writes BonJour, "it *is* an accident that the belief is true. And the suggestion here is that the rationality or justifiability of Norman's belief should be judged from Norman's own perspective rather than from one which is unavailable to him."[16] Thus, justification includes an element of subjective awareness or some sort of subjective assurance from the person's point of view that the belief is true.[17]

The primary features of epistemic justification are covered by the objective connection to truth and the subjective assurance requirement. In this light, a strong argument for Classical Evidentialism is that it provides the best way to satisfy both of these conditions for epistemic justification. Since Classical Evidentialism requires persons to be directly acquainted with their grounds for believing something to be the case as well as the truth-bearing relationship that holds between their belief and the grounds on which they hold it, Classical Evidentialism provides a natural mutual satisfaction of the objective and subjective requirements of epistemic justification.

Classical Evidentialism satisfies the objective connection to truth because properly basic beliefs must be true and any inferential connections from those beliefs must stand in objective truth-bearing relationships. Thus, every justified belief in the Classical Evidentialist's prescribed noetic structure has a nonarbitrary connection to truth. The subjective assurance condition is met by Classical Evidentialism because of its requirement that subjects must be directly acquainted with these features that objectively secure the truth of their beliefs. For instance, a person who is directly acquainted with his grounds for holding a belief and directly aware that his grounds logically entail the belief in question is in an excellent epistemic position to be aware of the justified status of his belief.

Other epistemic accounts have a difficult time adequately satisfying the objective and subjective components of epistemic justification simultaneously. On the one hand, externalist accounts fail to provide an account of epistemic justification that offers any nonarbitrary subjective assurance that any given belief is true. On the other hand, alternative internalist accounts of epistemic justification tend to disappoint in explicating how the first-person assurance they offer is related to an objective connection to truth.

In closing, alternatives to Classical Evidentialism must fall short in one of three ways: (1) deny that justification has an objective connection to truth; (2) deny that justification requires subjective assurance of truth; or (3) affirm weaker and *ad hoc* ways to meet these features of justification. Classical Evidentialism is truly unique in how well and how naturally it meets the objective and subjective requirements of epistemic justification.

Other accounts of religious epistemology fall short compared to Classical Evidentialism.

Classical Evidentialism and Natural Theology

After defining and defending Classical Evidentialism, next I shall spell out some of the applications of Classical Evidentialism to important issues in religious epistemology, beginning with its approach to natural theology. After that, I will briefly explain how my version of Classical Evidentialism addresses the problem of divine hiddenness and peer disagreement.

Natural theology, in contrast to revealed theology, describes the project of acquiring knowledge of the existence and attributes of God from nature. Excepting the possibility that persons could be directly acquainted with God,[18] Classical Evidentialism entails that belief in God cannot be properly basic.[19] Theism, therefore, in order to be justified needs supporting evidence. At this point, it is instructive to correct some potential misconceptions about evidentialism's use of natural theology.[20] First, it might be tempting to think that Classical Evidentialism maintains that a requirement for justified religious beliefs is that people know and defend the traditional theistic arguments, like some specific version of the ontological, cosmological, or teleological arguments. Setting aside whether there are any defensible accounts of these arguments,[21] the evidentialist is not saddled with this requirement. For one reason, the average person might hold justified religious beliefs on some simpler grounds, such as the testimony of respected members of one's religious community.[22] A second yet more important reason is that many people may possess sufficiently strong evidence that grounds their religious beliefs, yet they may not be able to express their grounds for holding their religious beliefs in ways that are conceptually scrupulous and luminous.[23] In my experience of probing common folk in Protestant Christian churches, they often express some reasons for believing in God like a crude version of one of the traditional arguments for theism. In many cases, it is clear that given more time and conceptual resources the nascent ideas held by the common folk could be expressed more fully in ways that are more logically rigorous. What matters for the standards of epistemic justification touted by Classical Evidentialism is that these folks possess good reasons for their religious beliefs; not necessarily that they can immediately and spontaneously express their reasons in carefully articulated ways.

A second misconception about the role of natural theology in Classical Evidentialism is that one argument must serve as the evidential basis for a person's religious belief. Many philosophers, including some devout theists, claim that, since no single argument for theism can establish its truth, it follows that no evidential argument for theism can be given. Even if it is granted that no individual argument succeeds in demonstrating the truth of theism, it does not follow that no evidential case for theism can be made. The possibility remains that the evidence from several arguments, each of which is insufficient to validate the truth of theism taken individually, jointly constitutes a strong evidential case for theism.[24] Furthermore, the way in which the accumulation of multiple independent arguments for a belief can rapidly raise its probability is often considerably underappreciated.[25] Moreover, multiple lines of argument may provide a fuller understanding of one's religious beliefs. For instance, the cosmological and teleological arguments may underwrite the notion that God is the omnipotent creator of all reality, the argument from morality that God is supremely good, and the argument from miracles that God is loving and gracious.[26]

A third misunderstanding about Classical Evidentialism and natural theology is that theistic arguments must achieve absolute certainty in order to justify religious beliefs or ground any religious knowledge. It is notoriously difficult to achieve absolute certainty about anything besides beliefs about one's immediate psychological states, basic mathematics, and propositions that are true by definition. My view, in line with many in the Classical Evidentialist tradition, holds that knowledge does not require absolute certainty. A justified true belief that is rendered much more probable than not on a person's evidence counts as knowledge.[27] This standard does not prejudice the "ground rules" of epistemology for or against any particular religious beliefs. The same standards of epistemic justification for theistic beliefs apply to atheistic (affirming that God does not exist) or agnostic (affirming that God's existence is unknowable) religious claims. In other words, no religious or antireligious belief gets a free lunch on the standards prescribed by Classical Evidentialism.

With these clarifications in mind, I don't see any reason to think that Classical Evidentialism is inherently inimical to religious believers.[28] Indeed, I believe that this epistemology is preferable precisely because it places an equal evidential onus on every religious position to determine which beliefs are justified, and the requirements it places on individuals are not unattainable for any reflective individual. Any other practice allows too much room for beliefs to count as justified without the subject having any real basis for thinking that his belief is true.

Classical Evidentialism and the Problem of Divine Hiddenness

One complaint often raised against Classical Evidentialism, especially by theistic philosophers, is that its epistemic standards are too high.[29] If justified religious beliefs require people to be directly acquainted with strong supporting evidence, then many people who hold religious beliefs are going to fail to meet this standard. It seems awfully narrow-minded of Classical Evidentialists to maintain that all of these people hold their religious beliefs without justification, according to these critics. Even worse, they might add that a loving God would not make it so difficult for people to acquire justification for believing that He exists.

Some unbelievers have concluded that the evidence for God's existence is at best ambiguous. Significant numbers of intelligent, well-informed people have reviewed the evidence for God and found it wanting. Surely a morally perfect God would not leave people without sufficient evidence of His existence. Some unbelievers argue that since reasonable unbelief occurs and God (who is necessarily morally perfect) would not allow reasonable unbelief to occur if He exists, then it follows that God does not exist. This argument against theism is commonly referred to as the problem of divine hiddenness.[30] While antievidentialist religious epistemologies might attempt to escape this problem by maintaining that evidence and epistemic justification are not intrinsically related, evidentialists must grapple with this problem differently.

The theistic Classical Evidentialist appears to be in the unpopular position of responding to the problem of divine hiddenness by stating that reasonable nonbelief does not occur.[31] Briefly stated, my evidentialist solution to the problem of divine hiddenness is to note that belief in God may be strongly evidenced, yet nonobvious. The argument's misstep occurs by assuming that since many people do not find belief in God to be obviously true, it must follow that the evidence for theism is no good. However, there are many beliefs that are strongly evidenced, yet not obviously true—such as that plate tectonics are responsible for seismic activities on earth, that the earth is spherical, and that the sun is large enough to fit over one million earth-sized planets in it. There are many reasons why intelligent and well-informed people may not be acquainted with the abundant evidence for theism. One reason is that they may have no interest in honestly examining whether theism is true.[32] Such negligence constitutes grounds for thinking that their failure to believe in theism is not entirely innocent. A second way there could be nonbelief with abundant available evidence for theism is that the nontheist may be aware of the evidence for theism while not appreciating its strength. As noted above, the cumulative force of many lines of evidence can powerfully confirm the truth of a given belief. It would not be surprising to discover that some people are aware of abundant evidence for theism, and yet they have not realized the accumulated case for theism is quite strong.

But why would a perfectly good God remain epistemically hidden and distant from those He created, especially if He loves them? This sort of divine hiddenness might be necessary for persons to be in a position to enter into a genuine loving relationship with their Creator. God, of course, could overwhelm His creatures with an obvious awareness of His transcendent existence, but to present Himself in this way would limit their ability to respond to Him freely. John Hick explains that creatures who are placed in a world where the existence of God is obvious and unambiguous

> will not be able to *choose* to worship God, or to turn to Him freely as valuing spirits responding to infinite Value. In order, then, to give them the freedom to come to Him, God creates them at … an epistemic distance. He causes them to come into existence in a situation in which He is not immediately and overwhelmingly evident to them…. In a phrase with which Bonhoeffer has made us familiar, the world is *etsi deus non dare tut,* as if there were no God. That is to say, it is systematically ambiguous, capable of being interpreted either theistically or naturalistically. In such a world the awareness of God takes the form of the cognitive choice which we call faith.[33]

This idea is eloquently expressed by Blaise Pascal in his typical aphoristic style: "There is enough light for those who desire only to see, and enough darkness for those of a contrary disposition."[34] On the assumption that God desires each person He creates to enter into a genuine loving relationship with Him freely, it may not be surprising to discover that He has created a world where the evidence of His existence is strong but not obvious.[35]

Classical Evidentialism and Peer Disagreement

Responding to the problem of peer disagreement has piqued the interest of epistemologists recently, and some readers might wonder how Classical Evidentialism can respond to this growing issue in social epistemology. In brief, the problem of peer disagreement is that for any given significant religious belief every person is probably aware of at least one epistemic peer (a person with approximately equal intellectual capacities) who possesses the same relevant evidence for that religious belief, yet who has drawn a contrary conclusion. In light of peer disagreement, it seems we should suspend judgment on these significant religious beliefs. Let's begin by illustrating the problem of peer disagreement with a nonreligious example.

> Suppose you and an epistemic peer are working out a lengthy addition problem entirely in your heads (no scratch paper!) involving three numbers each of which has seven digits. Before comparing answers, you might feel highly confident that you have summed the numbers correctly. However, upon checking with your peer, you discover that he has reached a sum slightly different than yours. In light of this disagreement, many people are inclined to believe that your justification for believing that you summed correctly is diminished, if not completely undermined.[36]

If peer disagreement is sufficient to undermine the mathematical sum given above, contend some advocates of peer disagreement, then it seems like a strong analogy for discounting religious beliefs as well.[37]

I am not convinced that peer disagreement is as easy to come by for religious beliefs as detractors think.[38] The evidence for believing in God will often involve multiple lines of evidence that may be drawn from unique life experiences and might depend on important presuppositions or background beliefs. Aligning all of these conditions seems much harder for religious beliefs than for the mundane examples often given to illustrate the principles that underlie the problem of peer disagreement.

Nonetheless, Classical Evidentialism offers some insights on responding to the problem of peer disagreement.[39] Consider a case where two epistemic peers have the same evidence, yet due to the differing ways they base their beliefs, the impact of disagreement on their justification will vary. Suppose that Cindy believes that the sum of the prime numbers between zero and ten is seventeen. Her friend and epistemic peer, James, believes that the sum of the prime numbers between zero and ten is fifteen. Let's say that Cindy bases her belief on a direct awareness of her understanding of prime numbers and performing the basic addition operations. When the question is posed to James and Cindy playing on the same team in a trivia game, the disagreement surfaces. Under these circumstances, James's disagreement is less likely to sway Cindy in this situation. After all, Cindy is directly aware of good reasons that objectively indicate that her belief is true. Moreover, she might also see why James's answer has run afoul. Suppose she realizes that James's sum is short by two, which she can explain because she is aware of a common mistake in thinking about the prime numbers; James forgot to include the number two as a prime number. This mistake is common because two is the only even number that is a prime number. While James and Cindy both possess the same evidence, in this case Cindy has based her belief on her direct awareness of her reasoning that indicates her belief is true. Moreover, she is in a position to understand why James's belief is mistaken. In this case, Cindy is unfazed by James's disagreement.

Cindy's case is instructive because while James and Cindy both have the same evidence, Cindy is in a position to see that her reasoning is sound, and she can explain how James came to the wrong belief. Richard Fumerton describes situations like this as cases where a person has reason to believe he has better engaged the same evidence.[40] The upshot for the problem of religious disagreement is this: basing one's belief on one's direct awareness of the evidence strengthens the appropriateness of a believer's epistemic steadfastness when confronted with peer disagreement.

The application of this response to the problem of peer disagreement specifically for religious beliefs can be made explicit by considering that a large number of people hold their religious beliefs primarily on the indirect basis that the religion has been commended to them by their parents, peer group, or culture. Even assuming that justifying religious beliefs in this way is completely appropriate, it is apparent that this sort of justification does not provide people with ideal subjective awareness of the truth of their belief. Such people are not in a position to "see" directly that their religious beliefs have an objectively strong connection to truth. Thus, people in this situation are much more vulnerable to losing their initially justified religious beliefs when confronted with peer disagreement since their religious beliefs are not secured tenaciously. Perhaps one important application for religious groups that wish to safeguard the justified beliefs of their members is to raise the awareness of good evidential arguments for their beliefs among their members, rather than teaching that the truth of a religious tradition is exclusively a matter of participating in the narratives of one's family, peers, or culture.

Faith and Evidence

One final objection to Classical Evidentialism that I wish to address is that religious faith by its nature is opposed to evidence. What I am requiring of religious beliefs, some might say, is like asking oil and water to mix. Knowledge acquired through evidential arguments, they claim, cannot be a matter of faith.

At the heart of this objection is an assumption about the nature of faith, namely that faith is an act of belief without evidence or even against evidence. I reject this view of faith. Faith is better understood (at least in part) as the dispositional characteristic to trust and persevere in one's religious beliefs. Faith is a virtue that allows believers to remain steadfast in their religious beliefs *because* they have good reason to do so. My view of faith aligns with that of C. S. Lewis who wrote,[41]

> When we exhort people to Faith as a virtue, to the settled intention of continuing to believe certain things, we are not exhorting them to fight against reason. The intention of continuing to believe is required because, though Reason is divine, human reasoners are not …. If we wish to be rational, not now and then, but constantly, we must pray for the gift of Faith, for the power to go on believing not in the teeth of reason but in the teeth of lust and terror and jealousy and boredom and indifference that which reason, authority or experience, or all three, have once delivered to us for the truth.[42]

The virtuous exercise of faith is necessary not because of the absence of evidence. Rather, faith is helpful as a check to the irrational influences that threaten to dislodge a religious believer's justified religious convictions.

By recognizing that faith's epistemic work is essentially about trust and perseverance, the objection that faith is contrary to evidence vanishes. Consider an analogous case: my faith in my wife's fidelity is in no way diminished because I have abundant evidence of her trustworthiness. To the contrary, it is because I have evidence of her fidelity that I have faith in her. Thus, if I should encounter some weak evidence of my wife's infidelity (e.g., baseless rumors), it is my evidentially grounded trust in her that empowers me to remain steadfast in appropriately believing in her faithfulness. Likewise, a religious believer appropriately exercises faith when he has good reason to trust a source of religious belief, especially when it is difficult to do so.

Conclusion

Classical Evidentialism is the approach to religious epistemology that allows evidence to determine what religious beliefs are justified or not. If the acquisition of knowledge, which is a specific type of justified true belief,[43] is the goal of epistemic practices, then the right approach to religious epistemology will include epistemic principles that align with this goal. I have argued that Classical Evidentialism is preferable for precisely this reason. The principles that underwrite this approach to religious epistemology prescribe epistemic practices that require a justified belief both to possess an objective connection to truth and to provide persons with subjective awareness of the belief's truth. Both requirements are essential to the goal of acquiring knowledge. Watering down these requirements for religious beliefs invites error and falsehood where the truth is of utmost importance.

Notes

1. Michael Peterson et al., *Reason and Religious Belief: An Introduction to the Philosophy of Religion*, 2nd ed. (Oxford: Oxford University Press, 1998), 147–8.
2. For a similar account of evidence, see Timothy J. McGrew, "Evidence," in *The Routledge Companion to Epistemology*, ed. Sven Bernecker and Duncan Pritchard (New York: Routledge, 2011), 58–67.
3. For the ease of my readers I will omit the parenthetical phrase "or likely to be true" throughout the rest of this essay. For those who are interested in these technicalities, keep in mind that when I speak of evidence implying that a belief is true, I always intend the qualifier "or likely to be true."
4. Note two distinct ways we can speak of evidence making another belief probable. The first way is by making the belief more probable than not. The second way is by raising the probability of a belief without necessarily making the belief more probable than not. In religious epistemology, this mirrors a distinction Richard Swinburne has made in relation to theistic arguments in terms of P-inductive arguments and C-inductive arguments. See Swinburne, *The Existence of God*, 6.

5. For a concise and accessible defense of classical foundationalism, see Timothy J. McGrew, "A Defense of Strong Foundationalism," in *The Theory of Knowledge: Classical and Contemporary Readings*, ed. Louis Pojman, 3rd ed. (Belmont, CA: Wadsworth, 2003), 194–206.

6. The reason for the quotes around "begins," "above," and "higher" is to stress the metaphorical nature of these relational descriptions between beliefs. The metaphors are intended only to elucidate the justificational relationship between beliefs. Some have misconstrued foundationalism by taking these relations in some other unintended senses (e.g., temporal).

7. The rumors of classical foundationalism's demise have been greatly exaggerated; among its supporters today include Paul K. Moser, *Empirical Justification* (Dordrecht: D. Reidel, 1985); Timothy J. McGrew, *The Foundations of Knowledge* (Lanham, MD: Littlefield Adams, 1995); Richard A. Fumerton, *Metaepistemology and Skepticism* (Lanham, MD: Rowman & Littlefield, 1995); Evan Fales, *A Defense of the Given* (Lanham, MD: Rowman & Littlefield, 1996); Michael R. DePaul, ed., *Resurrecting Old-Fashioned Foundationalism* (Lanham, MD: Rowman & Littlefield, 2001); Laurence BonJour, "A Version of Internalist Strong Foundationalism," in *Epistemic Justification: Internalism vs. Externalism, Foundations vs. Virtues*, ed. Ernest Sosa and Laurence BonJour (Malden, MA: Blackwell, 2003), 3–96; Earl Conee and Richard Feldman, *Evidentialism: Essays in Epistemology* (Oxford: Oxford University Press, 2004), see especially chapter 8; Timothy J. McGrew and Lydia McGrew, *Internalism and Epistemology: The Architecture of Reason* (New York: Routledge, 2007); Ali Hasan, "Classical Foundationalism and Bergmann's Dilemma for Internalism," *Journal of Philosophical Research* 36 (2011): 391–410; Ali Hasan, "Internalist Foundationalism and the Sellarsian Dilemma," *Res Philosophica* 90, no. 2 (2013): 171–84; Ali Hasan, "Phenomenal Conservatism, Classical Foundationalism, and Internalist Justification," *Philosophical Studies* 162, no. 2 (2013): 119–41.

8. See Augustine, *Against the Academicians and The Teacher*, trans. Peter King, reprint ed. (Indianapolis, IN: Hackett, 1995); Locke, *An Essay Concerning Human Understanding*; Bertrand Russell, *The Problems of Philosophy*, ed. John Perry, reprint ed. (Oxford: Oxford University Press, 1997); Clarence Irving Lewis, *Mind and the World-Order: Outline of a Theory of Knowledge*, reprint ed. (Mineola, NY: Dover, 1956); Roderick M. Chisholm, *The Foundations of Knowing* (Minneapolis: University of Minnesota Press, 1982).

9. See McGrew, *The Foundations of Knowledge*, 89–90.

10. Bertrand Russell, "Knowledge by Acquaintance and Knowledge by Description," *Proceedings of the Aristotelian Society* 11 (1910): 108.

11. Russell, *The Problems of Philosophy*, 46.

12. Fumerton, *Metaepistemology and Skepticism*, 73–9.

13. For more on epistemic justification's connection to truth requirement, see Moser, *Empirical Justification*, chap. 1; Conee and Feldman, *Evidentialism*, chap. 10; McGrew and McGrew, *Internalism and Epistemology*, chap. 2.

14. For a pointed argument in support of this claim, see BonJour, "A Version of Internalist Strong Foundationalism," 40.

15. Laurence BonJour, *The Structure of Empirical Knowledge* (Cambridge, MA: Harvard University Press, 1985), 41.

16. Ibid., 43–4. Emphasis in the original.

17. For a fuller account of the awareness requirement for epistemic justification, see John M. DePoe, "Bergmann's Dilemma and Internalism's Escape," *Acta Analytica* 27, no. 4 (2012): 409–23.

18. Actually for belief in God to be properly basic, Classical Evidentialism requires a person to be directly acquainted with God, directly acquainted with the belief that God exists, and directly acquainted with the evidential relationship between the belief and the direct awareness with God. Presumably these conditions could be satisfied with a sufficiently robust religious experience. However, I am personally doubtful that such experiences are common enough to merit the requisite philosophical defense in an essay like this one. Moreover, any person who has had such an experience would likely not be in any doubt of his belief's justification. Therefore, it is far more fitting for Classical Evidentialists to note this one possibility in a footnote and press on to the far more common nonbasic ways to justify belief in God.

19. While I refer to theism as not being properly basic, the same goes for atheism and agnosticism (understood as the belief that one cannot know whether God exists). All of these religious beliefs must be inferentially justified according to Classical Evidentialism.

20. For more on the uses of natural theology within an evidentialist framework, see John M. DePoe and Timothy J. McGrew, "Natural Theology and the Uses of Argument," *Philosophia Christi* 15, no. 2 (2013): 299–310.

21. Are there any good arguments for theism? For some recent examples of philosophically informed and rigorous arguments that answer this question affirmatively, see Swinburne, *The Existence of God*; William Lane Craig, *Reasonable Faith: Christian Truth and Apologetics*, 3rd ed. (Wheaton, IL: Crossway, 2008); and especially Craig and Moreland, *The Blackwell Companion to Natural Theology*.

22. Whether or not this sort of testimony should count as evidence is, of course, a matter of great controversy. My views do not depend on including this type of testimony as a source of evidence. I list it here merely as a possibility worth exploring. For what it's worth, Stephen Wykstra has defended something like this in a number of papers including

Stephen J. Wykstra, "Toward a Sensible Evidentialism: On the Notion of 'Needing Evidence,'" in *Philosophy of Religion: Selected Readings*, ed. William Wainwright and William L. Rowe, 2nd ed. (New York: Harcourt Brace Jovanovich, 1989), 426–37; Stephen J. Wykstra, "Not Done in a Corner: How to Be a Sensible Evidentialist about Jesus," *Philosophical Books* 43 (2002): 92–116.

23. I provide a more fleshed-out account of this idea in John M. DePoe, "What's (Not) Wrong with Evidentialism," *The Global Journal for Classical Theology* 13, no. 2 (September 2016), accessed August 1, 2017, http://www.globaljournalct.com/wp-content/uploads/2016/09/DePoe-Vol-13-No-2-Whats-Not-Wrong-with-Evidentialism.pdf.

24. Using a Bayesian model with some defined assumptions, this notion is lucidly applied to cumulative arguments in natural theology in Ted Poston, "The Argument from so Many Arguments," in *Two Dozen (or so) Arguments for God*, ed. Trent Dougherty and Jerry L. Walls (Oxford: Oxford University Press, 2018); see also Timothy J. McGrew, "Has Plantinga Refuted the Historical Argument?," *Philosophia Christi* 6, no. 1 (2004): 7–26.

25. In addition to the works cited in the previous footnote, see the following works for some general formal accounts of the impact of multiple lines of independent evidence: Branden Fitelson, "A Bayesian Account of Independent Evidence with Applications," *Philosophy of Science* 68, no. S3 (2001): S123–S140; Lydia McGrew, "Evidential Diversity and the Negation of H: A Probabilistic Account of the Value of Varied Evidence," *Ergo* 3, no. 10 (2016), http://hdl.handle.net/2027/spo.12405314.0003.010; accessed date December 24, 2018. Lydia McGrew, "Accounting for Dependence: Relative Consilience as a Correction Factor in Cumulative Case Arguments," *Australasian Journal of Philosophy* 95, no. 3 (2017): 560–72.

26. For more on the use of cumulative theistic arguments along these lines, see R. Douglas Geivett, "David Hume and a Cumulative Case Argument," in *In Defense of Natural Theology: A Post-Humean Assessment*, ed. Douglas Groothuis and James F. Sennett (Downers Grove, IL: InterVarsity, 2005), 297–329.

27. Veteran epistemologists will balk at the claim that knowledge is justified true belief because of the so-called "Gettier problem" where a justified true belief turns out to be accidentally true and clearly is not a case of knowledge. See the infamous Gettier, "Is Justified True Belief Knowledge?" Like many epistemologists from the past century, I think the Gettier problem is no problem as long as the inferential lines of justification that lead to knowledge do not include any false propositions. See the following sources that provide this type of solution (including one published 50 years before Gettier's paper): Russell, *The Problems of Philosophy*, chap. 13; Michael Clark, "Knowledge and Grounds: A Comment on Mr. Gettier's

Paper," *Analysis* 24, no. 2 (1963): 46–8; McGrew and McGrew, *Internalism and Epistemology*, chap. 1.

28. Nor do I think it is inherently inimical to nonbelievers. However, many who complain about the epistemic standards of Classical Evidentialism are often religious believers who think that evidentialism somehow places excessive and unreasonable encumbrances on religious beliefs.

29. Some prominent statements of this objection include Alvin Plantinga, "Reason and Belief in God," in *Faith and Rationality: Reason and Belief in God*, ed. Alvin Plantinga and Nicholas Wolterstorff (Notre Dame, IN: University of Notre Dame Press, 1983), 16–93; Kelly James Clark, *Return to Reason: A Critique of Enlightenment Evidentialism and a Defense of Reason and Belief in God* (Grand Rapids, MI: Eerdmans, 1990), 157–8; W. Jay Wood, *Epistemology: Becoming Intellectually Virtuous* (Downers Grove, IL: InterVarsity, 1998), 157.

30. The most influential contemporary account of the problem of divine hiddenness is John L. Schellenberg, *Divine Hiddenness and Human Reason*, reprint ed. (Ithaca, NY: Cornell University Press, 2006).

31. For a defense of this unpopular stance, see Douglas V. Henry, "Does Reasonable Nonbelief Exist?," *Faith and Philosophy* 18, no. 1 (2001): 75–92; Douglas V. Henry, "Reasonable Doubts about Reasonable Nonbelief," *Faith and Philosophy* 25, no. 3 (2008): 276–89.

32. Note that virtuous epistemic character ought to include intellectual curiosity to pursue answers to the important questions in life. As this applies to the evidence for theism, I commend C. S. Lewis, "Man or Rabbit?," in *God in the Dock*, reprint ed. (Grand Rapids, MI: Eerdmans, 2002), 108–13; see also my brief discussion in DePoe, "What's (Not) Wrong with Evidentialism," 13–14.

33. John Hick, *Evil and the God of Love*, 2nd ed. (New York: Harper & Row, 1978), 373.

34. Blaise Pascal, *Pensées*, trans. A. J. Krailsheimer, reprint ed. (New York: Penguin, 1995), 50.

35. Elsewhere I have argued that we should positively expect God to create a world where there is "epistemic distance" between God and created persons. See John M. DePoe, "The Epistemic Framework for Skeptical Theism," in *Skeptical Theism: New Essays*, ed. Trent Dougherty and Justin P. McBrayer (Oxford: Oxford University Press, 2014), 32–44; John M. DePoe, "Positive Skeptical Theism and the Problem of Divine Deception," *International Journal for Philosophy of Religion* 82, no. 1 (2017): 89–99.

36. I lifted this example (and other portions of this section) from John M. DePoe, "Hold on Loosely, But Don't Let Go: Evaluating the Evidential Impact of Religious Disagreement," *Philosophia Christi* 20, no. 1 (2018): 253–64.

37. For some recent defenses of the problem of peer disagreement to undermine theism, see Richard Feldman, "Reasonable Religious Disagreement," in

Philosophers without Gods: Meditations on Atheism and the Secular Life, ed. Antony Louise (Oxford: Oxford University Press, 2007), 194–214; Sanford C. Goldberg, "Does Externalist Epistemology Rationalize Religious Commitment?," in *Religious Faith and Intellectual Virtue*, ed. Laura Frances Callahan and Timothy O'Connor (Oxford: Oxford University Press, 2014), 279–98.

38. Compare Nathan L. King, "Disagreement: What's the Problem? Or a Good Peer Is Hard to Find," *Philosophy and Phenomenological Research* 85, no. 2 (2012): 249–72.

39. I have exposited my views on religious epistemology and peer disagreement at length in John M. DePoe, "The Significance of Religious Disagreement," in *Taking Christian Moral Thought Seriously: The Legitimacy of Religious Beliefs in the Marketplace of Ideas*, ed. Jeremy Evans (Nashville: Broadman & Holman Academic, 2011), 48–76; DePoe, "Hold on Loosely, But Don't Let Go."

40. Richard A. Fumerton, "You Can't Trust a Philosopher," in *Disagreement*, ed. Richard Feldman and Ted A. Warfield (Oxford: Oxford University Press, 2010), 91–110; more on how this response can apply to religious disagreement is explored in DePoe, "The Significance of Religious Disagreement," 68–9.

41. As a starting place on the nature of faith I highly recommend Lewis's writings. See C. S. Lewis, *Mere Christianity*, reprint ed. (New York: Touchstone, 1999) bk. 3, chs. 11–12; C. S. Lewis, "On Obstinacy in Belief," in *The World's Last Night: And Other Essays*, reprint ed. (San Francisco, CA: HarperOne, 2017), 11–30; C. S. Lewis, "Religion: Reality or Substitute?," in *Christian Reflections*, reprint ed. (Grand Rapids, MI: Eerdmans, 2014), 45–53.

42. Lewis, "Religion: Reality or Substitute?," 53.

43. For those concerned about this account of knowledge and the so-called "Gettier problem," see references in footnote 27.

Reponses to John M. DePoe

A Phenomenal Conservative Response to Classical Evidentialism

Logan Paul Gage and Blake McAllister

There is a lot of agreement between Classical Evidentialism and the Phenomenal Conservative approach we have defended.[1] Both are internalist. Both are evidentialist. Both are foundationalist. Both claim that properly basic beliefs are justified by evidence from a certain kind of mental state. (Indeed, if we weren't Phenomenal Conservatives, we might well be Classical Evidentialists in the vein of DePoe.) Our disagreement lies mostly at the foundations. DePoe claims that properly basic beliefs must be incorrigible—the sort about which you can't be mistaken—while Phenomenal Conservatives allow anything that seems true to be properly basic in the absence of defeaters. According to DePoe, basing everything on incorrigible beliefs helps maintain two desiderata:

(1) An objective connection between justification and truth, and
(2) The subjective assurance that justified beliefs are true.

In the following, we'll explain some problems for DePoe's view and why we think Phenomenal Conservatism is superior.

§1 An Objective Connection to Truth

DePoe thinks that justified beliefs are objectively likely to be true, and that Classical Evidentialism, because of its appeal to incorrigible beliefs, accounts for this feature of justification in a way that other internalist theories (like ours) do not. But what does it mean for a belief to be objectively probable? The most natural interpretation is that the belief is true in most nearby possible worlds. That is, in most situations similar to the subject's, that belief is in fact true. In this sense, not even Classical Evidentialism ensures that justified beliefs are objectively probable.

Consider a subject, let's call him "Unlucky," who is being deceived by Descartes's evil demon. From the inside, things appear to Unlucky exactly as they do to us. Starting from incorrigible beliefs, Unlucky makes all the same inferences about the world that we do: he believes that he has a body, that there is an external world in which his body is located, that the external world includes the planet Earth which existed long before he did, and so on. Unfortunately, Unlucky's beliefs are all false. He is a disembodied spirit, there is no external world, and everything came into existence right as Unlucky did. Unlucky's beliefs are all objectively improbable as well, since they remain false in all the possible worlds similar to his. Nevertheless, Unlucky's beliefs are justified. (Classical Evidentialists must affirm this on pain of skepticism, since our own beliefs are justified only if Unlucky's are. We all base our beliefs on the same evidence, after all.)

What this example shows is that, as soon as we stray beyond incorrigible beliefs, it doesn't matter how carefully we follow the evidence, we cannot thereby guarantee that our beliefs are objectively probable in the above sense. It is a mistake to demand such guarantees from justification. Thus, neither Classical Evidentialism nor the Phenomenal Conservative approach satisfies (1), so understood. We are just upfront about this fact.

Perhaps there is a different sense in which justified beliefs need to be objectively probable. Perhaps DePoe only means that the evidence one possesses needs to rationally support the content of your belief, making it *epistemically* probable, and that rational support of this sort is an objective matter (objective epistemic probability). Classical Evidentialism can account for the objective likelihood of justified beliefs in *this* sense, but arguably so can Phenomenal Conservatism. When something seems true, and there are no other relevant considerations, that experience makes its content objectively epistemically probable for the subject.[2] That is, the seeming bears an objective support relation to its content.

In summary, the only kind of objective connection that Classical Evidentialism provides is one that Phenomenal Conservatism can plausibly provide as well. Thus, there is no advantage for Classical Evidentialism here.

§2 The Subjective Assurance of Truth

We agree that part of justification is having some indication from the first-person perspective that the belief is true. We also agree that certain incorrigible beliefs have this in a supreme way. Consider the law of noncontradictions: it cannot be the case that p and $\sim p$ are both true at the same time and in the same way. What kind of subjective assurance do you have in this principle? First and foremost, that, when you consider it, it feels utterly obvious. We would describe this by saying it feels true in an especially strong way. There is a certain phenomenal character at play here—the feel of truth—which makes the content of a mental state evident. Incorrigible judgments are based on experiences that have this "truth-y" phenomenal character in a (virtually) maximal way, which gives us maximal subjective assurance in their truth.

You'll notice, however, that many other judgments are based on experiences with this same truth-y phenomenal character. For instance, perceptual beliefs are based on perceptual appearances in which propositions about our proximate physical environments are made evident. These perceptual appearances may not feel *as* true as the appearances underlying incorrigible judgments, but the difference is one of degree, not kind. Indeed, when we say that something "seems true," all we mean is that the subject has a mental state with this truth-y phenomenal character. Thus, *any* belief whose content seems true has the same sort of subjective assurance enjoyed by incorrigible beliefs, albeit to a lesser degree.

Now, Classical Evidentialists say that only beliefs with maximal subjective assurance—that is, incorrigible beliefs—can be properly basic. Why place the bar so high? One traditional motivation is this: if the foundations are guaranteed to be true, then surely anything properly based on those foundations is also guaranteed to be true, or at least true in most nearby possible worlds. In other words, demanding maximal subjective assurance at the foundations is supposed to secure the objective connection to truth. We saw in the last section, however, that such an idea is mistaken. Not even Classical Evidentialism can guarantee that justified beliefs are objectively probable in this sense.[3]

The other traditional motivation is that incorrigible beliefs enjoy a special kind of reflective assurance. That is, when you ask yourself whether an incorrigible belief is true, you are immediately able to see that it is, dispelling any doubts. The hope of Classical Evidentialists is that limiting the foundations to incorrigible beliefs will transfer this same kind of reflective assurance to anything based on those foundations. We could be certain, on reflection, that those non-incorrigible beliefs were objectively probable. Once again, the example in the previous section shows that nothing beyond incorrigible beliefs enjoys that kind of reflective assurance. We can never entirely get rid of the possibility that our beliefs are radically mistaken. We can, of course, reflect and give good reasons to think that our beliefs are mostly true. This more moderate form of reflective assurance is available on Phenomenal Conservatism as well. But neither theory can extend the special reflective assurance belonging to incorrigible beliefs to the non-incorrigible.

The emerging trend is that Classical Evidentialism is running a campaign on promises it can't keep. It asks us to restrict the foundations of our noetic structures to the incorrigible, promising that this will guarantee the probable truth of beliefs based on those foundations and allow us to dispel skeptical worries once and for all. These are things it cannot do. Nothing beyond the incorrigible can enjoy such security.

Once we realize this, there isn't any reason we can see to limit properly basic beliefs to the incorrigible. Indeed, it begins to seem quite arbitrary to say that incorrigible beliefs are properly basic because they seem true, but other beliefs are not properly basic even though they too seem true. These other beliefs might be less evident, but that just means we shouldn't hold them *as confidently* as we do incorrigible beliefs, not that we shouldn't hold them *at all*. The natural position is that our justification for basic beliefs should be *proportional* to the degree of subjective assurance we have in their content. This, of course, is just the view of Phenomenal Conservatism, which says that the degree of justification you have for a basic belief is proportional to how strongly its content seems true (other things being equal).

§3 Final Worries

We have already mentioned (in our defense of Phenomenal Conservatism) that we worry Classical Evidentialism leads to skepticism. This is because there doesn't seem to be strong enough arguments based solely on the incorrigible to justify our robust confidence in all matters of common sense. And even if there are, people don't actually base their beliefs on such arguments. They do not acquaint themselves with their ordinary judgments, acquaint themselves with how things appear to them, and then acquaint themselves with the connection between their judgments and how things appear, which is what Classical Evidentialism requires of them in order to be justified.

We should say, however, that such skeptical concerns are of less import in our thinking than the above sorts of considerations. Going back at least to Descartes, Classical Evidentialists limited properly basic beliefs to the incorrigible because this was supposed to provide special guarantees of truth to the rest of one's noetic structure. Once we realize this isn't the case, there just isn't any good reason we can see for limiting the domain of properly basic beliefs in this way.

Notes

1. Strictly speaking, Phenomenal Conservatism is just the single epistemic principle: If it seems to S that p, then, in the absence of defeaters, S thereby has at least some degree of justification for believing that p. But there are a cluster of additional epistemological theses that fit naturally with Phenomenal Conservatism. For convenience, we will often speak of "the Phenomenal Conservative approach" as though it incorporates these additional positions.
2. At least one of us openly endorses this. The other prefers to formulate Phenomenal Conservatism in terms of a more subjective form of epistemic probability.
3. Not unless they are willing to embrace skepticism and limit justified beliefs to the incorrigible.

A Proper Functionalist Response to Classical Evidentialism

Tyler Dalton McNabb

In John DePoe's well argued for essay, DePoe endorses Classical Evidentialism, which as I understand it is another phrase for classical foundationalism. For DePoe, in order for a belief to be properly basic, the belief needs to be incorrigible. If the belief isn't incorrigible, it must be properly based on a belief that is incorrigible. This means that, if belief that God exists isn't an incorrigible belief, belief that God exists couldn't be properly basic. This is why DePoe thinks that a subject possessing arguments for her religious belief is necessary for her religious beliefs to be justified or warranted.

DePoe argues that his Classical Evidentialism is more plausible than any of its epistemological competitors as it best can make sense of (1) there being an objective connection to truth and (2) there being a subjective assurance of truth.

By objective connection to truth, DePoe has in mind the need for a belief to have an intrinsic and nonarbitrary link to truth. This is similar to what I call a tight connection to truth. I defined it as there needing to be a tight connection between the belief produced from a subject's faculties and that belief being true. In reference to Classical Evidentialism meeting the objective connection requirement, DePoe states the following:

> Classical Evidentialism satisfies the objective connection to truth because properly basic beliefs must be true and any inferential connections from those beliefs must stand in objective truth-bearing relationships. Thus, every

justified belief in the Classical Evidentialist's prescribed noetic structure has a nonarbitrary connection to truth. The subjective assurance condition is met by Classical Evidentialism because of its requirement that subjects must be directly acquainted with these features that objectively secure the truth of their beliefs.

By subjective assurance of truth, DePoe has in mind an internal rationality requirement that the subject must meet in order for her belief to be justified. DePoe utilizes BonJour's Norman the Clairvoyant case to help make this condition plausible:

> Norman, under certain conditions which usually obtain, is a completely reliable clairvoyant with respect to certain kinds of subject matter. He possesses no evidence or reasons of any kind for or against the general possibility of such a cognitive power or for or against the thesis that he possesses it. One day Norman comes to believe that the President is in New York City, though he has no evidence either for or against this belief. In fact, the belief is true and results from his clairvoyant power under circumstances in which it is completely reliable.[1]

DePoe thinks that Norman's belief that the president is in New York fails to constitute knowledge. Even though it is produced from a reliable process, Norman displays severe internal irrationality. He lacks reason for trusting his faculty, and yet, he trusts the beliefs that are produced from it. Externalist conditions, according to DePoe, aren't sufficient for warrant.

What is a Proper Functionalist to make of all of this? In reference to DePoe's claims that Classical Evidentialism captures best what one has in mind by an objective connection to truth, I'm dubious that humans possess incorrigible beliefs. Typically, infallibilism is glossed in truth-maker terminology. For example, it can be said that S can't be wrong about her belief that p, given that she sees the relationship between the truth-maker and the truth-bearer. But, might we be wrong about "seeing" the truth? At least in part, what makes one think that they see the relationship between the truth-maker and truth-bearer is a certain phenomenology. But we know that phenomenology can be misleading at times. How do we know that our phenomenology isn't leading us to a false belief with respect to seeing the truth? Plantinga makes this point in discussing the famous Russell/Frege debate. Plantinga states, "Before Russell showed him the error of his ways, Frege believed that for every property there is the set of just those things that display the property; and he believed that *a priori*. But he didn't see that it is true; it isn't true."[2]

Perhaps DePoe would argue that the phenomenology that can mislead people is different from the phenomenology that accompanies actually "seeing" the truth. But why think this? What reasons do we have to believe that this is the case? And how would we know when we are actually "seeing" the truth? I take it that Frege really thought that he saw the truth too. But as history shows, he was wrong.

I have a more pressing concern, however. I don't think Classical Evidentialism captures what I have called a tight connection to truth. Even granting that some of our beliefs are incorrigible, it would seem like those beliefs would still fall prey to the problems that I lay out in my Proper Functionalism chapter. For example, Swampman can form beliefs about his own mental experiences, and yet, as I have argued for, Swampman would still lack knowledge about his mental experiences. I imagine DePoe wouldn't grant that someone's belief would lack a tight connection to truth if it were incorrigible. Fine. Even if that were the case, I think what the Swampman cases would show then is that non-incorrigible beliefs would still lack a tight connection, unless they were produced from a cognitive system that had a way in which it should operate. It seems like incorrigibility isn't enough.

Furthermore, I do have a concern that Classical Evidentialism won't be able to account for animals and young infants possessing knowledge. Do animals and young infants "see" the truth? Do they have arguments for their beliefs that rest upon the incorrigible beliefs? This all seems doubtful to me.

But, even if I am right about all of this, what is a Proper Functionalist to make of Norman the Clairvoyant? Plantinga's Proper Functionalism has a no-defeater clause.[3] This means that a subject can't continue to rationally believe that p, if S has a defeater for her believe that p. With this stated, perhaps the Proper Functionalist would endorse that it is epistemically possible that the design plan is such that, if an agent realizes that she lacks reasons for believing that her faculty F is reliable, then the agent has an undercutting defeater for her belief that F is reliable. If this were the case, given that Norman lacks reasons for thinking that his clairvoyant faculty is reliable, Norman would have an undercutting defeater for his beliefs that are produced from the clairvoyant faculty.

Notice, however, that there is no need to appeal to an internalist framework in order to argue that Norman is irrational. The Proper Functionalist has resources to consistently make this claim too. I imagine that DePoe will think that this move is *ad hoc* or perhaps due to its conditional nature isn't satisfying. I'll have to agree to disagree on this point and punt to my work elsewhere.[4]

Notes

1. BonJour, *The Structure of Empirical Knowledge*, 41.
2. Alvin Plantinga, *Warrant and Proper Function* (Oxford: Oxford University Press, 1993), 106.
3. Kenneth Boyce, "Proper Functionalism," ed. James Fieser and Bradley Dowden, *Internet Encyclopedia of Philosophy*, n.d., accessed August 26, 2016, https://www.iep.utm.edu/prop-fun/.
4. Tyler McNabb, "Proper Functionalism and the Metalevel: A Friendly Response to Timothy and Lydia McGrew," *Quaestiones Disputatae* (forthcoming).

A Covenantal Epistemology Response to Classical Evidentialism

K. Scott Oliphint

There is nothing much new in the essay on Classical Evidentialism (CE), which is nothing against it at all. It may well be that the best approaches are the "tried and true" ones, even when they seem to go out of favor, at least for a time.

A Covenantal Epistemology is replete with evidential entailments.[1] There is much, therefore, that (CE) and a Covenantal Epistemology will have in common. And, there is much in a Covenantal approach that (CE) will want to oppose.

First, according to (CE), "this account of evidence entails that for a belief to be justified a person must be aware of good reasons or grounds that support the truth of the belief." What might it mean for someone to "be aware of" something? Does it mean that such reasons or grounds must be at the forefront of my consciousness, directly "apparent" to me in my thinking? Likely, this is not what (CE) would affirm. Perhaps to "be aware" of reasons or grounds that support the truth of the belief means that the person could have access to those reasons or grounds just in case such things were required.

In line with the awareness criterion, (CE) prefers an internalist view of epistemic conditions. "The subjective requirement for epistemic justification is that it must provide assurance of the belief's truth to those who possess it." The "awareness" and "internalist" conditions are linked to Russell's notion of "knowledge by acquaintance." As we have seen, for Russell,

The main consideration is undoubtedly to be derived from remembering what "presence" actually is. When an object is in my present experience, then I am acquainted with it; it is not necessary for me to reflect upon my experience, or to observe that the object has the property of belonging to my experience, in order to be acquainted with it, but, on the contrary, the object itself is known to me without the need of any reflection on my part as to its properties or relations.[2]

Readers who have followed my responses thus far will recognize immediately what comes next. If "awareness" and "internalism" can be adequately described in the Russellian way, then we have a merger of (some form of) evidentialism with a Covenantal Epistemology.

For Russell, there are two primary conditions for something to qualify as knowledge by acquaintance. First, it is the notion of the "presence" of an object—that is, an object's being in my present experience—that results in our acquaintance ("awareness"?) of that object. Second, there is no need for our cognitive reflection in order for us to know something by acquaintance. This, perhaps, is close to the notion of knowledge in "Tradition-Based Perspectivalism" such that there obtains an adequation between the mind and its object. In knowledge by acquaintance, that adequation happens "automatically." The mere presence of the object demands (a noninferential) knowledge.

This, it seems to me, is close to what the apostle Paul describes for us in his account of the universal and unassailable true knowledge of God that all people possess. To be sure, the apostle is not concerned with philosophical criteria or descriptions as he explains what this true knowledge of God is. However, given that all people (as I understand him, all people who are self-conscious) have this knowledge, and given that this knowledge comes not from proper reflection, but is instead implanted in us by virtue of God's own activity (Rom. 1:18–19), there is, universally and exhaustively, a "knowledge by acquaintance" that is given in and through all of creation (including in and through each of us).[3]

In this way, the knowledge of God that all people have is, *by definition*, evidential. As a matter of fact, as Paul explains, the entire universe is evidence of God's existence, including as well His "eternal power and divine nature" (Rom. 1:20). Thus, as with (CE), our knowledge of God is evidentially rooted; apart from that evidence, there could be no such knowledge. It is not the case, therefore, that belief in God is properly basic. It is much stronger than that, according to Covenantal Epistemology. Not *belief*, but *knowledge* of God, has its roots in all that God has made, and it accrues to each of us without the need of any inference or reflection. To put it in the most concise way possible, we have knowledge of God because He implants it in us.

But there is a problem when we consider this universal knowledge of God. It is a problem that requires a kind of externalist condition; it is the problem of sin, which causes us, inevitably (apart from regeneration), to suppress, deny, and hold down the knowledge of God that we all possess. However, this externalist condition isn't as bleak as (CE) supposes. For (CE), externalist accounts of justification are "unsatisfying and practically useless because they describe epistemology from a perspective that in practice no one possesses. At best, they offer conditional or hypothetical 'solutions' without any guidance as to how an individual can have assurance that he meets those conditions."

There are two complaints about externalism from (CE) that do not obtain in this externalist condition. First, the externalist condition attached to our universal, but suppressed, true knowledge of God is not, in this case, "from a perspective that in practice no one possesses." With respect to our *sensus divinitatis*, even if we ourselves refuse to acknowledge we have it, we can recognize it because we have, in Scripture, *God's* perspective on it (and that perspective is given to us in His Word). Thus, the *sensus divinitatis*, as an externalist condition for the true knowledge of God obtaining in us, is affirmed, first, from God's perspective and then, following on that, when we agree to "think God's thoughts after Him."

Second, if the *sensus divinitatis* is an externalist condition, it includes the knowledge of God, which is ours even if we refuse to acknowledge it. In order to acknowledge it, certain "internalist" conditions must be met. There is clear guidance as to how one can have assurance that he meets those conditions. Put simply, we are meant to believe, in the first place, what God says about us, from Genesis to Revelation. If God says that we are made in His image, then the "guidance" as to how we can have assurance that we are so made is to trust what He says. If God says that all people know Him, then it is incumbent on us to acknowledge what He has said. In this case, we are to *acknowledge* the *knowledge* that God Himself gives to His creatures made in His image.[4]

The advantage of our approach, contra (CE), is that we have been given, by God's grace, a perspective on who we are and what the world is that transcends the conditions of human knowing. We are not bound to consider rationality or truth from the perspective of this world alone. Instead, we are to recognize that God Himself is absolute rationality—He is the truth—and then all rationality and truth flows from and must be consistent with who He is and what He has said.

As (CE) notes, truth is not determined by counting noses. The position of Covenantal Epistemology will not win by majority vote. What it does hope to do, however, is to take God at His Word and then note how doing so will have strong and substantive implications for epistemology. If the above is true with respect to a Covenantal approach, then Christian philosophers should recognize that all of our beliefs are downstream from *knowledge*, and not, in the first place, prerequisites for knowledge. God has so constituted us that we will, always and everywhere, know *Him* in and through the evidences given over all creation. If what we believe about the world and ourselves comports with, and does not deny, that knowledge, then the task of epistemology is firmly rooted and can proceed without the specter of skepticism looming.

Notes

1. Briefly, for reference, a Covenantal approach to epistemology recognizes (1) that all people are related to God by virtue of His revelation (natural and special) and (2) that all people *know* the true God and thus, by virtue of that knowledge, are responsible properly to respond to him (Rom. 1:18–32). Thus, knowledge is, first of all, *given* in and through God's revelation in creation and is, for most people, enhanced and supplemented by hearing or reading God's special revelation in Scripture. Since all of creation reveals God, there is evidence, in every fact, of His existence.
2. Bertrand Russell, *Logic and Knowledge: Essays 1901–1950* (New York: Macmillan, 1956), 167.
3. In a Covenantal, Reformed context, the knowledge of God that we all possess was historically distinguished as *cognitio insita* (implanted knowledge) and *cognitio acquisita* (acquired knowledge).
4. A question that comes naturally from this is just *how* we can know that Genesis to Revelation is God's Word. The best, short, answer to that question is that, in the Protestant tradition, the Word of God is taken as a basic *principium*. To see this articulated, see the *Westminster Confession of Faith*, chapter one, sections four and five. For more on this, see K. Scott Oliphint, "Because It Is the Word of God," in *Did God Really Say?: Affirming the Truthfulness and Trustworthiness of Scripture*, ed. David B. Garner (Phillipsburg, NJ: Presbyterian & Reformed, 2012), 1–22.

A Tradition-Based Perspectival Response to Classical Evidentialism

Erik Baldwin

DePoe's religious epistemology is characteristically Modern. Against this way of doing epistemology, I might modify and extend my arguments against the encyclopedists, but I think it's easy enough to see how that'd go. I shall rather explicate and gesture toward the defense of a characteristically Aquinian alternative approach to epistemology that is consistent with my rationality of traditions approach, omitting any direct application to religious epistemology.

Aquinas maintains that "truth is defined by the conformity of intellect and thing; and hence to know this conformity is to know truth."[1] In contemporary terminology, Aquinas affirms direct epistemological realism: the object of knowledge is not an idea, representation, or mental state, but rather the thing itself.[2] He assumes there is an external world that has objective features independently of what any created mind thinks about it.[3] What is of primary importance is not our judging that particular propositions are true, but rather our ability to grasp real essences of things. For instance, the intellect (a power of a soul, and not its very essence[4]) grasps immediately truths that are self-evident to us, namely, judgments in which "the predicate is included in the essence of the subject, as 'Man is an animal,' for animal is contained in the essence of man."[5] The proposition *humans are animals* is self-evident to us only insofar as we have true cognitions of the essences, or natures, of man, rationality. MacIntyre writes,

> on Aquinas's type of account [of truth], a particular person's intellect is adequate to some particular subject matter with which it is engaged in its thinking, it is what the objects of that thinking in fact are which makes it the case that that person's thoughts about those objects are what they are—and, in respect of the content of that thought, nothing else …. This adequacy of the intellect to its objects—and its primary objects are, for example, the actual specimens of sodium or chlorine about which the chemist enquires, or the actual strata about which the geologist enquires, not, as in so many later accounts of mind, ideas or presentations of those specimens or strata—is expressed in the making of true judgments about those objects. And true judgments are uses of sentences which satisfy the truth-conditions for those sentences.[6]

Aquinas's views are characteristically externalist; what grounds the truth of a judgment is not a matter of epistemic agent having privileged access to or awareness of features of his or her mental states, but rather the intellect's conformity to extra-mental objects, a view that assumes that a subject's cognitive faculties have been well-designed and are functioning properly.[7]

DePoe maintains that epistemology is essentially a first-person activity. For the Aquinian, it is a third-person activity, for each inquirer is but one among many, and self-knowledge must be "integrated into a general account of souls and their teleology." Insofar as one moves toward truth successfully, one's intellect becomes adequate to the objects it knows and "responds to the object as the object is and as it would be, independently of the mind's knowledge of it."[8] On this view, metaphysics is prior to epistemology. I can't give a fully satisfactory defense of that thesis here, but I can gesture in the general direction. Jacques Maritain eloquently writes,

> Aquinas makes knowledge *absolutely dependent* upon what is. To know, in fact, is essentially to know *something*, and something which … measures it and governs it, and thus possesses its own being, independent of my knowledge … the object of knowledge … must, by its very nature of known object, be that which a thing is—a thing other than myself and my subjective activity … The entire specification of my act of intelligence comes, therefore, from the object *as something other*, as free from me. In knowing, I subordinate myself to a being independent of me; I am conquered, convinced and subjugated by it. And the truth of my mind lies in its conformity to *what* is outside of it and independent of it.[9]

Consider now some points about justification. For Aquinas, the truth of some propositions can be self-evident to all: "If therefore, the essence of the predicate and subject be known to all, the proposition will be self-evident to all." Such truths include the first principles of demonstration, "the terms of which are common things that no one is ignorant of."[10] For example, the principle *a whole is greater than its parts* is grasped immediately by the intellect on account of its cognition of the relevant natures involved in it.[11] A belief is *evident to the senses* if it directly involves one or more of the five senses. Examples include the beliefs that some things in the world are in motion, that some things are caused to exist, and that some things come to be and then go out of existence.[12] The belief that one sees a duck flying overhead involves input from the senses, but the object of intellectual cognition is not the sensory input or some feature of our mental states of which we are aware, but rather the duck itself.

Essential to DePoe's account of justification is that the mind must be aware of some feature that provides a subjective ground for thinking that a proposition is true. In contrast, for the Aquinian, what ultimately grounds the truth of a proposition is a mind being in direct cognitive contact with an extra-mental object of perception, which can and usually does occur without a person being consciously or self-reflectively aware of what's going on. As we begin to know things, we don't start with a theory of epistemic justification and then determine whether our beliefs conform to its criteria, but rather we find ourselves coming to know all manner of things on account of our participating in various belief-forming practices. Children feed ducks at the park to watch them fly away and thereby come to understand things about them. As they mature, some go on to learn what it is about birds that makes them capable of flight. We typically give rational justifications of such things only when some controversial truth-claim is at issue, which motivates us to inquire more deeply into the natures of things. For instance, starting with general knowledge of the nature of birds, evolutionary biologists inquire into how it could be that they are the evolutionary descendants of dinosaurs.[13] MacIntyre writes, "Practices of rational justification are thus devised and are only fully intelligible as parts of all those human activities which aim at truth: questioning, doubting, formulating hypotheses, confirming, disconfirming, and so on."[14]

For the Classical Evidentialist, first principles (e.g., the *cogito*—"I am; I exist") are grasped immediately and prior to inquiry. For Aquinas, we don't begin with first principles, but with *endoxa*, as I explained earlier. Truth is the aim of inquiry, and when an enquiry reaches its end, our understanding of a matter is perfected, and we are able to "say how things are, rather than how they seem to be from the particular, partial, and limited standpoint of some particular set of perceivers or observers or enquirers."[15] Our inquiries into truth take place, "in the context of the conceptual framework of some more or less large-scale theory."[16] We make progress toward truth by transcending and correcting for the distortions and limitations of our starting points. It is only after a lengthy process of inquiry that we are able to look backward and give a full justification of truth-claims in terms of first principles. In sum, for the Aquinian, substantive philosophical first principles, in both epistemology and metaphysics, are the fruit of philosophical inquiry, not its seeds.

I've sketched an Aquinian way of doing epistemology that is very much out of step with DePoe's. While much more could be said, I take it that what I have said (taken together with what I said in my chapter) provides an adequate enough defense of why I take it to be preferable to Classical Evidentialism.

Notes

1. Thomas Aquinas, *Summa Theologica*, trans. Fathers of the English Dominican Province, 2d., 1920, http://www.newadvent.org/summa/, 1, q. 16, a. 2.
2. See Anthony J. Lisska, *Aquinas's Theory of Perception: An Analytic Reconstruction* (Oxford: Oxford University Press, 2016).
3. Eleonore Stump, "Aquinas on the Foundations of Knowledge," *Canadian Journal of Philosophy* 21, no. suppl. 1 (1991): 144.
4. Thomas Aquinas, *Summa Theologica*, 1, q. 54, a. 3 and 1, q. 19, a. 1.
5. Ibid., 1, q. 2, a. 1. Note that Aquinas argues that the specific essence of a thing is that which is expressed by its definition in 1, q. 3, a. 3.
6. Alasdair MacIntyre, "Moral Relativism, Truth and Justification," in *The Tasks of Philosophy: Volume One* (Cambridge: Cambridge University Press, 2006), 66. See also Thomas Aquinas, *Questiones Disputatae De Veritate*, trans. Robert Mulligan, reprint ed. (Indianapolis, IN: Hackett, 1994), 1.1.
7. John I. Jenkins, *Knowledge and Faith in Thomas Aquinas* (Cambridge: Cambridge University Press, 1997); and Stump, "Aquinas on the Foundations of Knowledge."
8. Alasdair MacIntyre, "First Principles, Final Ends, and Contemporary Issues," in *The Tasks of Philosophy: Volume One* (Cambridge: Cambridge University Press, 2006), 149.

9. Jacques Maritain, "The Range of Reason," accessed December 21, 2018, https://maritain.nd.edu/jmc/etext/range01.htm.

10. Thomas Aquinas, *Summa Theologica*, 1, q. 2, a. 1.

11. Ibid., 1, q. 1, a. 1.

12. Ibid., 1, q. 2, a. 3.

13. Generally, Thomists aren't all that concerned with many contemporary epistemological problems, puzzles, and concerns. MacIntyre writes, "the refutation of skepticism will appear to [the Thomist] as misguided an enterprise as it does to the Wittgensteinian." MacIntyre, "First Principles, Final Ends, and Contemporary Issues," 148.

14. MacIntyre, "Moral Relativism, Truth and Justification," 58.

15. Ibid.

16. MacIntyre, "First Principles, Final Ends, and Contemporary Issues," 147–8.

Classical Evidentialism: Response to Critics

John M. DePoe

Reviewing my critics' responses, I am delighted and, in some instances, surprised to discover that there is much agreement between my view and the others. Although, it is clear that we have our fair share of disagreements as well. In what follows, I have decided to address major themes from my critics taken collectively since there are significant intersections in their responses to my position. Rather than taking a strictly defensive posture, I will also use this opportunity to spell out some problems (or at least critical questions) for the other views that struck me as I read their responses.

Incorrigibility or Bust?

A common issue raised from all of the respondents concerns the issue of incorrigibility. Gage and McAllister think that incorrigible beliefs are attainable but constitute too thin of a foundation for an adequate structure of knowledge. A much more extreme position is taken by McNabb who is dubious that one can reliably tell whether a given belief is incorrigible. Baldwin altogether rejects the notion of commencing empirical knowledge from the basis of mental states, incorrigible or not.

First, I shall address Gage and McAllister's concerns. While they acknowledge that incorrigibility provides a connection to truth, they also believe that it is an unnecessarily high standard for basic beliefs. The reason why incorrigibility is the appropriate standard for foundational beliefs is that it is the only way to guarantee that one's noetic structure has a connection to truth. To put this another way, incorrigibility is the tether to reality for one's thoughts. Allow me to elaborate on this point by reviewing a common reason why foundationalists often reject coherentism.[1] Coherentism is the theory of justification where all the beliefs in a person's noetic structure provide mutual support for each other's justification. In a coherentist's epistemic structure, no beliefs are more basic or foundational than another. The whole network of beliefs support and justify each other as long as they cohere or "fit" together in the right way. A persisting problem for coherentism known as the isolation objection is that there could be large sets of beliefs that cohere in all the ways prescribed by a coherentist's theory of justification but which remain entirely divorced from reality. For instance, what if someone who was reading J. R. R. Tolkien's *Lord of the Rings* decided to adopt the beliefs of Tolkien's fantasy novel as if they were describing reality? Couldn't such a person assemble a large set of coherent beliefs that failed to describe anything in the real world?

At the heart of the isolation objection is a commitment to the proposition that a sound epistemic structure should have some bond to reality and truth. Coherentism is often judged as inadequate because it fails in this respect. However, those foundationalists who accept moderate standards for basic beliefs do not have a better alternative than coherentism since they permit basic beliefs that have no connection to truth. After all, it is possible to compile a system of completely false beliefs to describe reality following a moderate foundationalist's epistemic principles. Without incorrigibility, there is no assurance that any belief in a person's noetic structure corresponds to reality. Foundationalists who marshal the isolation problem against coherentists should not be content with epistemic theories that permit properly basic beliefs without some guaranteed connection to truth.

What Gage and McAllister are missing in their critique is that only the Classical Evidentialist's structure of justification has any claim to truth for a person's whole noetic structure since it is the only view that has a guaranteed connection to truth *whatsoever*. Starting with uncertain foundations, Phenomenal Conservatism (like all forms of moderate foundationalism) suffers from the same defect as coherentism—it permits creating a whole system of putatively justified beliefs that may be entirely divorced from truth and reality. Properly basic beliefs require a higher standard for justification because they have one of the most important roles in a theory of justification; that is, they ensure that at its genesis a person's noetic structure is bound to reality and truth. The point, in other words, is that without a connection to truth at the most basic level, there can be no justification imputed to those beliefs inferred in the nonbasic levels. After all, justification is a feature of a belief that indicates that the belief is likely to be true, which can only be given when at the most basic level there is a guaranteed connection to truth.[2]

McNabb's doubts about my incorrigibility standard are more severe. He alleges that no one can ever be certain whether a belief is incorrigible because it is always possible for one's belief to be overturned by new evidence or insight. McNabb takes incorrigibility to be founded upon a certain type of phenomenology, a strong feeling of assurance. Gage and McAllister concur and state that incorrigible judgments are founded upon experiences with a "truth-y" phenomenological character. Yet, this feeling can be misleading, causing us to believe something is certain when in fact it is demonstrably false. To support his case, McNabb cites Plantinga who draws upon the famous episode of Russell correcting Frege about set theory. No less of a mind than Frege's misled him to believe that each property has a corresponding membership in a set. The lesson we should take from this, according to McNabb, is that we may never be in a position to know for sure that our beliefs are incorrigible.

Interestingly, the target of McNabb's borrowed example from Plantinga is some form of *a priori* justification or knowledge, not incorrigibility. However, McNabb is reappropriating it to highlight a potential problem with my account of incorrigibility. My response to the Frege example is to concur with McNabb at least in saying Frege's belief was clearly not incorrigible. Incorrigible beliefs are, after all, by definition beliefs that are held by someone in such a way that they are uncorrectable with respect to its truth. Frege's belief turned out to be correctable by Russell, so it wasn't incorrigible. When someone believes that he is experiencing a severe headache, for instance, that person cannot be corrected by anyone with respect to the belief that he is experiencing a headache. The same can be said for a multitude of other experiences because the experience is formed in direct reference to the experience. There is no possible slippage between the possession of the belief and its truth.

So, what happened in the case of Frege? The first thing to note about Frege's belief about properties having corresponding sets is that he did not hold this belief because he thought that it was incorrigible, certain, or unassailably self-evident. Frege describes his adherence to this principle writing, "I have never disguised from myself its lack of self-evidence that belongs to the other axioms and that must properly be demanded of a logical law."[3] Thus, it turns out that Frege's problem was not that he wrongly held that his belief was incorrigible. To the contrary, his mistake could be diagnosed as a case of holding a belief, while he was aware of its uncertainty. Indeed, he never had any phenomenal experience of the belief being incorrigible or absolutely self-evident.

McNabb's point presents an opportunity to elaborate on incorrigibility since it is an oft-maligned, yet commonly misunderstood, characteristic. While I think that there is a distinct phenomenology that accompanies virtually all conscious states of mind,[4] it would be a mistake to reduce incorrigibility to some phenomenological sensation. Incorrigible beliefs are those whose truth necessarily follows when they are believed. Incorrigibility cannot be conferred on a class of beliefs uncritically, such as maintaining that all beliefs about one's own mental states must be incorrigible or that all *a priori* justified beliefs are incorrigible. Some beliefs about one's own mental states or appropriately held *a priori* beliefs may be incorrigible, while others may not. How is a person made aware that one of his beliefs is incorrigible? I believe that it follows from a direct acquaintance with *both* the belief's truth-maker *and* the correspondence relation that holds between the belief and its truth-maker. Like all mental states, there is a unique phenomenology that accompanies it, but this phenomenology is not the essential distinguishing feature of incorrigible beliefs. Incorrigible beliefs can be recognized through a direct awareness of the belief's truth-maker and its correspondence to the truth-maker.

The Specter of Skepticism

Gage, McAllister, and McNabb all raise skeptical concerns with my religious epistemology. Even if I can guarantee truth at the most basic level, what have I to say about attaining knowledge among nonbasic beliefs? Do Gage and McAllister's "Unlucky" case or McNabb's revised Swampman case represent an insurmountable challenge for my view? For the sake of space, regrettably I will have to ignore some of the details of their particular skeptical challenges and sketch how I generally respond to skeptical worries. The first thing to note is that no epistemology can provide absolute certainty to guarantee the truth for one's beliefs about the external world. In this respect, Classical Evidentialism is no different from the others in neither claiming nor requiring that level of justification to possess knowledge of the world at large. Second, I believe that it is the unprincipled epistemologist who gerrymanders the standards for knowledge to accommodate commonly held beliefs when he discovers that his otherwise reasonable standards do not include those beliefs. All too often the approach of Classical Evidentialism is rejected because it is thought to hold standards so high that many commonplace beliefs fail to meet those standards. My practice has been to discover sound epistemic principles and to apply them fairly letting the chips fall where they may. There is, after all, no *a priori* reason to believe that external world skepticism is necessarily false. In fact, I tend to be suspicious of the integrity of epistemological views that dispense with the possibility of skepticism without providing a good reason to think it is false.

In brief, Classical Evidentialism can overcome external world skepticism because our incorrigible beliefs provide a stronger confirmation for the view that there is an external world than that we are victims of a wide-ranging skeptical situation, like a Cartesian deceiver.[5] Skeptical scenarios by their nature are always exceptionally less probable in comparison to their nonskeptical counterparts. This is due to a number of factors, such as that skeptical scenarios tend to be far more complex in explaining the evidence of incorrigible belief and that skeptical scenarios typically mimic nonskeptical ones. Using the Cartesian deceiver as an example, as Timothy McGrew explains,

> The existence of the deceiver over and above these particular causes of our experiences is a "fifth wheel." Though we may grant his existence is logically possible, it is perfectly reasonable for us not to take it seriously since we have at hand a simpler, more plausible, and therefore better-confirmed explanation for our experience: that we inhabit a real world of mind-independent objects.[6]

In short, what distinguishes Classical Evidentialists on skepticism is that they believe that skepticism must be addressed and refuted, while the others typically do not. The other views often believe skepticism will succeed if given a fair hearing and that the only way to avoid skepticism is to manipulate their epistemic principles and practices to dispense with it without a fair fight.

A Covenantal Merger?

In his response to Classical Evidentialism, K. Scott Oliphint raises the possibility that much of my approach could be merged with his. Oliphint believes that all people have first and foremost a knowledge of God. He supposes that this inherent divine knowledge is known through direct acquaintance, but it's suppressed as a result of the effects of sin. The merger could occur by incorporating much of my views about knowledge through direct acquaintance along with his theological framework affirming humans' knowledge of God.

I am intrigued by this merger, although I see some significant differences in our views that make it unlikely to succeed. In the first place is a difference between our views about knowledge and belief. Oliphint theorizes that knowledge of God is the primary epistemic starting point and all other beliefs follow from it. For reasons that I give in my response to his view, I don't think that this is a plausible approach.

Another significant difference regards our interpretations of Rom. 1. Oliphint appears to read this as a statement that God has bestowed some form of innate knowledge of Himself in all humans. This alone raises many questions. Is it dispositional or occurrent knowledge? Is this knowledge propositional or experiential (or something else)? Does this innate knowledge include Christian theology, like the Trinity? Do infants and the mentally challenged have this knowledge too?

But a more important difference here is that I see Rom. 1 describing Paul's views on natural theology. The knowledge of God is made evident, according to Paul, not through some innate knowledge, but rather because this knowledge is "clearly perceived, ever since the creation of the world, *in the things that have been made*" (1:20 ESV, my emphasis). My convictions align with the traditions that interpret this passage as describing the tremendous evidence for theism through natural theology.[7] This comports with my overall response to the problem of divine hiddenness that affirms that the knowledge of God is abundant but not obvious. Ultimately, for the possibility of merging Covenantal Epistemology and Classical Evidentialism, this means that without significant revisions, our positions will remain separate.

A Few Parting Shots

In closing, I would like to register some final critical remarks in light of my critics' comments. First, I was stunned to read McNabb's response to the case of Norman the Clairvoyant where to rebut the concerns that externalist approaches to justification lack any subjective assurance of truth, he suggests the principle that "if an agent realizes that she lacks reasons for believing that her faculty F is reliable, then the agent has an undercutting defeater for her belief that F is reliable." This principle is just shy of adding an awareness requirement for his account of Proper Functionalism. Plantinga himself does not claim to show that his account of warrant is true, but only that "if Christian belief is indeed true, then the model in question or one very like it is also true."[8] Indeed, he says, "I don't know how to do something one could sensibly call 'showing' that either of these *is* true."[9] Does this mean McNabb would say that since Plantinga himself is unaware of reasons for thinking his cognitive faculties are reliable that he has an undercutting defeater for thinking his faculties are reliable?

Baldwin states that he follows Aquinas's direct realist approach to empirical knowledge whereby knowledge of the external world occurs by "a mind being in direct cognitive contact with an extra-mental object of perception." But this approach is untenable since there is no way to distinguish between veridical experience and non-veridical ones (like hallucinations, dreams, and illusions).[10] After all, it is possible for a person to have the exact same experiences of feeding ducks at the pond whether the person is truly feeding ducks at the pond, the person is having a vivid and realistic dream of feeding ducks at the pond, or the person is having a vivid and realistic hallucination of feeding ducks at the pond. Since these experiences are indistinguishable, why assume the first is correct without some further reason? Indirect realism, the position that relies upon inference from beliefs based upon sense experiences to arrive at contingent beliefs about the physical world, provides a non-question-begging way to justify perceptual beliefs.

Perhaps Baldwin's objection is actually that this is simply not how people do in fact reason about the empirical world.[11] He says, "we don't start with a theory of epistemic justification and then determine whether our beliefs conform to its criteria." This seems to confuse the object level of epistemology with the meta-level.[12] I believe that ordinary people, maybe even young children, can satisfy my standards for justified belief in practice. It is no requirement of my approach that anyone should have conscious awareness about theories of justification and knowledge and then apply these to their epistemic practices in order to possess these epistemic goods. My view is that the right inferential structures must be in place to justify beliefs, whether or not those who are justified take the time to reflect on their epistemic practices to become fully aware that these structures are in place. Most often these inferences take place quickly at a subconscious level, which mercifully spares us the tedium of consciously rehearsing each step of inference when forming justified empirical beliefs.

A final problem with Baldwin's view is that he takes Aristotle's *endoxa* as epistemic starting points. However, this is not truly possible since one must employ epistemic principles in order to discover what are Aristotle's *endoxa*. Even supposing one was in full agreement with Baldwin, he would need to rely on sense perception and basic forms of reasoning to read Aristotle's works and understand them. Clearly, the *endoxa* are not the origins of epistemic principles and practices. At best, they are intermediary authorities for belief that we discover by applying more fundamental epistemic principles.

My Final Plea

I'd like to conclude by making a final plea to my readers. As you study the different approaches to religious epistemology, I hope that you will conform your approach to the one that offers principles and practices that will help individuals align their beliefs with what is true. I believe that Classical Evidentialism is the best approach because it is the only view that can mutually satisfy both an objective connection to truth and a subjective assurance of truth. When it comes to regulatory principles for religious beliefs, we should not compromise these features for convenience or comfort.

Notes

1. See, for instance, BonJour, "A Version of Internalist Strong Foundationalism," 53.
2. I have sympathies for an argument against moderate foundationalism that argues that in order for a belief to be probable, there must be some belief that is certain. I haven't included it due to space considerations. Inquiring minds can consult McGrew, *The Foundations of Knowledge*, chap. 4; concisely argued in McGrew, "A Defense of Strong Foundationalism," 197.
3. Gottlob Frege, *The Foundations of Arithmetic*, trans. J. L. Austin (Oxford: Basil Blackwell, 1950), 234, quoted in McGrew and McGrew, *Internalism and Epistemology*, 109.
4. For those interested in this debate, see the philosophical literature spawned by David Pitt, "The Phenomenology of Cognition or What Is It Like to Think That P?," *Philosophy and Phenomenological Research* 69, no. 1 (2004): 1–36.
5. For a concise version of this argument see McGrew, "A Defense of Strong Foundationalism," 205; for an argument with more details see Jonathan Vogel, "The Refutation of Skepticism," in *Contemporary Debates in Epistemology*, ed. Mattias Steup, Ernest Sosa, and John Turri, 3rd ed. (Malden, MA: Wiley-Blackwell, 2014), 108–19; and for a more extensive

account of this argument see McGrew, *The Foundations of Knowledge*, chap. 7.

6. McGrew, "A Defense of Strong Foundationalism," 205.

7. In Greek, the verbs commonly translated "having been clearly perceived" are more literally rendered "[nooumena] being understood [kathoratai] are perceived." The first verb [nooumena] refers to a purely intellectual activity and the second verb [kathoratai] refers to physical sight. The implication is that Paul is describing the inferential reasoning from experience that is typical of natural theology. See Frederick Fyvie Bruce, *The Letter of Paul to the Romans: An Introduction and Commentary*, 2nd ed. (Grand Rapids, MI: Eerdmans, 1985), 80.

8. Plantinga, *Warranted Christian Belief*, 169.

9. Ibid., 170.

10. An excellent introduction to these issues is Ali Hasan, *A Critical Introduction to the Epistemology of Perception* (New York: Bloomsbury, 2017), especially chs. 3 and 9.

11. For my views about how the standards of Classical Evidentialism are achievable to common folk, see John M. DePoe, "Indirect Realism with a Human Face," *Ratio* 31, no. 1 (2018): 57–72; DePoe, "What's (Not) Wrong with Evidentialism."

12. See McGrew and McGrew, *Internalism and Epistemology*, 57–66.

2

Phenomenal Conservatism

Logan Paul Gage and Blake McAllister

Introduction

From an early age, we thought it important to approach our Christian beliefs rationally. Through C. S. Lewis and contemporary Christian apologetics, we encountered various arguments in support of the Christian worldview. Later we discovered the latest and greatest arguments of natural theology, many of which we found convincing. In light of these arguments, we were tempted to endorse a Classical Evidentialist approach to religious epistemology: belief in God or Christianity is justified if and only if it is supported by good arguments.[1] This made sense, for we wanted our beliefs to be grounded in solid reasons rather than wishful thinking or tribal prejudice.

As we read more philosophy during our undergraduate years, however, we encountered the growing movement of Reformed Epistemology in the writings of Alvin Plantinga, Nicholas Wolterstorff, and others. We came to believe that the Classical Evidentialist approach did not adequately account for the ability of people without PhDs to hold justified religious beliefs. Furthermore, when we assessed the foundations of our own beliefs, we realized that, though we possessed arguments, our beliefs did not absolutely *depend* on those arguments. Thus, we found Reformed Epistemology's critique of Classical Evidentialism deeply attractive.

Nevertheless, we couldn't shake the conviction that evidence matters to the justification of our beliefs. Only in our graduate studies did we come to see that a third option—the Phenomenal Conservative approach—offers a more satisfying synthesis of the good-making features found in both Classical Evidentialism and Reformed Epistemology.

In this essay, we set forth the basics of Phenomenal Conservatism (PC) and defend it against common objections. We then use PC to develop an overall approach to the justification of religious belief. Several advantages of this approach emerge, which allow it to walk a middle road between Classical Evidentialism and Reformed Epistemology. Most prominently, PC acknowledges that experiences can directly provide evidence for belief. Thus, a religious belief can be justified by *evidence* even if it is not based on *arguments*. Given our backgrounds, we will limit our discussion to theistic and Christian beliefs. However, almost everything we say could apply to other forms of religious belief as well.

Phenomenal Conservatism

A well-formed belief structure is like a sturdy house. Some bricks may be supported by other bricks, but underlying them all is a foundation. The foundation of the house is supported not by other bricks but by the ground, which has the unique ability to support the elements on top of it without itself requiring support. In the same way, some beliefs may be justified by other beliefs, but ultimately our belief structures must rest on properly basic beliefs that are noninferentially justified. These foundational beliefs are not based on other beliefs but on experiences, which have the unique ability to justify beliefs without themselves requiring justification.[2]

If (like most epistemologists in history) we accept this picture, the question becomes: What kinds of experiences are capable of noninferentially justifying belief? Philosophers like Descartes and Hume said that only introspection and rational intuition could justify basic beliefs. These sorts of experiences, they thought, deserved the benefit of the doubt. Perceptual experiences, on the other hand, had to be proven reliable before they could be trusted. By the end of the Early Modern period it was clear that such a view led to skepticism. Reason and introspection provide too meager of a foundation to support the existence of the external world or other matters of common sense.[3]

To account for the justification of common-sense beliefs, we must extend the benefit of the doubt to other kinds of experiences. Following in the footsteps of the "common-sense" tradition of epistemology from Carneades (in the second century BC) to Thomas Reid (in the eighteenth century) to Roderick Chisholm in our own time,[4] Michael Huemer has proposed the following principle:

(Phenomenal Conservatism): If it seems to S that p, then, in the absence of defeaters, S thereby has at least some degree of justification for believing that p.[5]

PC extends the benefit of the doubt to everything that seems true to us. For example, intuitions, introspections, perceptions, and memories are all different types of experiences in which something seems true. PC says that all of these experiences—these "seemings"—are capable of justifying basic beliefs.[6]

It is imperative to see that PC is a principle of *noninferential* justification. If there seems to be a tree in front of me, then I immediately have justification for believing this. I do not need to make the second-order observation *that* I am being appeared to treely, and then *infer* that there is a tree that is making things appear this way.[7] It just seems to me that there is a tree, I am moved to believe it, and (assuming I have no defeaters or substantial counterevidence) this belief is justified.[8]

Beliefs based on seemings can be justified to different degrees depending on the seeming's strength. Something that seems exceedingly obvious, say, that everything is identical to itself, might thereby be justified to a degree sufficient for knowledge, whereas something that only slightly seems true might be justified to a much lesser degree. The important point is this: seemings provide positive reasons for belief.[9]

Seemings can sound technical, but we all have them constantly. A seeming is simply a conscious experience in which a proposition is presented to the subject as true—that is, a conscious experience with assertive propositional content. We call seemings "assertive" because they feel as though they are asserting something to be true of the world. In contrast, when you merely imagine that something is true, it doesn't feel as though the state of affairs being entertained is representative of the way things actually are. Thus, imagination lacks this assertive quality.[10]

Chisholm helpfully distinguished the epistemic sense of "seeming" from the comparative sense in which something looks the way such things typically look.[11] A stick in water, for instance, might seem bent in the comparative sense without it seeming epistemically that the stick is truly bent. In the epistemic sense of "seeming," it will not seem to the experienced rower that a submerged oar is bent (even if it looks that way in the comparative sense). Seemings, then, are not mere "looks" but rather the way things seem to us to be in reality.

Some suggest that seemings are reducible to beliefs or inclinations to believe.[12] But we think this reduction should be resisted.[13] First, seemings provide nontrivial explanations for our beliefs and inclinations to believe.[14] Seemings explain *why* we believe or are inclined to believe, and so cannot be identified with those beliefs or inclinations. Second, something can seem true without one believing (or feeling inclined to believe) that it's true, such as when you see a tree in passing but pay it no mind. There are also cases where seemings conflict. Say *p* seems true to you, but then, on the basis of expert testimony, you have a second experience in which *p* seems false. You will likely withhold judgment for at least a short time until you figure out how to resolve the conflict. But if seemings *just are* beliefs, we would have to uncharitably say that, while deliberating, you irrationally believe both *p* and not-*p*.

We also think, against some accounts,[15] that seemings must be distinguished from sensations. Typically, when we have sensations, they are accompanied by seemings. For instance, when I bite into an apple it might taste tart and, simultaneously, seem to me that it is tart. But the sensation and the seeming are distinct. An infant might have the very same sensations that an adult would have while looking at a picture above her crib, but it won't *seem* to her that there is a van Gogh print on the wall (as it would to an adult). Importantly, as we gain new concepts and background beliefs, we begin to experience the world in deeper ways. There is a sense in which art experts *see* more when viewing paintings. The expert has "thicker" experiences in which things seem to him to be the case that would never occur to the novice.

Seemings, then, are assertive experiences with propositional content.[16] On reflection, we think it apparent that most (really *all*) of our beliefs are based on the way things seem, at least somewhere down the line. What PC claims is that seemings can serve as the ultimate source of justification for those beliefs.

Consider now the notion of justification. Epistemic justification is an evaluative notion; that is, it involves an assessment or evaluation of our beliefs. There are two major schools of thought on justification: internalism and externalism. Roughly, internalists hold that epistemic justification rests on features the subject is or can be aware of. They evaluate whether your belief is fitting or sensible or permissible *given the information available to you*.[17] Externalists hold that justification largely depends on features of which the subject may be unaware, such as whether the belief is formed by an objectively reliable process or by properly functioning mental faculties.[18]

Say you were briefly abducted by aliens, who then wiped your memories and replaced them with false memories of a quiet evening at home. As a result, you believe that you spent yesterday evening reading a book by the fire. Given internalism, this belief is justified, since it best fits the information within your first-person perspective. Given externalism, this belief is likely unjustified, since it is unreliably formed and improperly caused.

PC is a thesis about internalist justification. It says that when something seems true to you, and you have no reason to think that this experience is misleading, then, from your perspective, it is sensible for you to believe it. Even if your experience is misleading, this does not affect the internal justification of your belief so long as this fact remains unknown to you.

It is also important to understand that PC is an internalist view of *justification* rather than a view of *knowledge*. Internalists (like ourselves) think internalist justification is necessary but insufficient for knowledge. Advocates of PC might even include accounts of virtue, reliability, and/ or proper function in their account of knowledge. But we think this focus on justification is crucial. While we can't control the nature of the external world (e.g., whether we live in Descartes's demon world), and hence we can't fully control whether we have knowledge, we can all do our level best to believe according to our evidence.

Having clarified the nature of internalist justification, PC can seem almost obvious. If something seems true and we genuinely have zero reason to doubt it, why should we be rationally prohibited from believing it—especially if we hold that belief provisionally and are open to correction? All that matters for internalist justification is whether, from the first-person perspective, it makes sense to believe something when it seems true and one has no reason to doubt it. In such conditions, we think belief is justified. After all, what else are we *supposed* to believe but what seems true from our perspective?[19]

Consider the alternative. If we cannot base belief on anything that seems true until we have first proven seeming to be reliable, then we will quickly find ourselves mired in skepticism. Any argument you could give for the reliability of one seeming would inevitably rely on other seemings; but you would need to give arguments for the reliability of *those* seemings, which would rely on further seemings, and so on. So, we must give the benefit of the doubt to at least some seemings.

Classical Evidentialists might suggest that we initially trust only those seemings whose content is incorrigible, or unmistakable in some way; all others must be proven reliable before we base beliefs on them. This would mean that only a few rational and introspective judgments could be properly basic. Alas, this too, we think, would result in pervasive skepticism about matters of common sense, both in principle and in fact. It would lead to skepticism *in principle* because, as we learned from the Early Moderns, there doesn't seem to be any good argument for things like the existence of the external world, the existence of other minds, the reality of the past, and so on, based solely on incorrigible judgments—at least, no such argument is good enough to justify the supreme level of confidence we place in those common-sense beliefs.

The Classical Evidentialist approach would also lead to skepticism *in fact* because, even if there is a good argument from incorrigible propositions for, say, the existence of the external world, ordinary people do not actually base their beliefs on this sort of argument. It just seems that there is an external world and people believe it. Indeed, many adults (not to mention toddlers) may not be able to even understand the argument, much less work it out for themselves. So, unless we are willing to embrace pervasive skepticism about matters of common sense, we must extend the benefit of the doubt to a wider variety of seemings. For instance, we must allow the perceptual seeming that there is an external world to immediately justify belief.

Putting aside the threat of skepticism, it seems arbitrary to give the benefit of the doubt to some seemings but not others, as Classical Evidentialism recommends. For instance, why would it be rational to trust introspective seemings without verifying their reliability but not other kinds of seemings? Introspective seemings may be incorrigible, but we do not *know* this to be true about introspective seemings until we have reflected on those experiences and intuited or argued for their incorrigibility; and, for the reasons described above, we cannot require this sort of reflective process prior to placing trust in those seemings on pain of total skepticism. So, any confirmation of the reliability of introspective seemings only comes *after* we have already placed our trust in them.

The fact of the matter is that we initially trust in the testimony of our introspective seemings for no other reason than that their content *feels true* to us. But all seemings have this same assertive phenomenal character, though often to a lesser degree. If that assertive character is sufficient to justify belief, absent defeaters, in the case of introspective seemings, then it should be sufficient to justify belief, absent defeaters, in the case of other seemings (albeit to a lesser degree). In a nutshell, if it is rational to believe in the content of some seemings just because that content feels true—something that must be the case if we are to rationally believe anything—then it should be rational to believe in the content of *any* seeming whose content similarly feels true. Thus, consistency demands that we trust all seemings to a degree proportional to the strength of their assertive phenomenal character. And this is just what PC maintains.

Common Objections to PC

PC, however, faces two obvious challenges. First, isn't PC too permissive? That is, doesn't PC allow all beliefs to be justified—even crazy beliefs—so long as they seem true to the subject? Well, PC is undoubtedly more permissive than some theories of justification. It allows a wide variety of beliefs to be noninferentially justified. But why think that justification is difficult to obtain? Outright irrationality is surely less common than partisan talking heads claim. Indeed, we think it an advantage that, on PC, two equally intelligent and thoughtful individuals might rationally disagree about an issue. Sometimes perfectly reasonable disagreements arise because (given differences in genetics, environment, past experiences, current beliefs, and a host of other factors) people experience the world in different ways. An adequate theory of justification should, like PC, acknowledge this fact.

But couldn't belief in a flat earth be justified by PC so long as earth seems flat to the believer? Well, yes and no. If it were truly the case that the world seemed flat to some tribesman in the middle of nowhere—a person with no contact with modern science and who is focused on gathering food to survive each day—then, sure, perhaps that tribesman could have a justified false belief in a flat earth. Why should we expect him to hold beliefs from *our* perspective rather than his own? Similarly, only the hardest of the hard-hearted would judge a child's belief in Santa Claus epistemically unjustified when every adult she trusts tells her that Santa brings gifts on Christmas Eve. Her justification, we insist, depends on the information *she* possesses.

However, it would be very difficult for someone in our society to justifiably believe in a flat earth, since they are extremely likely to be aware of defeaters for that view (e.g., pictures from outer space, scientists' testimony). Far from troubling PC, this objection highlights the fact that PC rightly acknowledges the perspectival nature of rationality. What we are rational in believing isn't some fixed set of beliefs but depends on the information we possess at a given time. PC gets exactly the right answer, then: we'd be unjustified, but the tribesman might be justified, in believing in a flat earth.

A second objection arises from the growing awareness that our perceptions of reality can be heavily influenced by nonrational factors. How can PC claim that beliefs based on seemings are innocent until proven guilty if seemings can stem from wishful thinking, confirmation bias, or eating spicy peppers? The worry is that our seemings can be "tainted" by these nonrational factors and rendered incapable of justifying belief. This is known as the cognitive penetration objection.[20]

While it may appear strong at first, we think this objection is ultimately mistaken. As we've already indicated, given the perspectival nature of rationality, what matters for justification is the evidence one possesses—not evidence from a third-person perspective. So long as S is not aware that the reason it seems to him that p is because of wishful thinking, then this has no bearing on S's justification for believing p. But if S knows that the reason it seems to him that p is wishful thinking, then S has a defeater and is not justified in believing that p.[21] To turn the question around: if it strongly seems to S that p, and S is unaware of the tainted source of this seeming, then wouldn't it be irrational for S to flout his experience and fail to believe p?

Far from revealing flaws, then, these objections showcase how PC gives just the right answers vis-à-vis permissiveness and cognitive penetration.

Theism and Noninferential Justification

We argue that PC shows that many theistic beliefs are likely justified. (Christian belief specifically will be the focus of a later section.) The story here will sound very much like the one Reformed Epistemologists typically tell. There are numerous people to whom it seems God exists when they are out in nature, when they pray, in their moments of joy and sorrow.[22] Indeed, it is not uncommon for believers to undergo periods of time in which God's existence appears woven into the very fabric of existence—they see His fingerprints everywhere. In these moments, God's existence can seem nearly as apparent as the existence of other human beings. The very idea of a world without God feels absurd. In accordance with PC, these theistic seemings provide noninferential justification for believing that God exists.[23] Defeaters (discussed more in the next section) can arise, which removes this justification. But until they do, such believers appear well within their epistemic rights to believe that God exists, even if they are mistaken.[24] What else are they supposed to believe in light of their experiences?

Of course, not everyone finds God's existence so apparent. Some have tried to turn this into an objection to theism, called "the problem of divine hiddenness," arguing that there wouldn't be any reasonable doubt about God's existence if theism were true. There are convincing objections to this line of reasoning that are independent of (but also available to) PC. For example, at most we have evidence for the *temporary* hiddenness of God, and there are plenty of ways that temporary periods of nonbelief might prepare people to submit to God or help them grow in His likeness. But PC may offer some special insight here. Given PC, it is natural to think that what is reasonable for someone to believe is largely (if not entirely) a function of what seems true to him; but what seems to be the case can be influenced significantly by both communal and individual resistance to God.[25] Such resistance might prevent God's existence from being apparent, or even make God seem silly or absurd.[26] In this case, the nonbeliever is reasonable—his nonbelief is in accordance with what seems true to him—and yet things only seem thusly because of human sin. In those cases, the obstacle to reasonable belief would be located in human freedom, not in God.

There are many nonbelievers today. Still, the number of people with theistic seemings across times, places, and cultures is striking. Why does it seem to so many people that God exists?[27] Notice first that the experiences that produce theistic seemings tend to have a rational structure. It isn't as though theistic seemings are produced whenever one sees yard kitsch or has indigestion. Rather, theistic seemings tend to be produced by experiences that, on some level, objectively appear to support God's existence. For instance, it may seem to one that God exists when he observes exquisite design or gratuitous beauty in nature, or when he thinks about why anything at all exists (even if he doesn't know terms like "contingency"). It makes sense to posit, then, that (many) theistic seemings result when the subject tacitly grasps the ways in which features of the world support God's existence.[28]

Studies by cognitive and developmental psychologists appear to show that we are built to notice signs of agency, and so will automatically come to believe in God at a very young age.[29] We seem to be built with mental modules or pathways along which we naturally think. These make it easy and natural for us to see the world as designed, as the product of intelligent agency rather than mindless forces. Our natural tendency to draw these sorts of logical connections can be thought of as a kind of cognitive mechanism or faculty, sometimes called the "*sensus divinitatis.*"[30] While some have sought to argue that our natural tendency toward theism means religious belief is a trick of our evolved brains, what the science really shows is that we are built for it to seem to us like God exists.[31] Isn't this exactly the way God would build us if He wanted us to be aware of Him and hold justified beliefs about His existence?

Usually, subjects only recognize the support for God on a tacit level. Cognitive science tells us that we are quite adept at this sort of subconscious processing, especially when it comes to detecting signs of agency.[32] Thus, the subject is not making any sort of conscious inference or argument. Nevertheless, the logical connections that one intuitively grasps are the sorts of things that, if consciously articulated, would construct theistic arguments.

This marks a point of contrast between our view and Plantinga-style Reformed Epistemology. Like us, Plantinga posits the existence of a *sensus divinitatis*, but unlike us, the structure of the world is only accidentally involved in triggering the *sensus divinitatis*. As Plantinga writes, "the experience is the *occasion* for the formation of the beliefs in question."[33] If our experiences only serve as occasions for the formation of theistic belief, and nothing more, then there is no in-principle reason why *any* kind of experience—such as the experience of yawning or tying one's shoes—couldn't trigger the *sensus divinitatis*. In contrast, in our view, the experiences of the world that reveal God to us bear an *evidential* relation to God (à la Rom. 1:18-20), not merely a *causal* relation to theistic belief.

Plantinga's conception of the *sensus divinitatis* seems to be that of a special religious faculty—a mechanism that is designed to produce exclusively theistic beliefs and that wouldn't exist if God didn't.[34] Positing a special religious faculty runs contrary to the findings of cognitive science of religion, which suggest that belief in God typically results from standard kinds of cognitive mechanisms. Our view, on the other hand, models theistic belief as arising from standard cognitive abilities that are independently confirmed through reflection and cognitive science. It thus avoids the appearance of special pleading and harmonizes well with this growing body of research.

What is especially exciting is that the Phenomenal Conservative approach offers us the above advantages while retaining what is best about Plantinga-style Reformed Epistemology. Plantinga was concerned to show how ordinary believers might reasonably hold religious beliefs even though they do not know the ins and outs of classical theistic arguments.[35] Their beliefs could, Plantinga argued, have positive epistemic status even without arguments. We think that this is exactly right, and PC successfully captures this fact.[36]

Often, however, Plantinga went well beyond claiming that theistic beliefs could have positive epistemic status without *arguments*; he implied that theistic beliefs could have positive epistemic status even without *evidence*.

Along with Classical Evidentialism, we think this a mistake. We think a broader and more humane understanding of evidence than that offered by many evidentialists is what is missing. It is not only arguments but experiences that constitute evidence.[37]

In this way, PC gives us the best of both worlds vis-à-vis Reformed Epistemology and Classical Evidentialism. Classical Evidentialism was right to emphasize the role of evidence in epistemic justification but wrong to insist that, in the case of theistic belief, this evidence must consist in arguments. Reformed Epistemology was right in its insistence that ordinary theistic beliefs might be noninferentially justified but wrong to detach this justification from evidence. PC, then, incorporates the best of both views and leaves their weaknesses behind.

Theism and Inferential Justification

It is important to see that PC is a principle of *prima facie* justification.[38] It claims that seemings justify, all other things being equal. So even if God's existence seems apparent, this can't be the end of the story—at least for most ordinary people in our culture—as theists will almost inevitably encounter all manner of potential defeaters. You don't have to be an academic to wonder how a good God could allow children to suffer, whether theism can be reconciled with contemporary science, and so on. Such challenges, if left unanswered, can be enough to defeat the noninferential justification provided by one's theistic seemings. Thus, mature theists will likely need to address such questions in order to achieve secure, sustainable justification for their beliefs.[39]

Now, the defeaters one encounters are not always that sophisticated, and hence one's defeater-defeaters don't always need to be that sophisticated either. We shouldn't pretend that everyone is (or should be) an academic. But neither should we naively think that a one-off seeming that God exists can and should carry one's theistic belief fully justified throughout adulthood. The mature theist will likely need to build up a coherent and mutually supporting system of beliefs around her theism in order to remain justified.

Building up a worldview is something we rational creatures do naturally. We wonder at the world, and this leads us to gather evidence about its various features. Since God's existence bears on nearly everything, the theist will frequently need to assess how this evidence fits with theism. This process typically plays out over a considerable period of time, moving in fits and spurts. How exactly this process unfolds and what comes of it will depend greatly on the specific individual.

On the micro-level, the theist will focus in on specific items of evidence (other things that seem true) and evaluate how well theism explains that evidence. We suspect that the ordinary theist will find numerous instances in which her observations are explained especially well by theism. Perhaps the theist has witnessed a remarkable transformation in her own life and in the lives of others that is hard to make sense of apart from God. Perhaps the theist feels in herself a deep yearning for something beyond this world and judges this yearning best explained by God. Or, if she is more philosophically minded, she might find that her belief in objective morality fits better with theism than with naturalism, or that theism better explains the existence of contingent beings. In such instances, the individual gains inferential support for her theistic belief.

One source of inferential justification worth emphasizing is testimony. Testimony provides inferential support for its content if one has evidence for the reliability of the testifier—be it a person, organization, or sacred text.[40] Obviously, this evidence of reliability *can* take the form of arguments, but, given PC, it needn't. As Dougherty argues,[41] an appearance of credibility in the testifier is enough to provide support for the content of that testimony. Thus, if one hears testimony of God's existence (from one's parents, the Church, the Bible, etc.), and the source seems credible, then one will have additional support for theism, absent defeaters.

There may also be times when theism seems to fit poorly with other things that seem true. These are potential defeaters. In these moments, the theist must assess, first, whether there is any genuine discord between theism and what seems true, and, if there is, whether it is more reasonable to live with the poor fit, alter beliefs in those areas of discord, or abandon theism. In any case, the support for theism is diminished to some degree.

These small-scale evaluations aid the subject in making a single large-scale evaluation of which worldview, or system of beliefs, best makes sense of her experiences on the whole. We seem to be built to make exactly these sorts of macro-level judgments about where the weight of probability lies.[42] Making these sorts of evaluations needn't be an overly formal (or fully conscious) process. As we noted earlier with regard to the origins of theistic seemings, we are quite adept at drawing logical connections on a tacit level. What the subject will experience is the impression that the theistic belief system, and the picture of the world that it represents, just makes sense.

Thus, if all goes well for theism (which is not guaranteed), the mature theist will be left with a coherent system of beliefs centered around her theism that, overall, seems to make better sense of reality than the relevant alternatives. As a result, her theism will no longer be justified solely by her initial theistic seeming. Her theistic belief will also receive a measure of inferential support by virtue of its presence in this explanatorily virtuous belief system.

The theism of mature believers, then, will likely enjoy both inferential and noninferential support. This inferential support is, in many cases, subsequent and complementary to one's noninferential justification. Hence, one can start from a position of noninferential justification and then secure or bolster one's justified beliefs with further inferential support. In the end, theistic belief may be justified before the possession of inferential support but typically not without it.

The typical adult theist is thus armed not merely with a bare theistic seeming but with a larger worldview in which God is deeply entrenched. This makes the robust nature of most theistic beliefs—even in the face of counterargument—intelligible. At times atheists have written as though ordinary theists are unjustified if they don't have a sophisticated response to some atheistic argument. But we think this a mistake given the way that our belief networks hang together in a complicated fashion. Many mature theists, we believe, are justified not by a killer argument but by the interlocking belief network they've built up.

What about intelligent, informed people who come to a different conclusion? Should the existence of such individuals make theists abandon their worldview? We don't think so. The issue is too complicated to fully flesh out here, but we will note a few things. First, for a host of reasons, people experience the world in different ways. No two perspectives are exactly alike. Thus, PC leads us to expect reasonable disagreement on complicated issues like the existence of God. Endorsing theism commits you to thinking that atheists are mistaken, but it doesn't require you to think that they are stupid or irrational. Perhaps they just have different experiences. Second, a fully worked out theistic belief system (especially a Christian one) will usually contain some explanation for why people have misleading experiences. As we said earlier, communal or personal resistance to God might distort one's perspective on the world. Lastly, even if there is no forthcoming explanation for why some people see the world differently, it is not clear that one should therefore withhold trust from one's own perspective. Take some horrifying account of child abuse from the news. It seems obvious that those who perpetrate such abuse have done something objectively wrong, and yet there are intelligent people who genuinely disagree. It seems to them that what is occurring is distasteful to Western sentiments—highly unfashionable in present society—but not objectively wrong. Even if we were at a loss as to why their perspective is distorted, it appears reasonable for us to continue to endorse what seems supremely evident to us: that such abuse is objectively wrong.[43] Rationality does not demand that we automatically abandon the obvious just because others, for unknown reasons, cannot see it. Peer disagreement should give us pause, but it does not force one to relinquish theistic belief.[44]

Beyond Theism to Christian Faith

Much of what we have said about theism will apply with minimal changes to Christian belief. If Christian doctrine seems true (either of its own accord or because of the special work of the Holy Spirit), then, given PC, one will possess noninferential justification for believing it, absent defeaters. Of course, the Christian will also need to go through a worldview-building process similar to the theist, and (assuming all goes well for Christianity) thereby supplement his belief with inferential support.

On our version of the Phenomenal Conservative approach, whether a religious belief is justified ultimately comes down to whether it is, on balance, supported by what seems true. The two-fold process we've described thus far bears this out: first, look at whether the religious proposition itself seems true (and to what extent), and, second, look at how it fits with other things that seem true. But what seems true to an individual is not a static thing. One's perspective can change quite radically over time. What seemed apparent at one stage can seem ridiculous at another, and vice versa.

Now, a deep commitment to theism or Christianity can't help but affect the way one views the world. After taking a course in psychology, for instance, you may begin to view ordinary interactions through the lens of various psychological theories—identifying confirmation of these theories in ways that would otherwise have gone unnoticed. Just so, the believer may find newfound appreciation for the ways in which Christian revelation makes sense of things. More generally, the believer will begin to experience the world in light of her religious framework. Some people watch a nature documentary and say, "Nature's powers are more amazing than I thought!" But the Christian might instead perceive God's handiwork.

Some see tragedy and decry the world's indifference. But the believer might see an opportunity to be God's hands and feet and help those in need. This perspective-shift can be pervasive, systematically reorienting how one sees the world.

Though confirmation bias is always a worry, there's nothing inherently irrational about a belief influencing one's perspective in the way we've described. Your perceptual seemings, for instance, are completely saturated by belief in the external world. When you look around you, it doesn't seem that there are certain arrangements of color sensations, but rather that there are objects—books, furniture, buildings—existing within a mind-independent world. A primary purpose of education is to help us see the world in light of new concepts. That said, it is important to reflect critically on our experiences, questioning whether our newfound perspective is accurate. If such reflection only confirms the reliability of one's perspective, then what else is one to do but continue to trust it?

The ability to see God in the world can seemingly be honed through prayer and practice, aided by grace (Eph. 1:15-19). In the Christian tradition, believers are told to pray unceasingly (1 Thess. 5:17), to have the mind of Christ (Phil. 2:5), to reason out of spiritual maturity (1 Cor. 13:11), and to be transformed by this renewal of their minds (Rom. 12:2). That is, Christians are told to think like God in all they do—to view the world the way He does—and let this transform their lives. If Christianity is true, there is a kind of intellectual virtue involved here—a habit of thinking in line with the truth, conforming our minds to reality, of seeing the world as it actually is with respect to God. Possessing this disposition seems like part of what it is to have Christian faith.[45]

If faith involves this sort of shift in perspective, then faith has the potential to bolster the justification for one's religious beliefs. Remember that, in our approach, justification depends on whether the position itself seems true and whether it fits with whatever else seems true. By helping one see the world in light of Christian truth-claims, faith increases one's justification for holding these positions.[46] This adds a new layer of meaning to C. S. Lewis's profession, "I believe in Christianity as I believe that the Sun has risen, not only because I see it, but because by it I see everything else."[47]

This way of thinking about faith is quite different from the popular misconception of faith, described by Mark Twain as "believing what you know ain't so." Based on something like this misconception, Huemer, the father of PC, thinks of religious beliefs as being at odds with the justification conferred via PC. Huemer is worried about a blind leap of faith in which it seems to S that not-p, but because of the teaching of some religious authority (the Scriptures or the Magisterium) S believes p.[48]

We agree that believing against what seems true is a great way to have unjustified beliefs. However, Huemer fails to understand the perspective of the typical believer. Because of her faith in the religious authority, which the believer normally has reason to trust, there is typically no conflict between the believer's seemings and the religious teaching. The teaching (like all education) affects the very way she sees the world. For instance, when she prays or worships, it is not usually the case that it seems to her that God is absent and then she must will to believe that He is present. Rather, the spiritually minded person just sees God as present in the first place.[49]

We have been focusing on the intellectual dimensions of faith thus far, but one must remember that Christian faith goes beyond seemings and beliefs— after all, even the demons believe (Jas 2:19).[50] Faith, as we understand it, involves a disposition (by grace) to trust and commit one's entire self to God. It is typically a commitment in the direction of one's theistic evidence and is thus in concert with reason: grace building on nature. But it is a comprehensive commitment—not only epistemic but also affective and volitional. As in a marriage, it is a commitment of the entire person to the beloved, holding nothing back; it is a total self-gift.[51] This comes with a commitment to action: to deepen one's relationship with God, to live life in light of this commitment to God.

People with such intimate faith can find it difficult to talk about "evidence" for God. That language can feel cold and reductionistic. They think they see God and experience Him every day. If we started talking to you about the evidence for your best friend's existence, you might see it as beside the point.[52] This is how many people of faith feel. They know the person of Christ, and so talk of evidence can seem inappropriate. Their confidence is so strong, their experience so overwhelming, that academic arguments and evidence seem irrelevant.

As we have sought to show, however, they have evidence nonetheless: the noninferential evidence of the way things seem to them as well as their (likely) inferential evidence in the way of a large-scale explanatory judgment that God's existence makes the most sense of the totality of their experience. Evidence in this sense is a natural companion to the kind of personal knowledge of God that the person of faith enjoys. Therefore, seeking evidence for God and seeking relationship with him are not only compatible but mutually reinforcing. This has been so not only in our academic work but also in our personal lives.

Notes

1. Classical Evidentialism would also maintain that these arguments must be founded on propositions that are incorrigible.
2. This position is called "foundationalism." The alternatives to foundationalism are infinitism, which says that justification requires an infinite regress of beliefs, and coherentism, which drops the linear conception of justification altogether and says that individual beliefs are justified by virtue of their presence in a coherent belief structure. See Peter D. Klein, "Human Knowledge and the Infinite Regress of Reasons," *Noûs* 33 (1999): 297–325, and BonJour, *The Structure of Empirical Knowledge* for classic defenses of infinitism and coherentism, respectively.
3. There are those who disagree. For an explanationist response to skepticism see Jonathan Vogel, "Cartesian Skepticism and Inference to the Best Explanation," *The Journal of Philosophy* 87, no. 11 (1990): 658–66.
4. On the history of this tradition see especially Roderick M. Chisholm, *Theory of Knowledge*, 1st ed. (Englewood Cliffs, NJ: Prentice-Hall, 1966); Logan Paul Gage, "Objectivity and Subjectivity in Epistemology: A Defense of the Phenomenal Conception of Evidence" (Ph.D. diss., Baylor University, 2014), chap. 4, and concerning Reid, Blake McAllister, "Re-Evaluating Reid's Response to Skepticism," *Journal of Scottish Philosophy* 14, no. 3 (2016): 317–39.
5. Michael Huemer, "Compassionate Phenomenal Conservatism," *Philosophy and Phenomenological Research* 74, no. 1 (2007): 30–55; This version of PC is slight (but importantly) revised from Michael Huemer, *Skepticism and the Veil of Perception* (Lanham, MD: Rowman & Littlefield, 2001).
6. For recent defenses of experience as evidence, see Gage, "Objectivity and Subjectivity in Epistemology"; Logan Paul Gage, "Can Experience Fulfill the Many Roles of Evidence?," *Quaestiones Disputatae* 8, no. 2 (2018): 87–111.
7. It is good that PC does not require this, for typically one lacks any second-order belief about oneself seeing a tree.
8. Notice that it could seem to you that there is a tree without you actually forming the belief that there is a tree. For this reason, PC is a principle of propositional justification rather than doxastic justification. That is, you have justification for believing p regardless of whether you in fact come to believe p.
9. In fact, one formulation of such a principle we like avoids potentially confusing justification language altogether: "(Reasons Commonsensism): If it seems to S that p, then S thereby has a pro tanto reason for believing p." Trent Dougherty, "Further Epistemological Considerations Concerning Skeptical Theism," *Faith and Philosophy* 28, no. 3 (2011): 333.

10. Huemer, *Skepticism and the Veil of Perception*, 77–9; Chris Tucker, "Why Open-Minded People Should Endorse Dogmatism," *Philosophical Perspectives* 24, no. 1 (2010): 530.

11. Roderick Chisholm, *Perceiving: A Philosophical Study* (Ithaca, NY: Cornell University Press, 1957), 44–7.

12. Richard Swinburne, *Epistemic Justification* (Oxford: Oxford University Press, 2001), 135–51; Jason Rogers and Jonathan Matheson, "Bergmann's Dilemma: Exit Strategies for Internalists," *Philosophical Studies* 152, no. 1 (2011): 55–80.

13. See Blake McAllister, "Seemings as Sui Generis," *Synthese* 195, no. 7 (2018): 3079–96 for a more complete presentation of the reasons to resist reduction.

14. Huemer, "Compassionate Phenomenal Conservatism."

15. William Tolhurst, "Seemings," *American Philosophical Quarterly* 35, no. 3 (1998): 293–302; Huemer, *Skepticism and the Veil of Perception*, 58–79.

16. Andrew Cullison, "What Are Seemings?," *Ratio* 23, no. 3 (2010): 260–74 thinks of seemings as *sui generis* "propositional attitudes." We prefer to talk of "experiences" because we do not want to give the impression that seemings are judgments, choices, or things we endorse. Seemings tend to be much more passive than this.

17. One should not assume with Alvin Plantinga, *Warrant: The Current Debate* (Oxford: Oxford University Press, 1993), 15; that internalist epistemic justification is deontological (involving praise and blame). Leading proponents of internalism like Conee and Feldman, *Evidentialism*, 61–4, deny that the view of justification they have in mind is deontic.

18. The most important externalist critique of internalism in recent years is Michael Bergmann, *Justification without Awareness: A Defense of Epistemic Externalism* (Oxford: Oxford University Press, 2006). For a recent reply from a PC perspective, see Logan Paul Gage, "Phenomenal Conservatism and the Subject's Perspective Objection," *Acta Analytica* 31, no. 1 (2016): 43–58.

19. See Huemer, *Skepticism and the Veil of Perception*, 104–5; and Matthew McGrath, "Phenomenal Conservatism and Cognitive Penetration: The 'Bad Basis' Counterexamples," in *Seemings and Justification: New Essays on Dogmatism and Phenomenal Conservatism*, ed. Christopher Tucker (Oxford: Oxford University Press, 2013), 226 for similar arguments. Perhaps the most extended articulation of this general line of thinking is in McAllister, "Seemings as Sui Generis."

20. It has also been referred to as the "tainted source" or "bad basis" objection, Chris Tucker, *Seemings and Justification: New Essays on Dogmatism and Phenomenal Conservatism* (Oxford: Oxford University Press, 2013), 12–16.

21. We should always be watchful for and responsive to indications that our experiences have been skewed by such nonrational factors. By no means does PC say we should dogmatically cling to our beliefs.

22. If we're being precise, it more often seems to people that God loves them or that he has forgiven them of their sins—things which obviously entail God's existence.

23. It is also possible, of course, to have strong seemings that God does not exist and thus to be epistemically justified in holding atheistic beliefs. See Trent Dougherty, "The Common Sense Problem of Evil," n.d.

24. This is a point of contrast with most versions of Reformed Epistemology, which pin the justification of basic theistic beliefs on the reliability and design of the faculty producing them and, so in turn, on the existence of God.

25. The role of communal sin is, we think, underplayed in these discussions. The rejection of truth by a few can easily infect the perspectives of the many by becoming a part of the dominant cultural narrative.

26. An interesting possibility here is that the fallen perspective may fail to appreciate the myriad ways in which God best explains the world around us. Thus, the evidence for God would be available in an objective sense, but one would fail to draw the relevant connections between those things and God. This resembles an idea suggested by Pierre Rousselot, *The Eyes of Faith* (New York: Fordham University Press, 1990).

27. The story we give here is not entailed by PC. We think it plausible and fitting, however.

28. Blake McAllister and Trent Dougherty, "Reforming Reformed Epistemology: A New Take on the Sensus Divinitatis," *Religious Studies* (2018) 1–21.

29. Justin Barrett, *Why Would Anyone Believe in God?* (Lanham, MD: Altamira, 2004).

30. The concept of a *sensus divinitatis*, in its most general sense, just seems to be that of a general cognitive faculty whereby we secure noninferential justification for belief in God's existence and basic divine attributes.

31. Michael Murray and Jeffrey Schloss, eds., *The Believing Primate: Scientific, Philosophical, and Theological Reflections on the Origin of Religion* (Oxford: Oxford University Press, 2009).

32. Barrett, *Why Would Anyone Believe in God?*

33. Plantinga, *Warranted Christian Belief*, 259.

34. Ibid., 187.

35. Plantinga, *Warranted Christian Belief*.

36. Furthermore, PC captures this fact without going overboard in the opposite direction. Plantingian Reformed Epistemology appeared to give arguments little role in the justification of theistic belief. This is odd. Surely arguments

have *some* significant role to play in the justification of theistic belief. Our approach allows noninferentially justified theistic belief while still ascribing an important role to arguments in the formation of those beliefs, as well as in their long-term justification (see the following section on the latter point).

37. We think, however, that Plantinga's project could be modified and ultimately harmonized with our view. See especially Chris Tucker, "Phenomenal Conservatism and Evidentialism in Religious Epistemology," in *Evidence and Religious Belief*, ed. Kelly James Clark and Raymond VanArragon (Oxford: Oxford University Press, 2011), 52–73; McAllister and Dougherty, "Reforming Reformed Epistemology."

38. We actually prefer the phrase *pro tanto*, because *prima facie* might lead one to think that when a defeater arises the initial belief was never justified in the first place. In reality, as the *pro tanto* language indicates, a defeater that arises later in time doesn't show one's initial belief never to have been justified but only outweighed at that later time.

39. Reformed epistemologists are starting to acknowledge this as well. See Andrew Moon, "How to Use Cognitive Faculties You Never Knew You Had," *Pacific Philosophical Quarterly* 99 (2018): 251–75.

40. Given PC, there is a sense in which testimony can operate noninferentially— by occasioning in the recipient a seeming in the content of the testimony— but we will leave that aside here.

41. Trent Dougherty, "Faith, Trust, and Testimony: An Evidentialist Account," in *Religious Faith and Intellectual Virtue*, ed. Laura Frances Callahan and Timothy O'Connor (Oxford: Oxford University Press, 2014), 97–123.

42. John Henry Newman, *An Essay in Aid of a Grammar of Assent*, reprint ed. (Notre Dame, IN: University of Notre Dame Press, 1992).

43. Alvin Plantinga, "Pluralism: A Defense of Religious Exclusivism," in *The Rationality of Belief and the Plurality of Faith: Essays in Honor of William P. Alston*, ed. Thomas Senor (Ithaca, NY: Cornell University Press, 1995), 181–2.

44. For a recent treatment of how PC might handle cases of peer disagreement, see Logan Paul Gage, "Evidence and What We Make of It," *Southwest Philosophy Review* 30, no. 2 (2014): 89–99.

45. Blake McAllister, "The Perspective of Faith: Its Nature and Epistemic Implications," *American Catholic Philosophical Quarterly* (2018).

46. For more on the epistemic implications of faith, see ibid.

47. C. S. Lewis, *The Weight of Glory*, reprint ed. (New York: Macmillan, 1996), 106.

48. Huemer, *Skepticism and the Veil of Perception*, 109–10.

49. Ibid., 109, considers the case in which a Catholic (or other high church member) receives the Eucharist. Huemer appears to think that the believer

has the seeming that the consecrated host is bread but believes against this seeming because of religious teaching. Huemer appears to be confusing the two senses of "seems" distinguished by Chisholm (above). The faithful Catholic sees the host as the body of Christ made present. (N.B.: Huemer may also be confused about Catholic teaching. There cannot be a conflict between the way the host looks and the fact that it seems to the believer to be the body of Christ since the Catholic Church teaches that the accidents [all the looks] of the bread remain post-transubstantiation.)

50. As Aquinas notes, the act of faith reaches beyond propositions and to the realities expressed propositionally by the articles of faith, Thomas Aquinas, *Summa Theologica* II-II.1.2.

51. Karol Wojtyla, *Love and Responsibility*, reprint ed. (San Francisco: Ignatius Press, 1993).

52. J. L. Austin, *Sense and Sensibilia* (Oxford: Oxford University Press, 1962), 115.

A Classical Evidentialist Response to PC

John M. DePoe

Gage and McAllister's account of PC as religious epistemology is lucid and personally engaging. I concur with their rejection of externalist approaches to epistemology, since these theories offer nothing to satiate the epistemic subject's perspective in ascertaining the truth of one's beliefs. Despite having some common ground, I have some serious misgivings about PC. My primary concern with PC is that it fails to provide a theory of justification that satisfies an objective connection to truth, but I also believe that it carries other liabilities.

Are Seemings Connected to Truth?

Do seemings provide any intrinsic, nonarbitrary connection to truth for the beliefs that they accompany? I don't see any reason to think that these psychological states inherently provide any link to true beliefs. It is possible, after all, to have false beliefs that seem true. Seemings, in and of themselves, have no tie to truth. For instance, I cannot reliably determine whether a painting is a forgery or the testimony of an eyewitness is true just by trusting what seems to be the case to me.

Not only do seemings fail to indicate true beliefs consistently, but seemings also often accompany false beliefs. A person on a jury might immediately form the belief that the defendant on trial is guilty solely on the grounds that "he seems guilty." Or an interviewer may decide that a new job applicant who has just walked into the room is unfit for the position just because "she seems like the kind of person we don't want for the position." In these cases, seemings are formed without any awareness of independently good reasons for thinking that the belief is true. Even after carefully attending to the entire trial, a juror may cast a guilty vote with nothing more to support his decision than that the defendant seemed guilty (supposing he judges the cases of the prosecution and the defense to be equal). Should we take that juror's seeming as evidence that tips the scales for appropriately believing that the defendant is guilty? That strikes me as paradigmatic reckless epistemology! Yet, it is licensed by PC since seemings have to be given intrinsic evidential weight. Indeed, Gage and McAllister have indicated that they find such epistemic practices are entirely admissible according to their account.

Since seemings inherently are neither reliably tethered to true beliefs nor are they averse to false beliefs, it implies that these psychological states cannot possess the intrinsic truth-indicative character that PC requires. Taken by themselves, seemings have no penchant for truth or aversion for falsehood. Consequently, a system of beliefs founded only upon seemings will have no objective connection to truth and thereby is not a sound theory of epistemic justification.

Another View of Seemings

There is another way to think about seemings as psychological states that is far more appealing in my view. Instead of taking seemings as psychological states with primary epistemic significance, seemings should be understood as secondary psychological states that have been caused by other epistemically significant factors. Consider that presently it seems to me that PC is false. This psychological state is not a self-defeating paradox. My seeming is not an epistemic state, but it is the psychological product of my mind when I contemplate my reasons for rejecting PC. Seemings by themselves do not carry evidential force, but sometimes (when they are caused by one's appreciation of a belief's evidence) what is strongly evidenced causes a person to experience its seeming to be true. My hunch is that what misleads many to think that seemings should be given some evidential significance is the conflation of seemings as primary epistemic states carrying intrinsic evidential significance with seemings that are secondary states caused by one's awareness of strong reasons to accept that a belief is true. Just because sometimes seemings are caused by one's awareness of good reasons to believe something is true, it does not mean that seemings themselves are good reasons to believe something is true.

On my alternative account of seemings, they are psychological states that can result from many different causes. Sometimes they are caused by other psychological states that are sensitively tuned to truth (e.g., awareness of good reasons); other times, they can be caused by psychological states that are indifferent to truth (e.g., prejudice and wishful thinking). For this reason, we should not look to seemings as the primary source of justification. Rather, we should look to the underlying causes of seemings to determine whether they have any epistemic significance. It is a backward epistemic theory that advises that what seems to be true is justified. The proper role of an epistemic theory is to provide evaluative principles that determine when a person is justified in believing what seems to be true or when a person should believe what does not seem to be true. Simply conferring some degree of epistemic justification on all seemings without some account of how these psychological states have an intrinsic connection to truth constitutes a theory of justification where the basic source of justification is groundless.

Conceptual Circularity

PC also fails to provide a robust theory of epistemic justification because it defines epistemic justification circularly.[1] Advocates of PC define epistemic justification as occurring when a belief seems to be the case to a person and the person has no defeaters for this belief. The circularity emerges when we unpack what is meant by the no-defeaters requirement. Defeaters are propositions that count against a belief's being justified. Defeaters must have some *justified* epistemic standing since only those beliefs that carry some evidential significance should disqualify a belief from being justified. In essence, then, Gage and McAllister have defined epistemic justification as occurring when a belief seems to be the case to a person and when there is no other proposition that the person is *justified* in believing that counts against it. Since they must rely upon the concept of justification to state their definition of justification, their definition is circular. Alternatively, they could accept that defeaters are not required to have justified epistemic standing, but such a liberal view of defeaters would invite more serious difficulties.

PC and Theism

In their application of PC to belief in God, Gage and McAllister claim to have captured the best of Classical Evidentialism and Reformed Epistemology by crafting a view that requires evidence for theism without necessarily employing arguments. If PC fails to meet the objective truth-connection requirement, however, then PC is no better than Reformed Epistemology in providing a person with reasons to believe theism. For example, suppose a person has carefully considered many arguments for and against theism and judges that the arguments for both positions carry equal evidential force, yet this person is nonetheless struck by its seeming to be the case that God exists. Should we conclude that this person is epistemically justified in believing that God exists? Answering affirmatively entails that this person's experience of seeming adds to his evidence for theism. Yet, for this state of seeming to count as evidence for theism, it would require that the state itself is intrinsically connected to the truth of theism. A person's being struck by its seeming that God exists (without any accompanying reasons), however, does not provide any objective evidence of God's existence. For instance, if a person claims to believe that the Great Pumpkin will return on Halloween solely on the grounds that it seems true (and when pressed this person cannot find an inkling of a deeper reason), then it is hard to see what this person's psychological state has to do with its being true. We certainly wouldn't allow these sorts of seemings to justify beliefs about renaissance history or molecular biology.

Finally, in my experience, it is evidence that must curtail the way things seem in religion. It often seems to me that there is no God or that God can have no moral justification for many of the evils in this world. I must cling to evidence and reason to remain steadfast in my theism if I do not wish to be carried away by the unfounded seemings that commend atheism to me. Thank God seemings are not a source of epistemic justification!

Since seemings do not intrinsically carry evidential force, PC cannot provide the happy compromise that Gage and McAllister propose between Classical Evidentialism and Reformed Epistemology. In trying to split the difference, Gage and McAllister's PC has failed to produce a religious epistemology that relates one's subjective assurance to an objective connection to truth.

Note

1. Richard A. Fumerton, "Epistemic Conservatism: Theft or Honest Toil," in *Oxford Studies in Epistemology*, ed. Tamar S. Gendler and John Hawthorne, vol. 2 (Oxford: Oxford University Press, 2007), 80–1.

A Proper Functionalist Response to PC

Tyler Dalton McNabb

Logan Gage and Blake MacAllister attempt to offer a "centrist" epistemological position of sorts. While they agree with the Reformed Epistemologist that belief in God needn't be based on argument, they also agree with the Classical Foundationalist that, in order for a belief to be justified, the belief needs to be based on evidence. The idea being that, we shouldn't see evidence as equivalent or reducible to an argument. Instead, Gage and MacAllister endorse that, in light of there being no defeaters, epistemic seemings are sufficient to count as good evidence for rationally believing a proposition.

It is easy to see how one would apply PC to religious belief. If due to a seeming, *S* believes that God exists and *S* lacks a defeater for this belief, then *S* is *prima facie* justified in believing that God exists. The same sort of move can be made to argue for how Christian belief can be justified. Far from disagreeing with the thesis of Reformed epistemology, as I understand the thesis of Reformed Epistemology, Gage and MacAllister argue for it.[1]

Where the main disagreement seems to be is in reference to their optimism insofar as how many people will need to utilize natural theology in order to rationally maintain theistic belief in light of attempted defeaters. For example, Gage and MacAllister state the following:

> So even if God's existence seems apparent, this can't be the end of the story—at least for most ordinary people in our culture—as theists will almost inevitably encounter all manner of potential defeaters. You don't have to be an academic to wonder how a good God could allow children to suffer, whether theism can be reconciled with contemporary science, etc. Such challenges, if left unanswered, can be enough to defeat the non-inferential justification

provided by one's theistic seemings. Thus, mature theists will likely need to address such questions in order to achieve secure, sustainable justification for their beliefs.

I'm more optimistic about the needs of "mature theists." I'm inclined to think that most theists, especially Christian theists, have extremely strong seemings that ground their theistic or Christian faith. In fact, as I have argued for, I think in part, the strength of the seeming can help deflect potential defeaters. Thus, assuming the design plan is such that the strength of the seeming is sufficient to help deflect attempted defeaters, the mature theist who isn't sufficiently moved by the attempted defeater can continue to rationally hold to her theistic belief, without utilizing the resources of natural theology. Let me clarify by stating that, I do think that natural theology offers resources that help us deflect potential defeaters, and such resources increase our warrant for believing. However, I'm just not convinced that natural theology is necessary for most mature believers.

Finally, it is important to note that while Gage and MacAllister do not give an account of warrant or knowledge, they do seem open to a Proper Functionalist account of warrant as they state, "Advocates of PC might even include accounts of virtue, reliability, and/or proper function in their account of knowledge." I agree. From my perspective, a Proper Functionalist about warrant can also endorse PC as it pertains to justification. One could, for example, think of justification in primarily deontological terms. And, it might seem sufficient to think that S has done her epistemic duty if she has a seeming that p and she has no defeaters for her belief that p. However, due to wanting to capture a tight connection to truth, the proper functionalist would think that something much stronger is needed for warrant.[2] If, in fact, the arguments that I laid out in my Proper Functionalist chapter are plausible, then we have good reason to strongly consider the proper functionalist constraints as what captures that tight connection to truth. And in saying this, I'll stop and invite Gage and MacAllister to think more seriously about endorsing Proper Functionalism as it pertains to warrant.

Notes

1. Specifically, they state, "Reformed Epistemology was right in its insistence that ordinary theistic beliefs might be non-inferentially justified but wrong to detach this justification from evidence."

2. This is, in fact, the view that I take. I endorse Phenomenal Conservatism in reference to justification, but, I'm a Proper Functionalist as it pertains to warrant. Given that I'm much more concerned about whether we know certain propositions than if I am in my right in believing a proposition, I approach epistemology from a Proper Functionalist framework.

A Covenantal Epistemology Response to PC

K. Scott Oliphint

If I have properly grasped the PC approach, there are some things that are useful about it, given a proper context, and other things that are troubling to me.

What is useful is the notion that "seemings" are involved in our beliefs. This, of course, is how much of the population around the world operates on a day-to-day basis. If the traffic light seems red, then I immediately believe that it is red and act accordingly. If it seems that there is a poisonous snake at my feet, then, without reflection, I believe there is and I act accordingly. In that way, "seemings" is a short-hand word for our everyday experiences of the world. There are general patterns of human behavior and experiences that provide strong support to the notion of "seemings."

The problems begin to surface, however, with PC's notion of justification and its relation to truth. The authors face this problem head-on and are comfortable with a "perspectival" notion of justification and of truth. Justification is in the eye of the beholder, they think, such that the truth of the matter in PC seems to me to be of secondary importance. By secondary, I mean that, if it seems to someone that the earth is flat, then he is justified in believing the earth is flat. Surely, they argue, we can't be blamed for believing something false if all our "seemings" point to such a belief.

If we evaluate the overall thrust of the PC approach from the perspective of a Covenantal Epistemology, the following points, at least, must be taken into consideration: First, any notion of foundationalism (on which PC relies) will crumble of its own weight unless the noninferential beliefs themselves are grounded. Because the universality of noninferential beliefs is wanting, those beliefs themselves can only be person-relative until and unless they can be supported by the nature of reality.[1]

It is incumbent on epistemology, therefore, and on *religious* epistemology more specifically, to recognize that the inextricable link between human beings and the world is established by God at creation.

> Genesis 1:26—Then God said, "Let us make man in our image, after our likeness. And let them have dominion over the fish of the sea and over the birds of the heavens and over the livestock and over all the earth and over every creeping thing that creeps on the earth."

Because people are made in God's image (which itself is a *covenantal* category), they are meant to be rulers, under God, over everything else that God has made. Thus, the inextricable link is established; one cannot rule over that which one does not know. As we have argued, God's revelation gets through to us. His revelation in and through creation (since the beginning, Rom. 1:20) is implanted in our hearts, and His Word, spoken and written, is self-attesting in its authority, so Adam and Eve hear it and know its author even as He speaks to them. So, for example, the Lord brings the animals to Adam and assigns to him the task of naming those animals. In order to name them he has to know them. There is, then, from the beginning, a covenantal connection between man—as male and female—and the universe. The Lord relates himself to Adam and Eve, in that relation are commands, and those commands have to do with their relationship to the Lord, and with how that relationship is lived out given their relationship to creation.

Not only so, but we learn in Rom. 1:18-32 that the world itself is the means by which the Lord reveals "his eternal power and divine nature" (Rom. 1:20, cf. Ps. 19:1-5). As the Lord reveals himself in and through creation, included in that revelation is the knowledge of that in and through which he reveals himself. That is to say, the revelation of the Lord's character shows *through*, and not in spite of, the facts of creation. If one is to know God by way of His natural revelation (which Rom. 1:18-32 affirms) then entailed in that knowledge of God is knowledge of the world. In revealing his character in creation, God reveals the things and facts of creation to us as well.[2] Thus, in this sense, "seemings" would be a natural part of living in the world that God has made. As His image, human beings are meant to be stewards of (and thus to know) the world God has given us.

But, and this is the second aspect of a Covenantal Epistemology that impinges on PC, because of the reality of sin, our "seemings" have been significantly skewed. Because of the entrance of sin, we suppress and hold down that truth of God's existence, a truth that He is always and everywhere revealing to all who are made in His image. How, exactly, is that truth suppressed?

Generally speaking, it is suppressed by exchanging what is patently obvious to us—the eternal power and divine nature of God—for a lie, for that which is false, so that we wind up worshiping and serving something that is an idol, rather than the true God whom we know. This worship, of course, will include our knowledge, and the way we think about it.

There is, therefore, a serious problem afoot given this statement:

> PC is a thesis about internalist justification. It says that when something seems true to you, and you have no reason to think that this experience is misleading, then, from your perspective, it is sensible for you to believe it.

When the authors allow the person "seeming" to be the judge of what is reasonable and what is sensible, they have, by definition, disallowed what God has said about us and our "seemings" to speak with authority. Just to put the sharpest possible point on it, if it seems to me that there is no God, and I have no reason to think that my experiences are misleading, then, from my perspective, it is sensible for me to believe it.

The problem, however, is that God Himself has said that we all know Him. And He has said that, in our knowing Him, we suppress that knowledge; we twist and turn it in ways that ensure that it will not be a part of our "seemings." In that case, at least from God's perspective (as He reveals that perspective to us in His Word), it is the height of irrationality, and anything but sensible, for someone to believe that there is no God, or that He has not made Himself known to all, or that we are not His creatures, responsible to Him, and so on.[3]

If it "seems" to us that there is no God, or that we cannot know if there is a God, then all beliefs downstream from there are significantly and substantially distorted by virtue of that. If it seems to us there is no God, then it would seem to us that we are not His creatures, that we owe Him no honor or thanks, that we have not violated His holy character, that this universe is not His, that He does not reign over the affairs of all, and so on. Any "seeming" then that did/does not have included in it the implications and entailments of our true knowledge of God could never be justified in any positive sense. The only "justification" that such "seemings" could produce would be a justification of their erroneous foundation. Such "seemings," in other words, would always and everywhere be contrary to the truth of the matter (as that truth is given to us in natural revelation, and expanded and confirmed for us in special revelation, i.e., Scripture).

If our "seemings" are going to be justified in a positive way, such that they are included in what we truly believe, then they will have to be located within a Christian-theistic context. In that context, knowledge is, in the first place, initiated, implanted, and guided by God Himself, who is always and everywhere revealing Himself to all people. Once we acknowledge that—which, because of the blindness of sin we cannot do apart from the grace of God—then it is up to us to ensure that our "seemings" are aligned with what God Himself has told us, about Himself, about the world He has made, about who we are, and about how we are supposed to live and think in His world.

This does not preclude the fact that superficial "seemings" can be accurate, as far as they go. It does, however, recognize that superficial "seemings" are tainted with deadly error, and thus no positive justification is available on the basis of them.

Notes

1. See George Marsden, "The Collapse of American Evangelical Academia," in *Faith and Rationality: Reason and Belief in God*, ed. Alvin Plantinga and Nicholas Wolterstorff (Notre Dame, IN: University of Notre Dame Press, 1983), 219–64.
2. The South African philosopher, Hendrik Stoker, argues for a *phanerotic*, that is, *revelational*, approach to knowledge, given these truths about natural revelation. See Hendrik G. Stoker, "Reconnoitering the Theory of Knowledge of Prof. Dr. Cornelius van Til," in *Jerusalem and Athens: Critical Discussions on the Theology and Apologetics of Cornelius van Til*, ed. E. R. Geehan (Phillipsburg, NJ: Presbyterian & Reformed, 1977), n. 36, 456; and; Hendrik G. Stoker, *Oorsprong En Rigting*, 2 vols. (Kaapstad: Tafelberg-Uitgewers, 1970).
3. For a development of the theme of the irrationality of unbelief, see K. Scott Oliphint, "The Irrationality of Unbelief," in *Revelation and Reason: New Essays in Reformed Apologetics*, ed. K. Scott Oliphint and Lane G. Tipton (Phillipsburg, NJ: Presbyterian & Reformed, 2007).

A Tradition-Based Perspectival Response to PC

Erik Baldwin

There is much overlap between Gage and McAllister's approach to religious epistemology and mine. As I understand things, our basic starting points for inquiry, *endoxa*, are or are analogous to epistemic seemings. I agree that rational belief in God can but needn't depend on arguments and that evidence matters to the justification of religious beliefs. I think that experiences, including epistemic seemings, can directly provide evidence that contributes to the justification of religious belief, and grant that epistemic seemings "are assertive experiences with propositional content" that don't reduce to beliefs or inclinations to believe. However, I don't think epistemic seemings can provide ultimate justification for beliefs. (I presume that when the authors say that epistemic seemings are ultimate, they mean that they can be fundamental, foundational, or "rock bottom" grounds that serve as "evidential regress stoppers" for beliefs, or something to that effect.[1])

Epistemic seemings aren't fundamental because we can ask what it is about an assertive experience with propositional content that makes it (or its content) seem true. Apparently, taking introspective seemings as paradigmatic, Gage and McAllister write, "we initially trust in the testimony of our introspective seemings for no other reason than that their content *feels true* to us" and they maintain that "all seemings have this same assertive phenomenal character, though often to a lesser degree." In my view, epistemic seemings don't float free and they aren't *sui generis*; we don't have bare epistemic seemings about which nothing more can be said to characterize them or their natures, and they admit of kinds, or types, that have particular features. (Perhaps Gage and McAllister would agree on this point.)

Introspective seemings have hard-to-describe phenomenological features of intentionality, directedness, and aboutness pertaining to awareness of one's mind and of self-reflexive thought about its contents. It's overly blunt to say that they feel true; when I introspect, I don't necessarily *feel* myself as a thinking thing. Rather, introspective experiences have the aforementioned phenomenological features, which are "that in virtue of which" makes their propositional content seem true. Memorial seemings, Alvin Plantinga notes, have hard-to-describe phenomenological features: "sensuous imagery, a sense of pastness, an aboutness with respect to the subject of the memory, and something like the recognition that it is a memory."[2] Having an experience with *those* features is what makes a memorial epistemic seeming seem true. Wouldn't such phenomenological reflection, Gage and McAllister might object, merely yield a more fundamental and more accurate descriptive catalog of epistemological seemings that serve as ultimate justifiers of beliefs? I don't think so. As I wrote in response to DePoe, for the Aquinian, that which grounds the truth of even self-evident propositions isn't some subjective experiential or mental state of which we are aware, but rather an intellect's grasp of the real essences or natures of things, something that can happen either with or without our being fully and explicitly aware of our thought processes. In other words, from a Thomistic perspective, epistemic seemings are not that which does "ultimate" justificatory work, but rather the fact that a mind has been made fully adequate to the objects of its cognition.

This leads to another reason for thinking that epistemic seemings aren't fundamental, namely, the fact that we can ask for and provide explanations of them. That memorial seemings have certain features goes toward explaining why they seem true to us. When we attend to our epistemic seemings with a critical eye, we discover that some don't withstand scrutiny. As such, they provide us with provisional or *prima facie* justification. In times past, it seemed to many people that astrology was sound science. Since at least the time of Augustine,[3] astrology has been systematically discredited, even though some people don't realize this. Astrology is a "fossil science," a "failed attempt on the part of man to try to elucidate the natural world."[4] While it still seems to some that their astrological readings are good indications of future events, those seemings are misguided and illusory. That people can be misled by epistemic seemings raises the question of whether and if so how one could discern which of their deeply held epistemic seemings might be similarly misleading and illusory. One way to proceed is to subject deeply held seemings to rational criticism and radical external critique. For instance, in response to the facts of religious diversity, one might wonder whether their religious experiences are veridical. Questioning the evidential force of their (apparent?) experiences of God, one may find oneself in an epistemological crisis, described by Alasdair MacIntyre as a situation in which one no longer knows what to treat as evidence for what or which evidential scheme to adopt.[5] For instance, Hamlet, the namesake of Shakespeare's play, doesn't know what to believe about the various events he witnesses, for he can't decide upon which conceptual schemes to interpret their meaning and significance. He doesn't know what to count as evidence for what.[6] An Italian scientist, a contemporary of Galileo, torn between the astronomical systems of Ptolemy and Copernicus, makes observations and calculations; however, lacking a coherent conceptual scheme within which to interpret their meaning and significance, he doesn't know what to make of things.[7] Over time, astronomers, using the scientific method, exposed the Ptolemaic system to critical tests it couldn't pass. Copernicanism was found to provide a more empirically adequate explanation of the relevant observations, and was able to explain the failure of Ptolemaic astronomy. Similar narratives explain the progression from Newtonian to Einsteinian science, and so on. This goes toward showing that, however things might feel from a subjective point of view, the justificatory force of some of our epistemic seemings— including those pertaining to the relative motions of heavenly bodies—isn't basic or fundamental but is rather rooted in traditions of inquiry, conceptual schemes, and belief-forming practices.[8]

Many of our "fundamental" epistemic seemings have been inherited, having been handed down to us by others. We are raised in particular communities and engage in certain belief-forming practices endemic to them; we are shaped by institutions that are themselves products of traditions of inquiry that have been developed by influential people over time. For instance, Christians go to Church, participate in worship services, take communion, and engage in various practices of prayer. Christians maintain that these activities put them in experiential contact with the God of Traditional Theism. Buddhists engage in meditative practices that lead them to maintain that all objects of experience have contingent existence and that ultimate reality is empty of persistent being. When these insights are adequately grasped, they maintain, they achieve enlightenment, or nirvana. Typically, practicing Buddhists and Christians find themselves believing what they do in virtue of participating in particular belief-forming practices, but these practices have narrative histories and theoretical underpinnings that may remain largely unknown, even to experts. Typically, participating in such practices is a fine and reasonable thing to do. However, problems arise for those who are concerned about which set of conflicting seemings is actually indicative of how things really are.

Consider a Buddhist contemplating converting to Christianity, or a Christian contemplating converting to Buddhism. Traditional Christians accept a metaphysics of being; Buddhists accept a metaphysics of *sunyata*:

> "*S* accepts the metaphysics of *sunyata*" = def. *S* accepts that there are particulars and affirms that they are not self-identical but "open" in that they radically project and inter-penetrate one another ontologically.
> "*S* accepts the metaphysics of being" = def. *S* accepts the substratum theory and accepts that there are (at least) two basic categories of existence: substances and properties of substances.[9]

Reflective Buddhists and Christians report that their metaphysical views are accurate. But, clearly, if the metaphysics of *sunyata* is true then the metaphysics of being is false, and *vice versa*. Practicing Buddhists and Christians who are fully aware of these facts don't *necessarily* acquire defeaters for their respective metaphysical views. Nevertheless, when it comes to determining which worldview is all-things-considered deemed to be most empirically adequate, it's not sufficient to rely on the very object-level seemings, the accuracy of which is called into question. This problem is all the more acute for those living in a "boundary situation," being culturally and linguistically "equally at home" within the worldviews of both Buddhism and Christianity.[10] In any case, determining which of two conflicting epistemic seemings is more reliable and trustworthy requires engaging in careful philosophical enquiry, sometimes over an extended period of time. We make progress toward truth by transcending and correcting for the distortions and limitations of our starting points, including how things epistemically seem to us. It is only after a lengthy process of inquiry that we are able to look backward and give a full or ultimate justification of what initially seemed true to us. In sum, I think that epistemic seemings, like *endoxa*, are fine starting points for philosophical inquiry, but I don't think they are the sorts of things that can ultimately justify our beliefs.

Notes

1. Trent Dougherty and Patrick Rysiew, "Experience First," in *Contemporary Debates in Epistemology*, ed. Mattias Steup, John Turri, and Ernest Sosa, 3rd ed. (London: Wiley-Blackwell, 2014), 17.

2. Plantinga, *Warrant and Proper Function*, 60.

3. Augustine, *The City of God*, trans. Marcus Dods, reprint ed. (Peabody, MA: Hendrickson, 2008), 1.4.

4. William A. Lessa, "Review of Mark Graubard's Astrology and Alchemy: Two Fossil Sciences," *American Anthropologist* 56, no. 6 (1954): 1162.

5. Alasdair MacIntyre, "Epistemological Crises, Dramatic Narrative and the Philosophy of Science," in *The Tasks of Philosophy: Volume One* (Cambridge: Cambridge University Press, 2006), 4.

6. Ibid., 4–6.

7. Ibid., 10–12.

8. Ibid., 15–23.

9. Erik Baldwin, *Fully Informed Reasonable Disagreement and Tradition Based Perspectivalism* (Leuven: Peeters, 2016), 84.

10. Alasdair MacIntyre, "Relativism, Power, and Philosophy," *Proceedings and Addresses of the American Philosophical Association* 59, no. 1 (1985): 7–10.

PC: Response to Critics

Logan Paul Gage and Blake McAllister

We thank the other contributors for raising several important objections to the PC approach to religious epistemology. They raise far too many issues for us to cover each in detail. Hence, we will limit ourselves to five key objections: (1) McNabb worries that PC requires an awareness of natural theology for most adults; (2) Baldwin worries that seemings can't be ultimate justifiers; (3) DePoe worries that PC is far too liberal and even allows stray hunches to be justified; (4) DePoe further worries that PC has a circularity problem; and (5) Oliphint, Baldwin, and DePoe all worry that PC doesn't have the right sort of connection to the truth. In what follows, we discuss each critique of PC in order.

The Natural Theology Objection

First, we argued that, while seemings provisionally justify beliefs, most adult theists in our culture encounter potential defeaters to their theistic seemings. For this reason, they will need to form a broader worldview in which, say, evil and religious disagreement make sense if they are to have robust justification for their beliefs. Tyler McNabb worries, however, that PC requires more of ordinary theists than is necessary. He thinks that our design plan is such that most serious believers will have *strong* theistic seemings that completely overwhelm potential defeaters. (To compare, you would likely dismiss out of hand any argument that purported to show that you do not exist.) So theists won't have to rely on the support of a broader worldview to dismiss potential defeaters.

In reply, we disagree about the strength of our initial theistic seemings. If a boy goes to church camp and it seems to him that God exists, that seeming, in and of itself, is probably not going to be strong enough to deflect all challenges for the rest of his life. Nor is that how it seems to work for most believers. For instance, the boy will, at some point, begin to question where this seeming came from and whether it was veridical. If he cannot assure himself that this seeming was a part of God's self-revelation, then he will have a defeater.

That said, we agree that most mature theists, once assured in their faith, will have robust theistic seemings. Such assurance is not a brute feature of their design plan, however, but stems from their broad range of evidence: having thought about the world, having grown closer to God in prayer, from hearing an apologetics lecture at church, from talking to other believers about the ways God redeems suffering, from witnessing God's transformative power in their own lives, and so on. Whether they realize it or not, they've built up a host of auxiliary beliefs that reinforce their theistic commitments and neutralize the defeaters they encounter. So we think that McNabb doesn't give ordinary theists enough credit.

Perhaps McNabb thinks that our approach requires most theists to rely on the formal arguments of natural theology. If this is the objection, let us state clearly that this is not so. We think ordinary people require broader worldviews to deflect potential defeaters, and that such worldviews can provide additional support for theism because the world as they see it becomes inexplicable without God. But we do not think theists need to be able to state formal *arguments*. There is a whole lot of ground between relying on random hunches and knowing Plantinga's modal ontological argument. Ordinary people, we suggest, have reasons that fall in between these categories—reasons that tend to make their religious beliefs reasonable.

The Seemings Aren't Ultimate Objection

Second, Erik Baldwin argues that seemings cannot be epistemically ultimate, bedrock, or foundational, as we claim. As we see things, our beliefs typically stem out of experiences we call "seemings." If you think about why you believe what you believe, you eventually trace your belief back to the fact that the world appears to you to be a certain way. So seemings, for us, are ultimate in some sense. Baldwin appears to think, however, that this means that on PC seemings can't be questioned—that we can't consider whether our seemings are truth-oriented or misleading.

But this is not the case. We must distinguish *prima facie* justification from *ultima facie* justification. We have only argued that seemings lend *prima facie* justification to one's beliefs. Seemings may certainly be questioned. They aren't fundamental in the sense of being unquestionable. When defeaters arise, for instance, we can and do question our initial appearances. This is what makes PC a version of moderate/modest foundationalism; the foundations need not be certain or indubitable, as Descartes would have it, but are open to question. The typical theist, as we suggested above, will encounter reasons to question his or her seemings. To obtain *ultima facie* justification, the totality of the theist's evidence must support theism. This will likely require a larger theistic belief system to address potential defeaters (a belief system that will be profoundly shaped by one's tradition).[1]

The Crazy Liberal Objection

Third, John DePoe chastises the PC view for being far too liberal. Even a stray hunch, DePoe claims, would be capable of justifying a guilty verdict in a court of law.[2] In response, note that normal adults have learned over many years how to tell the difference between a stray hunch and a reasonable judgment based on an overall impression of the world—even when they can't articulate all the features of the world that prompted the seeming. One need not be an epistemologist to notice that a seeming is out of the blue. It is psychologically implausible to us that people have the sort of random seemings DePoe describes with any regularity. We certainly don't. And those who do are likely to immediately recognize the seeming *as* a stray hunch. At any rate, it is implausible that such seemings would be of any strength, and thus would only lend the weakest support to any attendant belief.

Moreover, our claim is only that seemings increase one's rational support for believing a proposition *in the absence of defeaters*. While many worry that PC makes it too easy to gain evidence for dubious propositions, notice that PC also makes it extremely easy to gain evidence *against* dubious propositions. One has a weak seeming that some strange proposition is true; and then it immediately seems to one that this is no better than a strange hunch, and the seeming is defeated (counterbalanced, if not outweighed).

Consider also that we all have a great deal of experience with our own cognitive faculties—enough to know that we are in no position to have reliable seemings about the date that a certain tree was planted just by looking at it.[3] We know we possess no track record of success about such propositions and would naturally distrust any such seemings—seemings that, as we said above, we've certainly never experienced. Typical human beings are cautious about radically new or foreign experiences. We could say something similar about the juror who has a gut feeling that the defendant is guilty. We all know that such gut impressions are not reliable enough to place the defendant's guilt beyond a reasonable doubt, and it would be completely unreasonable for the juror to ignore such considerations. For this reason, we think the worry that PC allows nearly any proposition to be justified is off base, both because it posits hosts of strange seemings that we think ordinary people lack and because if ordinary people had such seemings they'd also possess defeaters. These supposed counterexamples to PC have whatever force they do precisely because all cognitively unimpaired adults immediately recognize the seeming as bizarre. In other words, typical persons would find such seemings bizarre given their background information and discount them for that reason.[4] We've now been accused by McNabb of being too demanding and by DePoe of being too liberal. Perhaps we truly have the Goldilocks view.

The Conceptual Circularity Objection

Fourth, DePoe also argues that PC provides a circular definition of epistemic justification. DePoe is incorrect for the simple reason that PC doesn't provide any definition of justification at all! PC merely states a sufficient condition for when a proposition has *prima facie* justification. PC does not claim that what it is for a proposition to be justified *just is* for that proposition to seem true and lack defeaters. Indeed, almost all proponents of PC, including ourselves, acknowledge other ways in which a proposition can be justified— for instance, through the inferential support provided by arguments. Thus, we have some prior understanding of justification in mind when we assert PC. Taking a closer look at that understanding of justification will clear up any remaining worries about conceptual circularity.

Justification, as we are conceiving of it, belongs to those propositions that one is permitted to believe given all that is indicated to be true from within one's first-person perspective.[5] On this approach, evidence for *p* can be understood as something that indicates the truth of *p* to the subject. Thus, a proposition is justified for a subject if it is permissible to believe given all of that person's evidence. When this is the case, we say that the proposition is "on-balance" indicated to be true for the subject.

On this framework, the heart of PC is just this: when *p* seems true to somebody, that person thereby has some indication of *p*'s truth. Even more simply, seemings indicate the truth of their content—the stronger the seeming, the more strongly the content is indicated to be true. It follows that, if *p* seems true, then *p* will be on-balance indicated to be true unless there is something in one's broader evidence to counter this. PC captures this implication by saying that *p* is justified in the absence of defeaters. We chose to frame PC in these terms to remain consonant with the literature and to make explicit the tie between having evidence for *p* and having justification for *p*, but perhaps it would be helpful to formulate it differently. We have done so in our other work. There we defended the following principles, which we take to be equivalent:

PC_R If it seems true to S that *p*, then S thereby has *pro tanto* good reason to believe *p*.

PC_E If it seems true to S that *p*, then S thereby has some evidence for *p* (the strength of that evidence being proportional to the strength of the seeming).

When laid out in this way, it should be especially plain that PC does not suffer from any kind of conceptual circularity vis-à-vis justification.

The Truth Connection Objection

Lastly, in perhaps the most serious challenge to PC, Oliphint, Baldwin, and DePoe all worry that the PC approach to religious epistemology does not contain a tight enough connection to the truth. The worry is that something can be justified in the sense that we have described and yet still be false. Indeed, you can be justified in our sense and still be *way* off the mark. In prehistoric times, for instance, people might have been justified in believing that the earth was flat, even though this isn't even close to the truth. Our critics seem to think that this constitutes an objection to our approach. It's not. Justification, properly understood, doesn't *intend* to provide any guarantee of truth or objective reliability. There are other positive epistemic statuses, like warrant, which concern themselves with guarantees of objective reliability. But the fact that justification is different from warrant is no objection. Nor does our choice to focus on justification suggest any lack of affection for truth. As we'll explain below, the love of truth should lead one to focus on justification. Before we get there, however, we must say more about the history of justification and its connection to truth. This will better position us to see why criticisms of this sort are misguided.

On our reading of the history, justification has always been—at least since the Early Modern period—about having good evidence. To be justified in believing something, the subject needs to have some on-balance indication that it is true. The evidence, moreover, cannot just be "out there"; it needs to be present within the subject's first-person perspective. Anything less was considered improper, irresponsible, a violation of one's epistemic duties in the pursuit of truth. A standard assumption accompanied this conception of justification:

> *The Objective Connection to Truth*—Necessarily, a justified belief is true or, at least, objectively reliable.

That is, following your evidence was thought to guarantee the reliability of your belief. Descartes went so far as to say that, so long as one carefully followed the evidence, one could never be mistaken!

Alas, Descartes was wrong. All of your current evidence (for things beyond the incorrigible) is logically compatible with any number of skeptical scenarios, such as the possibility that you are being deceived by an evil demon. And if you are in such a skeptical scenario, then your beliefs will neither be true nor objectively reliable (see our critique of DePoe for an example). It follows that no matter how carefully you follow your evidence, you can still be in error—gross error, in fact. In order for you to reach the truth, the world has to cooperate.

Thus, it turned out that the assumption accompanying justification was false. Justification does not guarantee that one's beliefs are objectively reliable. It is no objection to PC, then, that seemings can be misleading. *Evidence* can be misleading. Justification, history has taught us, just doesn't come with guarantees of truth.

Why, then, should we pay any attention to justification if it doesn't guarantee truth or even reliability? We want the truth, right? The answer is that following your evidence is the only sensible way of pursuing the truth. There's really no other option for fallible agents such as ourselves who, unfortunately, cannot snap our fingers and arrive at the correct answer. Take a situation in which all of your evidence points strongly toward p. What tolerable option is there but to believe p? Your alternatives are to disbelieve

p or to place the odds at 50–50—a stance sometimes called "withholding assent"—and neither of those makes any sense for someone who cares about securing the truth.

Thus, we see that being justified is about putting forth your best efforts in the pursuit of truth—about doing the best you can with the information available to you. This is really all you can do. You have no control over whether you live in an evil demon world or not and, hence, no control over whether your beliefs are reliable. All you can do is align your beliefs with that which your evidence indicates to be true.

Now, those called "externalists" have taken up the search for a positive epistemic status that can replace justification in providing the objective connection to truth. Unfortunately, some of these efforts have continued to use the term "justification" to describe this new epistemic status, though it bears little resemblance to justification as conceived throughout the Western tradition. Some, like Plantinga (and McNabb), have labeled the object of their search "warrant" rather than appropriating the term "justification" (much to our satisfaction). We do not disparage investigations into the nature of warrant. We want our beliefs to be warranted as well as justified. But notice that you do not have any direct control over whether your beliefs are warranted. No effort on your part can guarantee the reliability of your faculties. The only thing that *is* within your control is to take those actions that, given the evidence available to you, will maximize the chance that your beliefs are warranted. Justification, once again, proves indispensable.

To drive the point home, we might ask our critics why they hold the positions that they do. The answer had better be *because that is the position that our evidence indicates to be true*. If that's *not* the case—if their evidence points to the falsity of their own position or has nothing to say one way or the other—then they have no business believing it! If they really care about truth (as they all undoubtedly do), then they will be concerned to only believe those things that are indicated to be true by their evidence. Thus, every lover of truth should care about justification, even if justification does not guarantee success.

Conclusion

When the true nature of justification is made plain—when we see that it is about doing the best you can with the information available to you and not about guaranteeing success—PC becomes increasingly apparent. Of course appearances can be misleading. But what else are you supposed to do but follow them? We made this argument in our main essay. There we pointed out that if *p* seems true and you have absolutely no reason to doubt this, then it seems permissible to believe that *p*.

We extended the argument by looking at the alternatives. If you demand prior verification of everything that seems true, you're going to end up in complete skepticism. But if you can, at least some of the time, trust what seems to be the case without any prior verification, why would you not be entitled to do so all of the time? It would be arbitrary to extend the benefit of the doubt to some seemings but not others when, from the inside, there is no difference that could license such disparate treatment. Add to this the worry that, if you only give the benefit of the doubt to a limited number of seemings, you will once again end up in radical skepticism.

This argument was not contested by our critics. (Is it too optimistic to think that they found it exceedingly plausible?) Whatever the reason, the fact is that our main case for PC remains intact and unchallenged. Furthermore, we have shown above that none of the objections raised by our critics provides a strong reason to doubt the truth of PC. All considered, then, the evidence still points toward PC. And what else can you do but follow the evidence?

Notes

1. We think traditions have an indirect influence on what is reasonable to believe. They exert *indirect* influence by affecting how things seem to us; and how things seem to us, in accordance with tradition-transcendent standards, *directly* determines what we are justified in believing. For more, see our critique of Baldwin.
2. Most attorneys say that a guilty verdict requires >95% certainty of the defendant's guilt.
3. See Peter Markie, "The Mystery of Direct Perceptual Justification," *Philosophical Studies* 126, no. 3 (2005): 357.
4. Purported counterexamples to PC often just stipulate that the subject with the crazy seeming lacks defeaters. But once we are thinking about a subject that doesn't have any of the information normal adults have, it should no longer be obvious that the proposition that is crazy or unjustified relative to their information. See, for instance, the "Jod" example in Michael Tooley, "Michael Huemer and the Principle of Phenomenal Conservatism," in *Seemings and Justification: New Essays on Dogmatism and Phenomenal*

Conservatism, ed. Christopher Tucker (Oxford: Oxford University Press, 2013), 320.

5. Or, alternatively, those propositions that *fit with* what is indicated to be true. Internalists are split over whether to characterize justification deontologically, in terms of epistemic duties, or using a nondeontological notion of fittingness. We stick to deontological terminology for simplicity, but we wish to remain neutral on that debate here.

3

Proper Functionalism

Tyler Dalton McNabb

Reformed Epistemology: What It Is and What It Isn't

Reformed Epistemology is roughly the thesis that a subject *S*'s religious belief can be justified or warranted apart from argumentation.[1] That is, a Reformed Epistemologist advocates that religious belief can be what philosophers call properly basic. This isn't to say that Reformed Epistemology entails the rejection of natural theology or the idea that there are successful arguments for theism. Rather, Reformed Epistemologists are free to agree or disagree on whether the project of natural theology is successful and in what ways it can legitimately be utilized.[2] Notice also that this minimal thesis does not entail any view on predestination or God's sovereignty. You can be a Catholic or an open theist, and accept the aforementioned thesis. In fact, many philosophers think that you could be a follower of a non-Christian tradition and endorse Reformed Epistemology.[3] The reason why Reformed Epistemology utilizes the word "Reformed" is because the central idea of Reformed Epistemology can be most clearly seen in the thought of John Calvin. Calvin affirmed that there is something like a cognitive faculty that has an aim of producing theistic belief. Calvin states the following:

> That there exists in the human mind, and indeed by natural instinct, some sense of Deity, we hold to be beyond dispute, since God himself, to prevent any man from pretending ignorance, has endue all men with some idea of his Godhead, the memory of which he constantly renews and occasionally enlarges, that all to a man, being aware that there is a God, and that he is

their Maker, may be condemned by their own conscience when they neither worship him nor consecrate their lives to his service.[4]

Calvin isn't the only important religious thinker to endorse this thesis. Both the Doctor of the Catholic Church, Thomas Aquinas, and the esteemed Catholic theologian, Hans Urs von Balthasar, also seem to endorse the thesis. For example, Aquinas states that

> This is why it was necessary that the unshakeable certitude and pure truth concerning divine things should be presented to men by faith. Beneficially, therefore, did the divine Mercy provide that it should instruct us to hold by faith even those truths that the human reason is able to investigate. In this way, all men would easily be able to have a share in the knowledge of God, and this without uncertainty and error.[5]

In the context of this quote, Aquinas juxtaposes the idea of coming to possess knowledge of God by way of argument with coming to possess knowledge of God by way of faith. While arguments can certainly be sufficient to bring about genuine knowledge of Divinity, Aquinas takes it that coming to believe in God by faith is superior.[6]

According to Victoria Harrison, Balthasar, on the other hand, believed that humans are designed to instantiate holiness.[7] And because of this, humans will crave it. God has also set up human faculties in such a way that humans will recognize the holiness that is displayed by a Christian as Christians share in what Balthasar calls the Christ form. Such recognition might come about from seeing the Christian regularly attend mass, feed the poor, share the Good News, speak for the unborn, and catechize new converts. In the case of an unbeliever, the subject will see that the Christian's holiness is "right" and will be moved to participate in the Christ form as well.[8] Upon living a holy life in the Christ form, without the need for any argument, the subject will see that Christianity is valid or true.[9]

The most well-known defender of Reformed Epistemology is of course Alvin Plantinga. In his most mature work on religious epistemology, Plantinga argues that both theistic belief and Christian belief can be warranted apart from argumentation. Warrant for Plantinga is that ingredient which separates mere true belief from knowledge.[10] Or to put it slightly differently, warrant is that thing that when added to mere true belief turns mere true belief into knowledge. How does one achieve a warranted belief? Plantinga endorses an externalist theory of warrant called Proper Functionalism. Proper Functionalism goes as follows:

S's belief that p is warranted, *if and only if* ...

(1) The belief in question is formed by way of cognitive faculties that are properly functioning.

(2) The cognitive faculties in question are aimed at the production of true beliefs.

(3) The design plan is a good one. That is, when a belief is formed by way of truth-aimed cognitive proper function in the sort of environment for which the cognitive faculties in question were designed, there is a high objective probability that the resulting belief is true.

(4) The belief is formed in the sort of environment for which the cognitive faculties in question were designed.[11]

Since the theory is an externalist theory of warrant, one doesn't need to have access as to whether one's faculties are functioning properly or as to whether one is in the right environment. As long as the subject does have properly functioning faculties and as long as the subject is in the right environment, and so forth, the subject's belief can be warranted.

In *Warranted Christian Belief*, Plantinga argues for the epistemic possibility of humans possessing what Calvin called the *Sensus Divinitatis* (SD). Taking the possibility of possessing the SD, Plantinga utilizes his theory of warrant to argue for the thesis of Reformed Epistemology.[12] Echoing back to the sentiments of Aquinas and Calvin, Plantinga argues for what he calls the Aquinas/Calvin model (AC model). Roughly, the idea is that if belief that God exists is the result of the proper functionalist constraints being in place, then belief in God is warranted. It can be properly summed up as follows:

> AC Model: If S's SD produces theistic belief when it is functioning properly in the environment for which it was designed and the SD is aimed at truth with there being a high objective probability that the theistic belief it produces under these conditions will be true, then the theistic belief it produces will be warranted.

Plantinga doesn't stop with general theistic belief. He also argues that Christian belief can be warranted. But, before one can understand how Christian belief can be warranted, it's important first to understand that, according to Plantinga's story, the SD has been damaged by sin. It may work sufficiently well in most humans but it still doesn't work as it was originally designed. Humans were originally designed to perceive God and His activities in an analogous way to how humans perceive other minds. That is to say, humans were designed to believe in God without possessing any doubts whatsoever. But, sin has damaged the human capacity to become aware of God. And even in some, this capacity seems totally lost. However, Plantinga thinks that God is in the midst of overturning the noetic effects of sin. In part, God overturns such effects by His Spirit's repairing of the SD. In conjunction to the healing of effects of the Spirit's work, the Spirit is busy instigating and testifying to those who He is healing, to believe in the Great Truths of the Gospel.

For Plantinga, humans seem to have something within their cognitive structure that makes it such that there is a strong inclination to accept the testimony of others.[13] This is why you actually have to train young children not to accept everything they hear. When it comes to producing Christian belief, there is a special testimonial process that is in place. The Holy Scripture is a testimony written by both God's Spirit and human authors. And if a subject finds herself believing the testimony of the Gospel as the Spirit moves them to believe, belief that the testimony is true can be warranted apart from argument, at least, assuming that the aforementioned proper functionalist constraints are met. The model that he offers to help demonstrate this, he calls the extended AC model (EAC).

While there are numerous ways to argue for the thesis of Reformed Epistemology, including specifically Christian ways (of which I have given an example in the above text), in keeping with the thought of Plantinga, I will argue for Reformed Epistemology by arguing for Proper Functionalism. I will do this, first, by arguing for why each of Plantinga's conditions is necessary for warrant. Then, I will engage an objection aimed at showing that these conditions aren't jointly sufficient. Finally, I will engage two objections against Plantinga's Reformed Epistemology. The first objection that I will engage attempts to undermine Plantinga's Reformed Epistemology by way of arguing that the SD is unreliable. The second objection that I will engage attempts to discredit the Reformed Epistemologists' claims by way of the problem of Divine Hiddenness. I will argue that both of these objections fail.

Warrant as Proper Function

At the heart of Plantinga's Proper Functionalism is the proper function condition.

(1)   The belief in question is formed by way of cognitive faculties that are properly functioning.

But is such a condition plausible? Traditionally, the Swampman scenario has been given by those who argue that the condition isn't plausible.

> Suppose lightning strikes a dead tree in a swamp; I am standing nearby. My body is reduced to its elements, while entirely by coincidence (and out of different molecules) the tree is turned into my physical replica. My replica, The Swampman, moves exactly as I did; according to its nature it departs the swamp, encounters and seems to recognize my friends, and appears to return their greetings in English. It moves into my house and seems to write articles on radical interpretation. No one can tell the difference. But there is a difference.[14]

In this case, wouldn't Swampman know basic facts such as 2+2=4 or that Christopher Columbus sailed the Ocean Blue in 1492? Surely, if he can write articles on radical interpretation, he has to know at least some things, right? Yet, given that he came about from random conditions, it doesn't seem plausible to think that Swampman's faculties possess a cognitive design plan. If so, we have a genuine counterexample on our hands against the proper function condition. Swampman would possess knowledge, and yet, his faculties would lack cognitive proper function.

Recently however, proper functionalists have argued that the Swampman scenario gives us good reason to affirm the proper function condition. Kenneth Boyce and Andrew Moon think they have identified why most, at least at first, are inclined to think that Swampman possesses knowledge.[15] Implicitly, Boyce and Moon think something like (CI) is endorsed:

> (CI) If a belief B is warranted for a subject S and another subject S^* comes to hold B in the same way that S came to hold B in a relevantly similar environment to the one in which S came to hold B, then B is warranted for S^*.

Boyce and Moon then set up a counterexample to (CI). They imagine a young infant, Billy, who due to cognitive malfunction forms the belief that when unobserved, red objects cease to exist. They then invite the readers to imagine that Billy gets abducted by aliens. Billy is taken to the alien planet, where, due to strange quantum activity, red objects actually do cease to exist when they are not observed. Finally, Boyce and Moon invite the reader to compare Billy side by side with Zork, a young alien infant, whose faculties likewise produce the belief that red objects, when they are unobserved, cease to exist. Now, let's say that both Billy and Zork move away from a red object and both come to hold the belief that the red object no longer exists. While, both produced the same belief in the same way and in the same environment, it seems plausible to think that Zork possesses knowledge, while Billy does not. (CI) then seems to be refuted.[16] This not only takes away one's justification for thinking that Swampman possesses knowledge, but this scenario also gives us a plausible reason for thinking the proper function condition is plausible. For it seems to best explain why Zork seems to possess knowledge while Billy does not.

There is another argument for proper function that can be developed from the Swampman scenario. This argument has been defended by Boyce and Plantinga,[17] Bergmann,[18] and McNabb.[19] We will call this the Walking Gettier[20] Swampman argument.

In reference to figuring out what the jointly necessary and sufficient conditions for warrant are, epistemologists are after, what I have termed, a tight connection to truth. That is, epistemologists are trying to figure out what one needs minimally to establish a tight connection between the belief produced from a subject and that belief being true. But when we think about Swampman's beliefs, it seems like his beliefs lack such a connection. His faculties have no way in which they should operate. It isn't as if his faculties should or shouldn't produce a specific belief in a particular circumstance. It just so happens that his faculties do produce the right belief in the right circumstance. And all of this seems extremely serendipitous. So much so that there doesn't seem to be a tight connection between the beliefs produced from Swampman's faculties and those beliefs being true. What is missing in this case? Swampman has internal access and his faculties are reliable. It seems like what is doing the work in making Swampman look like a walking Gettier example is Swampman lacking cognitive proper function. Taking both of these Swampman arguments together, I think there is good reason to think that the proper function condition is plausible.

What about condition (2)? Is it plausible? Condition (2) again states:

(2)   The cognitive faculties in question are aimed at the production of true beliefs.

Imagine a subject whose design plan is such that whatever the subject wishes were the case, the belief that it is the case would be produced. We can call this design plan as that aimed at wish-fulfillment, and we can call this subject Brock. Imagine that Brock really wishes that a random beautiful woman would come up to him at t^2 and ask him to marry her. Brock has no reason as to why this would happen. Brock is a fairly normal looking guy, who lives on a modest income, and he lacks any celebrity status. Nonetheless, due to his design plan, Brock feels certain that a beautiful woman that he doesn't know will propose to him at t^2. Let's say that it just so happens that a beautiful woman did end up proposing to Brock at t^2. Are we to say that Brock's belief is warranted? This seems unlikely. Again, in order to capture a tight connection to truth, the design plan needs to be aimed at truth.

But this doesn't seem sufficient either. Imagine that there exists an incompetent deity who wishes to create rational creatures of his own. While the incompetent deity might intend that his subjects produce true beliefs, the design plan of his subjects might not be successful.[21] For example, though their faculties' design plan might be such that it is aimed toward truth, it might only successfully produce one true belief for every one hundred beliefs they have. Surely, even if a subject's faculties are functioning properly and are aimed at truth, the subject's one true belief that is produced shouldn't be considered warranted. The design plan is so unsuccessful statistically speaking that the subject's beliefs can't be said to have a tight connection to truth, even when they happen to be true. Scenarios like this one make the following condition plausible:

(3)   The design plan is a good one. That is, when a belief is formed by way of truth-aimed cognitive proper function in the sort of environment for which the cognitive faculties in question were designed, there is a high objective probability that the resulting belief is true.

But what about the fourth and final condition?

(4)   The belief is formed in the sort of environment for which the cognitive faculties in question were designed.

I think classic Gettier examples can make this condition plausible. Take, for example, the well-known Barn Façade case.[22] In this example, there is a person named Henry who is driving in rural Wisconsin. Of course, in such an environment, one would expect to see things like barns, hay, and tractors. Unbeknownst to Henry however, this isn't a normal environment. Unlike normal rural environments to which one would be accustomed, Henry finds himself in a town where some Wisconsinites have built dozens of fake barns alongside a real barn. Henry just so happens to walk by a real barn in the midst of the dozens of fake barns. Henry forms the belief that there is a barn nearby. Here, Henry is an individual who has faculties that are functioning properly and those faculties are aimed at truth and there is a high objective probability that belief being produced from these conditions will be true. And yet, given that the individual could have just as easily walked in any other direction and would then have run into a fake barn, there seems to be something significantly fortuitous about this situation. In order to prevent the luckiness of Henry's belief, it seems right to add that his beliefs can't be formed in an irregular epistemic environment, but rather, when his faculties do produce beliefs, they need to be producing beliefs in an environment for which they were designed.

So far, I have argued that the proposed proper functionalist conditions are all necessary for warrant. But are these conditions jointly sufficient? It seems that way to me. Imagine a man who is hardwired to believe that other minds exist. If his faculties are functioning properly in the environment for which they were designed and the faculties were aimed at the production of true belief with there being a high objective probability that the belief being produced under such conditions would be true, then it sure seems like the belief that other minds exist is warranted. This is so, even if there were no good argument for the existence of other minds. What more do you need?

Linda Zagzebski disagrees. She thinks that Proper Functionalism is susceptible to the Gettier problem.[23] That is, she thinks that a subject's belief could meet all of the proper functionalist constraints, and yet, due to something fortuitous in the scenario, the subject's belief could still lack warrant. She sets up her scenario as follows:

> Suppose that Mary has very good eyesight, but it is not perfect. It is good enough to allow her to identify her husband sitting in his usual chair in the living room from a distance of fifteen feet in somewhat dim light. She has made such an identification in these circumstances many times. Each time her faculties have been working properly and the environment has been appropriate for the faculties. There is nothing at all unusual about either her faculties or the environment in these cases. Of course, her faculties may not be functioning perfectly, but they are functioning well enough that if she's goes on to form the belief **My husband is sitting in the living room**, that belief has enough warrant to constitute knowledge when true and we can assume that it is almost always true.[24]

She moves on specifically to address how Proper Functionalism is susceptible to the Gettier problem.

> Suppose Mary simply misidentifies the chair-sitter who is, we'll suppose, her husband's brother, who looks very much like him. Her faculties may be working as well as they normally do when the belief is true and when we do not hesitate to say it is warranted in a degree sufficient for knowledge. It is not a question of their suddenly becoming defective, or at any rate, more defective than usual, nor is there a mismatch between her faculties and the

environment. No one is trying to surprise or fool her or anything like that. Her husband and his brother may not even know she is in the house, so the normal environment has not been doctored as it is in the fake barn case.[25]

So, though Mary forms the belief that her husband is in the room and her husband actually is in the room, given that she only believes that he is in the room because she sees his look-alike brother, there is something serendipitous about the situation such that it makes the belief seem unwarranted. And this is so, even granting that the belief was produced in light of the proper functionalist conditions being in place. If Zagzebski is right, then, though Plantinga's conditions for warrant are necessary, they aren't jointly sufficient.

But are all of the proper functionalist conditions actually met in this scenario? Zagzebski claims that there is nothing wrong with the environment but is this right? Plantinga makes a distinction between maxi- and mini-environments. Boyce summarizes the distinction:

> The maxi-environment … is the kind of global environment in which we live here on earth, the kind of environment for which our cognitive faculties were designed (or to which they were adapted). The mini-environment, by contrast, is a much more specific state of affairs, one that includes, for a given exercise of one's cognitive faculties E resulting in a belief B, all of the epistemically relevant circumstances obtaining when B is formed (though diminished with respect to whether B is true).[26]

In light of this distinction, Plantinga proposes what he calls the resolution condition:

> (RC) A belief B produced by an exercise E of cognitive powers has warrant sufficient for knowledge only if MBE (the minienvironment with respect to B and E) is favorable for E.[27]

It seems like the proper functionalist has a powerful retort that she can give to Zagzebski. Mary in the situation in question is in a favorable maxi-environment, but she isn't in a favorable mini-environment. Mary isn't designed to produce the belief about her husband's whereabouts in a room, when unbeknownst to her, his look-alike brother is around. This just simply isn't a favorable mini-environment. The resolution condition is clearly not met.

While I do not have the space to explore other objections aimed toward showing how Plantinga's theory isn't sufficient for warrant, for the sake of the constraints in this volume, I'll take it that I have sketched out a defense for thinking that it is. Moreover, if Plantinga's theory is sufficient for warrant, then it seems like one could successfully utilize it to argue for the thesis of Reformed Epistemology. There are, however, two objections that I will now move to engage, which attempt to put this move into question.

The SD and Reliability

Let's grant that one could apply Proper Functionalism to religious belief in order to demonstrate that religious belief could be warranted apart from argumentation. There still could potentially exist defeaters that could defeat the religious belief in question. Recently, there have been arguments from both cognitive science and religious diversity that attempt to show that the faculty responsible for religious belief (let's call it SD for our purposes) is unreliable. If a subject's SD is unreliable, then, so it's claimed, the subject would have a defeater for trusting the deliverances of their SD. I now move to more fully articulate both versions of this objection.

One popular story that's told in the field of cognitive science of religion for why humans naturally believe in the supernatural is that humans possess a hyper-agency detection device (HADD).[28] Roughly, humans detect agency even when it isn't there. Likely, humans possess HADD for the benefit of survival. For example, organisms that detect agency too much will likely have a better chance at surviving than an organism that doesn't detect agency enough. As Stephen Law has pointed out, it is likely that the SD/HADD has led people to believe in gods, ghosts, fairies, and psychic Sally.[29] Given that the SD/HADD (in others) has detected supernatural agency when it isn't there, shouldn't the religious believer think that, currently, it's likely that her SD/HADD is unreliable when it pertains to the production of her religious beliefs?[30]

As mentioned, there exist other reasons for thinking that the SD is unreliable. One might think that the existence of religious diversity is one such reason. Imagine a Jew, a Muslim, a Christian, a Daoist, a Hindu, a Buddhist, and a Confucian all walk into a bar.[31] Now, let's imagine that all of these believers roughly possess the same intellectual ability and all of the believers are equally informed about each religious view and why each believer thinks his or her religious view is correct. What should these religious believers do? Some would argue that they should all suspend belief.[32] The religious believers should realize that, at most, only one person's

SD could be functioning properly. Since there is no way to check on which faculty is functioning properly, each believer should remain religiously agnostic unless there are further developments. In most circumstances, we should view the SD as unreliable.

So, do the above arguments give us a defeater for trusting the religious beliefs produced from the SD? I think not. At the heart of each of these objections is something like the objective probability principle:

> (OP): When figuring out which proposition you should affirm; you should always affirm the proposition that is more probable according to the accessible and sharable evidence.

But proper functionalists have long denied (OP). Inspired by a similar example from Plantinga, McNabb and Taber give a counterexample to (OP):

> Say I am known for stealing philosophy books, in fact, there is even a picture of me, warning the clerks that I like to steal books. If, one day, the whole philosophy section of the library went missing and there were several witnesses saying they saw me steal a lot of books, the objective probability that I stole the books would be very high. Nonetheless, if I had a very distinct and highly warranted memory of myself at my house during the time that the books disappeared, would I have a defeater for my belief that I was at my house when the book snatching occurred? It doesn't appear to be the case that I would. As I hold to this belief with a sufficient amount of firmness (which is partly responsible for my level of warrant being high), the probability that I stole the philosophy books wouldn't play any significant role in my doxastic process.[33]

There are obvious cases where the probability, according to the accessible and sharable evidence, of a belief being false is high, and yet, the belief can be warranted. For a proper functionalist, the degree of warrant that a belief possesses depends on how firmly one holds to a proposition. Confidence that p is true is fundamental to beliefs being warranted, and to deflecting potential defeaters.[34]

Coming back to our own case, if the religious believer entertains the attempted defeaters and isn't significantly moved by them, then as long as her belief is the product of the aforementioned conditions, her belief is warranted. Given that the subject is hard-wired to produce p and there is a high objective probability (this should be understood in terms of frequency) that p is true (given it is produced from these conditions), the religious belief in question still has a sufficiently tight enough connection to truth, such that her religious belief can be warranted even in light of it being improbable, at least according to the accessible and sharable evidence, that her SD is reliable. More succinctly stated, the proper functionalist will likely endorse, what I call elsewhere, the Classic Plantingian Response (CPR):

> CPR: S's belief that p can deflect defeater D if S still believes p on the reflection of D and p is the product of properly functioning faculties which are successfully aimed at truth and there is a high objective probability [again, this should be understood in terms of frequency] that the belief produced under these conditions would be true.[35]

Divine Hiddenness and Reformed Epistemology

There is one other sort of defeater that I shall consider here. The problem of divine hiddenness is roughly the problem of why God is not more evident. You would think that a perfect being who has the power to write His name in the clouds or perhaps manifest Himself in physical form to let everyone know that He exists would do something extraordinary to make His existence beyond dispute. J. L. Schellenberg formalizes the problem like this:

(1)   If there is a God, He is perfectly loving.
(2)   If a perfectly loving God exists, reasonable nonbelief does not occur.
(3)   Reasonable nonbelief occurs.
(4)   No perfectly loving God exists.
(5)   There is no God.[36]

How might a Reformed Epistemologist respond? The Reformed Epistemologist likely won't think that God is hidden. God's existence is as obvious as the existence of other minds. But why don't we perceive it this way? We don't perceive it this way because of the noetic effects of sin. Remember, for Plantinga, sin has damaged the SD, and though while the SD might work sufficiently well to produce beliefs about God in most human beings, the SD still isn't working as it was designed to work. Taber and McNabb compare it to the following case:

> Having been handed over to the Russians to be tortured for killing Russian officials, Jack becomes both blind and deaf as he lies in a prison, awaiting a slow and agonizing death. However, unbeknownst to Jack, his good friend

Chloe has led a team to rescue him. Upon finding Jack, Chloe tries to talk to Jack so as to arrange his escape. And when she sees that Jack isn't responding to her, she begins to jump and to wave her hands to get his attention. Nonetheless, Jack is still unresponsive. Here it can be said that Jack isn't unresponsive due to a deficiency of objective evidence for Chloe. For it is rather the case that, due to the improper function of his own faculties, Jack lacks the epistemic ability to recognize Chloe.[37]

If the Reformed Epistemologist defines what is reasonable by way of the belief being produced from proper functionalist conditions, then it seems like she can deny (2). Properly functioning individuals who are in the environment for which they were designed perceive the existence of God as obvious. To deny the existence of God under such conditions just wouldn't be reasonable.

Now, one might formulate a new question. Why, if God is all loving and all powerful, would God not immediately fix or repair everyone's cognitive faculties and make it such that everyone is always in a favorable epistemic environment? To this, a Reformed Epistemologist could respond that God isn't interested in His creatures possessing mere propositional knowledge of His existence. God desires a transformative relationship. Perhaps, God does start to fix unbelievers' SD, but some of the unbelievers refuse to trust in the transformative light that they possess. God might see no need to continue to repair their faculties if the unbelievers are refusing to transform given what they already know.[38] At the end of the day, however, a Reformed Epistemologist can always endorse (CPR), and, if upon reflecting on the defeater from divine hiddenness, the Reformed Epistemologist still firmly believes in God, then, as long as that belief is produced from the aforementioned proper functionalist conditions, the belief will still be warranted. The Reformed Epistemologist has the resources to handle the problem of divine hiddenness.

Summary

In this chapter, I have argued for the plausibility of the thesis of Reformed Epistemology. I did this by arguing for Proper Functionalism. Specifically, I gave different scenarios that show plausible each condition of Proper Functionalism and then I engaged an objection aimed toward discrediting Proper Functionalism as a sufficient theory of warrant. Finally, I entertained and then responded to two objections aimed against the Reformed

Epistemologist. Having done all of this, I have laid out a plausible case for Reformed Epistemology, at least, I think a sufficiently enough plausible case such that my fellow contributors will have to take this project seriously.

Notes

1. See Andrew Moon, "Recent Work in Reformed Epistemology," *Philosophy Compass* 11, no. 12 (2016): 879–91.
2. Plantinga thinks that there are roughly two dozen or so arguments for God's existence. For more on this, see Trent Dougherty and Jerry L. Walls, eds., *Two Dozen (or so) Arguments for God: The Plantinga Project* (Oxford: Oxford University Press, 2018).
3. For example, see Rose Ann Christian, "Plantinga, Epistemic Permissiveness, and Metaphysical Pluralism," *Religious Studies* 28, no. 4 (1992): 553–73; David W. Tien, "Warranted Neo-Confucian Belief: Religious Pluralism and the Affections in the Epistemologies of Wang Yangming (1472–1529) and Alvin Plantinga," *International Journal for Philosophy of Religion* 55, no. 1 (2004): 31–55.
4. John Calvin, *Institutes of the Christian Religion*, trans. Henry Beveridge, reprint ed. (Grand Rapids, MI: Eerdmans, 1990), 43–4.
5. Thomas Aquinas, *Summa Contra Gentiles: Book One: God*, trans. Anton C. Pegis (Notre Dame, IN: University of Notre Dame Press, 1991), I, 4, 5–6.
6. Perhaps, one is inclined to see Aquinas's argument against belief in God being self-evident (see Summa Theologiae Question 2, Article 1) as evidence that Aquinas didn't endorse the thesis of Reformed Epistemology. This would be a mistake, however. While self-evident beliefs are basic beliefs, there are also basic beliefs that are not self-evident. Moreover, according to Brian Davies, Aquinas does not reject the thesis of Reformed Epistemology. In fact, Davies argues that Aquinas would endorse that by a special act of God, some individuals could rationally believe that God exists apart from argument. See Brian Davies, *Thomas Aquinas's Summa Theologiae: A Guide and Commentary* (Oxford: Oxford University Press, 2014).
7. Victoria S. Harrison, "Human Holiness as Religious Shape Apologia," *International Journal for Philosophy of Religion* 46, no. 2 (1999): 63–82.
8. Ibid., 70.
9. Ibid., 64.
10. Plantinga, *Warrant*, 3.
11. Boyce, "Proper Functionalism." For the original articulation of this theory, see Plantinga, *Warrant and Proper Function*.
12. Plantinga, *Warranted Christian Belief*.

13. Plantinga, *Warrant and Proper Function*, 79–80.
14. Donald Davidson, "Knowing One's Own Mind," *Proceedings and Addresses of the American Philosophical Association* 60 (1987): 441–58.
15. Kenny Boyce and Andrew Moon, "In Defense of Proper Functionalism: Cognitive Science Takes on Swampman," *Synthese* 193, no. 9 (2016): 2987–3001. A summary of this can also be found in Erik Baldwin and Tyler Dalton McNabb, *Plantingian Religious Epistemology and World Religions: Prospects and Problems* (Lanham, MD: Lexington Books, 2018), and Tyler Dalton McNabb, *Religious Epistemology* (Cambridge: Cambridge University Press, 2018).
16. For a recent defense of this scenario, see Tyler Dalton McNabb, *Religious Epistemology* (Cambridge: Cambridge University Press, 2018).
17. Kenny Boyce and Alvin Plantinga, "Proper Functionalism," in *The Continuum Companion to Epistemology*, ed. Andrew Cullison (London: Continuum, 2012), 130–1.
18. Bergmann, *Justification without Awareness*.
19. Tyler Dalton McNabb, "Warranted Religion: Answering Objections to Alvin Plantinga's Epistemology," *Religious Studies* 51, no. 4 (2015): 477–95. Also see Baldwin and McNabb, *Plantingian Religious Epistemology and World Religions*, and McNabb, *Religious Epistemology*.
20. Gettier examples are counterexamples developed by Edmund Gettier to demonstrate that the traditional tripartite theory of knowledge is insufficient. See Edmund Gettier, Gettier, "Is Justified True Belief Knowledge?"
21. See Michael Bergmann, *Justification without Awareness* (New York: Oxford University Press, 2006), 135.
22. Alvin Goldman credits the Barn Façade case to Carl Ginet in Alvin I. Goldman, *Philosophy Meets the Cognitive and Social Sciences* (Cambridge, MA: MIT Press, 1992), 102.
23. Linda Trinkaus Zagzebski, *Virtues of the Mind: An Inquiry into the Nature of Virtue and the Ethical Foundations of Knowledge* (Cambridge: Cambridge University Press, 1996).
24. Ibid., 285–6.
25. Ibid., 286.
26. Boyce, "Proper Functionalism."
27. Ibid.
28. Justin L. Barrett, *Cognitive Science, Religion, and Theology: From Human Minds to Divine Minds* (West Conshohocken, PA: Templeton Press, 2011), 100–2.
29. Stephen Law, "The X-Claim Argument against Religious Belief," *Religious Studies* 54, no. 1 (2018): 15–35.
30. Stephen Law develops this sort of argument in ibid.

31. This scenario is essentially taken from Tyler Dalton McNabb and Erik Daniel Baldwin, "Divine Methodology: A Lawful Deflection of Kantian and Kantian-Esque Defeaters," *Open Theology* 3, no. 1 (2017): 293–304.

32. David Christensen, "Epistemology of Disagreement: The Good News," *The Philosophical Review* 116, no. 2 (2007): 187–217.

33. Tyler Taber and Tyler Dalton McNabb, "Is the Problem of Divine Hiddenness a Problem for the Reformed Epistemologist?," *The Heythrop Journal* 59, no. 5 (2018): 783–93, 789.

34. I make a similar point in McNabb and Baldwin, "Divine Methodology." Also see Baldwin and McNabb, *Plantingian Religious Epistemology and World Religions*, and McNabb, *Religious Epistemology*.

35. McNabb and Baldwin, "Divine Methodology," 300–1.

36. Schellenberg, *Divine Hiddenness and Human Reason*, 83.

37. Taber and Dalton McNabb, "Is the Problem of Divine Hiddenness a Problem for the Reformed Epistemologist?", 788.

38. We suggest this in ibid., 790.

A Classical Evidentialist Response to Proper Functionalism

John M. DePoe

Tyler McNabb and I share common ground since we both affirm the importance of having an objective connection to truth for beliefs to possess positive epistemic status (warrant, justification, or knowledge). Where we differ is on the significance of subjective awareness as a requirement for positive epistemic status. My critical remarks will focus on this point of disagreement before turning to some other concerns with Proper Functionalism's applications in religious epistemology.

Epistemology without Subjective Awareness

The Proper Functionalist account is a paradigm case of an externalist approach to epistemology—that is, a theory that doesn't require any first-person or subjective awareness for beliefs to possess any positive epistemic standing. In other words, the epistemic externalist affirms that a person can know that *p* even if the person isn't in a position to be aware (in any sense of the word) of any reasons for believing that *p*, just so long as that person satisfies a number of conditions that are external to his perspective. For example, externalists accept that a person can *know* that the radius of the moon is 1,079 miles without being aware of any reasons why he believes this is so; all that matters is that the belief was produced in the right way by the appropriate external conditions. Externalists maintain that positive epistemic status doesn't need to involve the first-person, subjective awareness of one's evidence for believing things are this way. Unfortunately, this fundamental component of externalism is a poor foundation for constructing a healthy epistemology.

In the first place, an epistemology that rejects any subjective awareness is practically useless. If the conditions for epistemic goods like justification, warrant, and knowledge have nothing to do with conditions that reside within the purview of my awareness, how can I check my practices to tell if they are acquiring these epistemic goods? Supposing that I am interested in determining whether my belief that the moon's radius is 1,079 miles is warranted, in practice Proper Functionalism has nothing to say whether I can have subjective assurance that I meet the standards for warrant. At best, a proper functionalist can offer me the conditional claim that *if I meet the external requirements, then my belief is warranted*. When pressed how I can know whether I meet the external requirements, the proper functionalist has no reassurance for me except that I could have knowledge of these too *if I meet the appropriate external requirements*. In practice, then, Proper Functionalism has no conditions for warrant that assure the subject that he possesses any epistemic goods.

By eliminating the requirement for subjective awareness, externalist approaches to epistemology tend to dehumanize the role of persons in acquiring epistemic goods. Instead of positive epistemic states involving the exercise of the rational and reflective powers of human agents, they are analyzed in terms of complex mechanistic causes and effects. Most people tend not to think of their own epistemic practices this way. Richard Fumerton points out that when one is wondering whether a specific momentous belief is justified, "it is difficult to imagine, … , that what she wants is merely to be programmed so as to respond correctly. To get justification now for the belief is not to be in a situation in which one stands merely in certain nomological relations to stimuli."[1]

From the traditional view of humanity, epistemology must address the role of personal agency to avoid dehumanizing the human agent as nothing more than a mundane relata in the cause-and-effect machinery of the world. Even when Reformed Epistemology adds theological elements to the nomological sequences that are supposed to yield epistemic goods, ultimately the human agent is downgraded from being a person with active powers of rationality to a passive cog that is at the mercy of causes beyond one's control and awareness for acquiring those epistemic goods.

Natural Theology and Reformed Epistemology

McNabb identifies the central thesis of Reformed Epistemology as the claim that "a subject's religious belief can be justified or warranted apart from argumentation." By itself, this is a strange characterization as it might include radical fideistic approaches to religious beliefs, such as those that claim that any application of reasoning or evidence is contrary to the nature of religious beliefs. It seems consistent with K. Scott Oliphint's Covenantal Epistemology and Erik Baldwin's Traditions Approach. Moreover, this characterization is compatible with the Phenomenal Conservative approach to epistemology given by Gage and McAllister who also describe their approach as justifying theistic belief without argumentation. In fact, my own view of Classical Evidentialism may even satisfy this broad statement of McNabb's depending on how rigidly one defines "argumentation."

I take it that what McNabb means is that a person can have justified or warranted religious beliefs without him being aware of any reasons or evidence for them, just so long as one doesn't have any undefeated reasons to disbelieve them. McNabb isn't opposed to people having evidence to support their religious beliefs, but they are superfluous to determining whether one's religious beliefs have positive epistemic standing. At best, a person's reasons for holding religious beliefs become relevant only when addressing defeaters for one's religious beliefs. Religious beliefs can be justifiably held without reason, but Reformed Epistemologists aren't prepared to say that it is appropriate to hold religious beliefs against reason.

Reformed Epistemologists maintain that when a belief has been produced in a properly basic way, then it is appropriate to hold that belief unless one has an overriding reason not to believe it. Here the problem is that since there is no subjective assurance built into the account of properly basic beliefs in Reformed Epistemology, it follows that individuals aren't in a position to tell whether one's beliefs are properly basic or not. In other words, there is no way to tell from one's own perspective which basic beliefs have been produced in accordance with proper function. Suppose a person finds herself believing that God exists, but upon careful reflection she cannot discern any reason whatsoever for this belief. She just finds herself struck by the fact that she believes in God. Is her belief properly basic? Reformed Epistemologists conclude that the belief is properly basic *only if she meets a series of conditions that are outside of her purview of awareness.* From her perspective, a properly basic belief and an improperly basic belief are indistinguishable, given the epistemic standards of Reformed Epistemology.

Even Alvin Plantinga can only offer a conditional claim about the positive epistemic state of Christian belief: "If Christian belief is true, then very likely it has warrant."[2] Of course inquiring minds wonder, is it true? At the end of his book, Plantinga's answer to this question is terribly unsatisfying, "here we pass beyond the competence of philosophy .... Speaking for myself and of course not in the name of philosophy, I can say only that it does, indeed, seem to me to be true."[3] Ultimately, the best Reformed Epistemology has to offer when one asks whether his religious beliefs are held appropriately is that *possibly* his religious beliefs can meet the criteria for warrant and knowledge, *if* a host of conditions are met of which one cannot ascertain their obtaining. This is hardly blessed assurance!

Finally, I would like to raise a version of the Great Pumpkin Objection. This objection voices the concern that Reformed Epistemology opens the door to granting proper basicality to a wide range of paradigmatic beliefs that shouldn't count as properly basic. As its namesake example goes, Linus may believe fervently that the Great Pumpkin will return on Halloween, although without any supporting reasons. If Linus's cognitive faculties were designed by the Great Pumpkin to produce true beliefs in his environment and he has no defeaters, then Linus's belief would be properly basic. When questioned about his devotion to the Great Pumpkin, Linus can respond like Plantinga—that if there is a Great Pumpkin, then very likely his belief has warrant. Similar responses are available to a number of different belief traditions ranging from the mainstream (Christianity, Hinduism, Islam, Mormonism, etc.) to the eccentric (the Church of Jimi Hendrix, Westboro Baptist members, etc.). Consequently, religious disagreements can boil down to: "I'm right, if I'm right; and you're wrong, if you're wrong." This is hardly fertile ground for productive religious dialogue. While advocates of Reformed Epistemology point out that not all of these different worldviews are amenable to Proper Functionalism, I seriously doubt that they can successfully show incompatibilities with Proper Functionalism in all of them. Ultimately, without criteria for determining whether basic beliefs are warranted or justified that are accessible from the first-person perspective, Reformed Epistemology cannot help anyone ascertain whether his religious beliefs have positive epistemic standing.

Notes

1. Fumerton, *Metaepistemology and Skepticism*, 118.
2. Plantinga, *Warranted Christian Belief*, 285.
3. Ibid., 499.

A Phenomenal Conservatist Response to Proper Functionalism

Logan Paul Gage and Blake McAllister

We must begin by noting that we endorse Reformed Epistemology, defined by McNabb as the claim "that a subject S's religious belief can be justified or warranted apart from argumentation." This is, of course, because we think that subjects are justified in believing propositions that seem true to them so long as they lack defeaters (regardless of whether they are capable of mounting arguments for such propositions—let alone arguments that others would find satisfactory). McNabb, on the other hand, supports the thesis of Reformed Epistemology by defending a Plantingian proper functionalist account of warrant. And it is toward this Plantingian version of Reformed Epistemology that we will offer two concerns. First, we question the sufficiency of the proper functionalist account of warrant. Second, we argue that even if this account of warrant were satisfactory, Phenomenal Conservatism retains an important dialectical advantage over this account.

§1 An Objection to Proper Functionalism

McNabb and Plantinga's proper functionalist account of warrant (warrant being understood as whatever turns true belief into knowledge) claims that S's belief that p is warranted if and only if (i) S's belief that p results from a properly functioning cognitive system, (ii) the cognitive system is operating in a similar environment to the one for which it was designed, (iii) the cognitive system is aimed at the production of true beliefs, and (iv) the system's design plan is such that there is a high objective probability that p is true. We think, however, that a subject could have a true belief that p meet conditions i–iv, and yet not know that p. That is, we think conditions i–iv insufficient for warrant.

Imagine a subject named Skyler. Skyler has a newfound belief in God's existence. The experience that triggered Skyler's theistic belief was, oddly enough, the observing of yard kitsch—in particular, those iconic plastic pink flamingos designed by Don Featherstone in 1957. To Skyler, there is nothing about these flamingos that indicates God's existence. This new belief feels like a random hunch to her. Let us add that Skyler took a psychedelic drug earlier that she knows can induce random beliefs of just this sort. From Skyler's perspective, there is simply no indication that her belief is likely to be true. Realizing this, Skyler tries to stop believing but finds she cannot rid herself of this apparently baseless conviction. Despite all of this, Skyler's belief was not produced by the drug, nor was it entirely random. In actual fact, God designed Skyler to form an irresistible belief in His existence whenever she encounters that precise sort of yard kitsch. Thus, Skyler's belief meets conditions i–iv and, according to Proper Functionalism, is thereby warranted.[1] But, contra Proper Functionalism, Skyler's belief does not seem to constitute *knowledge* that God exists.

What is lacking is some indication from Skyler's own perspective that her belief is true. There needs to be some intelligible connection between the content of her belief and that on which it is based. Skyler's belief, however, is based on an experience whose content bears no discernible relation to God's existence. What we are proposing is that a fifth condition is necessary for warrant—namely, that the belief is based on a body of evidence that, on-balance, indicates the truth of that belief from the first-person perspective. A belief must result from proper functioning *and* be based on good evidence in order to constitute knowledge.

Phenomenal Conservatism explains how this fifth condition can be met by basic beliefs, even though they are not based on evidence from other propositions. On Phenomenal Conservatism, the subject's seeming that p gives the subject evidence for p. Thus, if it seems to you that *the Steelers just scored a touchdown*, then you have some evidence that *the Steelers just scored a touchdown*. Assuming you have no evidence to oppose this, a belief based on that seeming will satisfy the fifth condition on warrant. The key is that the content of your belief (unlike Skyler's) is intelligibly connected to the experience on which it is based.

Now, on Plantinga's model, the content of the triggering experience doesn't ultimately matter. His *SD* is a simple "input–output device" in which certain experiences are designed to trigger theistic belief.[2] Given the right design plan, then, any experience could lend warrant to a theistic belief. It is telling, however, that the stock Plantingian examples are of starry skies, majestic mountains, and tiny flowers. These experiences all seem to bear an intelligible connection to theistic belief: such beauty and apparent design evidence (at least weakly) an intelligent designer. We suspect that, had Plantinga chosen yard kitsch as his go-to example, fewer people would have intuited that the resulting beliefs were warranted. Instead, he chose experiences that bear an intelligible connection to God, allowing the fifth condition on warrant to go unnoticed.

§2 A Dialectical Advantage

Even if our first critique is mistaken, and the proper functionalist account of warrant does not need a fifth condition, there remains a weakness in McNabb's defense of Reformed Epistemology. Reformed Epistemology, once again, is to be understood as the claim that certain religious beliefs can be warranted or justified apart from argumentation.

McNabb's defense of Proper Functionalism, if successful, establishes the following conditional:

(1)   If God exists and has given us a *sensus divinitatis*, then theistic belief can be warranted apart from argumentation.

Notice that this conditional does not assert the truth of Reformed Epistemology. It says that Reformed Epistemology is true *if* we have a God-given *SD*. Defending this conditional was useful for Plantinga's purpose: to defend religious belief against the claim that it is epistemically subpar even if God exists. For, in light of this conditional, you cannot show that theistic belief is unwarranted without showing that it is false. McNabb, on the other hand, is trying to argue that Reformed Epistemology is *true*. Thus, to complete his defense, McNabb needs to provide evidence for both (i) that God exists and (ii) that God gave us an *SD*.[3] We think that the case for (1) is strong and that there is much to be said for (2), but until he provides evidence for these claims, McNabb has not established Reformed Epistemology's assertion that theistic belief can be warranted without arguments.

This problem highlights a serious dialectical advantage of the Phenomenal Conservative approach. On Phenomenal Conservatism, even an atheist could agree that theistic beliefs are sometimes noninferentially justified.[4] If it seems to someone that God exists, and she does not possess lasting defeaters for these strong seemings (challenges arise, we can imagine, but reflection repeatedly assuages her doubts), then Phenomenal Conservatism says that her theistic belief is justified without argumentation, even if God does not exist. Accordingly, Phenomenal Conservatives can argue for Reformed Epistemology without the burden of establishing God's existence (or His bestowal of a special religious faculty).[5] If, however, we seek to support Reformed Epistemology by an appeal to Proper Functionalism, then it becomes incumbent to argue that God exists and that He is likely to give us something like the *SD*. For on current proper functionalist models, atheists should not agree that religious beliefs can be warranted apart from arguments.[6] Phenomenal Conservatism, therefore, makes it considerably easier to argue for Reformed Epistemology than McNabb's Proper Functionalist approach.

Notes

1. Notice that Skyler's knowledge that her theistic belief may be the result of a psychedelic drug does not constitute a defeater given Proper Functionalism. This is because Skyler's continued belief in light of that knowledge is a part of the reliable, truth-aimed design plan given to her by God.
2. Plantinga, *Warranted Christian Belief*, 174–5.
3. He may also need to show that our typical theistic beliefs are actually the result of the *sensus divinitatis* rather than some other cognitive process.
4. You'll notice that Phenomenal Conservatism is about justification, not warrant. This shift in focus is part of why Phenomenal Conservatism possesses the dialectical advantaged spelled out here.
5. To see this approach in action, see McAllister and Dougherty, "Reforming Reformed Epistemology."
6. Plantinga states that if God does not exist, then belief in His existence is probably not warranted. See Plantinga, *Warranted Christian Belief*; however, if Proper Functionalists adopt the model of the *sensus divinitatis* developed in McAllister and Dougherty's "Reforming Reformed

Epistemology" then they might be able to maintain that religious beliefs have some degree of warrant—albeit a degree falling sort of that which is required for knowledge—even if God does not exist. See footnote 21 of the aforementioned article.

A Covenantal Epistemology Response to Proper Functionalism

K. Scott Oliphint

I would like to focus my brief response on the notion of the SD in Proper Functionalism (PF). According to (PF),

> it's important first to understand that, according to Plantinga's story, the SD has been damaged by sin. It may work sufficiently well in most humans but it still doesn't work as it was originally designed. Humans were originally designed to perceive God and His activities in an analogous way to how humans perceive other minds. That is to say, humans were designed to believe in God without possessing any doubts whatsoever. But, sin has damaged the human capacity to become aware of God. And even in some, this capacity seems totally lost.

As (PF) takes its cue from Plantinga, it may help to note Plantinga's own assessment of the (SD). Plantinga recognizes that Calvin's affirmation of the (SD) comes from the apostle Paul. Having quoted Rom. 1:18-20 and select passages from Calvin, Plantinga tells us just exactly how he understands the (SD). The (SD) is a disposition or set of dispositions to form theistic beliefs in various circumstances, in response to the sorts of conditions or stimuli that trigger the working of this sense of divinity.[1]

The central problem in the (PF) use of the (SD) is the ways in which (PF) redefines the (SD), which adds confusion to (PF) in those areas where the (SD) is central. To summarize some of what was in my original essay: the (SD) is neither a capacity *simpliciter* nor is it damaged by virtue of the noetic effects of sin.

There are two general points that the apostle Paul wants to make about (what Calvin calls) the (SD). The first point is that this *sensus* that all people have *is actual knowledge of God* (see Rom. 1:19-21). It is not the case that some have beliefs in God by virtue of the (SD) and some do not; nor is it the case that the (SD) lies dormant or empty until properly stimulated by experience. Paul's point is that, by virtue of all people being made in the image of God, all people inevitably know the God in whose image they are made. It is this knowledge, says Paul, that renders us all without excuse before the judgment seat of God (Rom. 1:20). So, the first point that any (PF) epistemology should recognize is that the (SD), as a matter of fact, functions properly—in all people, at all times. This is Paul's first point.

The second point that Paul, and Calvin following him, wants to make is that the power of sin in our hearts is evidenced in the suppression of this knowledge that God continues to give to us, as his creatures, throughout His creation, both within us and outside of us. This, too, has deep implications for a (PF) epistemology. In effect, the reality is that our cognitive faculties, while still able to navigate and assess, on a superficial level, the facts around us, nevertheless, *do not* function properly; they do not work as they were created to work in the first place. Instead, due to our sin, "we exchange the truth of God for a lie, and worship and serve the creature, rather than the Creator, who is blessed forever. Amen" (Rom. 1:23).

This egregious exchange (of the truth of God for a lie) has implications across the entire spectrum of knowledge, not simply with respect to theism (or atheism). It means, for example, that rather than seeing ourselves as those who are meant to "image" the character of God, we see ourselves as the product of chance, for example, or as nothing but material substances. To misunderstand who we are has extensive ramifications for what we think knowledge is.

Not only so, but it is not the case that one who moves from atheism to (some kind of) theism is one in whom the (SD) has now been properly engaged or activated. Instead, a movement from atheism to anything but Christian theism is a move toward idolatry. Since it is the case that we all truly know the true God, and since our sin moves us to suppress that truth, false religions are products, not of ignorance, nor of an activated (SD), but of the suppression of the knowledge that God gives to us all.

What this means for (PF), and for epistemology in general, is that instead of thinking of knowledge as downstream from our beliefs, we should see, instead, that God has created us as creatures who inevitably *know* and know Him, at the outset. To the extent that we are self-conscious, we are God-conscious. Since that is the case, it would be more fruitful for epistemology if we learned to assess our various and sundry beliefs in light of the true and certain knowledge that God Himself gives to all people everywhere.

This would mean, of course, that the knowledge that comes to all people by virtue of God's revelation in creation would necessarily be coupled with the knowledge that God gives in his special revelation, the Bible. While the Bible is certainly not a textbook on epistemology, it does give us the basic foundations on which epistemology (and all other disciplines) ought to proceed.[2]

Furthermore, as Plantinga admits, a (PF) epistemology is essentially Reidian. That is, it depends on some version of Common Sense Realism. But, as George Marsden has argued, the fundamental problem with a Reidian approach to knowledge, on which (at least some) (PF) proponents stand, is that "common sense could not settle a dispute over what was a matter of common sense."[3] The reason it could not settle such a dispute is that it could not carry the weight that fundamental *principia* are required to carry. What common-sense, or properly basic, beliefs need is a foundation by which they can be properly measured and assessed. That foundation can be found (1) in a proper understanding of the (SD) as true knowledge of the true God and (2) in a proper acknowledgement of the (SD) that can come only by way of repentance from sin and a turning to Christ. Thus, both general revelation and special revelation are required to ground any epistemology that wants to assert and assess the proper functioning of our deliverances of reason.

Notes

1. Plantinga, *Warranted Christian Belief*, 173.
2. For a fascinating assessment of the relationship of philosophy to theology and its principles, see Stoker, "Reconnoitering the Theory of Knowledge of Prof. Dr. Cornelius van Til."
3. Marsden, "The Collapse of American Evangelical Academia," 244.

A Tradition-Based Perspectival Response to Proper Functionalism

Erik Baldwin

I agree with McNabb on many things. So long as the Plantingian is willing to concede that Plantingian religious epistemology counts as a tradition of inquiry, the main thesis of Reformed Epistemology is consistent with my MacIntyrean rationality of traditions approach to religious epistemology. I don't disagree that proper function is necessary for warrant, nor do I dispute the claim that conditions (1)–(4) are necessary for warranted (or justified) belief. McNabb responds well to Zagzebski's objection, and I don't see any problems with his response to the objection regarding the reliability of the SD and his argument that divine hiddenness doesn't present special problems for the Reformed Epistemologist is plausible enough. However, there are, I think, some serious problems with the Plantingian approach to religious epistemology. Specifically, while I accept that conditions (1)–(4) are necessary for warranted belief, I don't think that they are jointly sufficient (at least not always so). Second, I don't think the traditional Plantingian view that all (potential) defeaters can be dealt with in a way that readily preserves the properly basic status of Theistic and/or Christian Belief is plausible.

According to McNabb, a person's religious beliefs are warranted just in case conditions (1)–(4) obtain. I maintain that, sometimes, a person's beliefs aren't internally rational unless he or she has and exercises intellectual virtues. For instance, it is implausible to suppose that all cases of disagreement between Plantingians about just which of several viable extensions of the standard AC model is true can be dealt with in reasonable manner just in case the disputants' cognitive faculties are functioning properly. Rather, I think that warranted religious belief in this sort of a case requires one to believe in accord with the meta-cognitive virtue of reasonableness. Elsewhere, I have proposed the following condition on reasonable belief:

Approximately, S (fully) manifests the meta-cognitive virtue of reasonability if:

(i) S, *qua* epistemic agent, is functioning well epistemically by having and exercising the epistemic virtues that underlie the manifestation of reasonability, including the intellectual virtues of the love of knowledge, firmness, courage and caution, humility, autonomy, generosity, and practical wisdom;

(ii) S is responsive to reasons; for example, S is willing to correct his/her views in light of criticism, willing to provide others with reasons, has a measure of good judgment that is incompatible with perversely bad judgment, and is to some degree self-critical, at least in the sense of being disposed to think about and correct tendencies that have gotten them into trouble;

(iii) S is minimally rational with respect to his/her desires and is not subject to serious affective disorders (e.g., extreme apathy or severe clinical depression) and is appropriately concerned about his/her own well-being; and

(iv) S is appropriately conscientious and reflective regarding the truth of his/her beliefs, especially when those beliefs are challenged.[1]

In addition to conditions (1)–(4), therefore, I think that internal rationality sometimes requires that (i)–(iv) also be satisfied. In other words, sometimes, one's belief that p is internally rational only if he or she manifests the meta-cognitive virtue of reasonability with respect to holding that p, if not fully, then at least to an adequate degree.

A traditional Plantingian might object that that one can manifest the meta-cognitive virtue of reasonability in virtue of being internally rational. Plantinga characterizes internal rationality as a matter of "forming or holding the appropriate beliefs in response to experience, including both phenomenal imagery and doxastic experience."[2] Internal rationality involves making inferences and deductions, realizing various connections between the beliefs one holds, looking for evidence as appropriate, being responsive to criticism, and the willingness to be corrected when wrong. It also pertains to dealing appropriately with epistemic defeaters for one's beliefs. I grant that if one is internally rational then (ii)–(iv) hold, but the requirements on reasonableness are more demanding. For (i) to hold, an epistemic agent must have and exercise certain epistemic virtues, something that doesn't happen just in case S's cognitive faculties are functioning properly, and so on. As Roberts and Wood write:

> Someone who takes this approach [the approach of the virtue epistemologist] has given up the spirit of a faculty epistemology ... Faculty epistemologists who are willing to accord to character traits a major and essential role in the acquisition of some epistemic goods have wandered far from the original idea of a faculty epistemology, because what is doing the work in the new permutation of their view is no longer just the faculties but, in the upper-end cases at least, the epistemic agent who *uses* the faculty virtuously for his or her purposes. The epistemologist may wish to keep the virtues in the humble role of supplementing the functioning of faculties, but in reality he has reduced the faculties to appliances in the hands of a person.[3]

A second problem I have with McNabb's account stems from the fact that some believers, having been exposed to evidence that counts against the truth of some core religious belief, or otherwise vexed by either the Problem of Evil or the Problem of Divine Hiddenness, are in a position of doubt. For instance, a believer who becomes aware of experience-based testimony from honest and sincere believers who belong to other religious traditions may no longer take himself to have a good reason for taking oneself to be in an epistemically superior position to those who hold other (and inconsistent) beliefs, and thereby acquire a defeater for their experience-based religious beliefs. In the context of how to rationally deal with testimony and counter-testimony from two sincere and honest religious believers from different religious traditions, Faith and Victor, Michael Thune and I argue that:

> a thorough knowledge of the facts of religious experience implies an awareness that there are millions of epistemically virtuous people who report transformative experiences upon which they come to form mutually exclusive religious beliefs. This spreads the quality of testimony across a larger quantity of testifiers, through different religious traditions. Even if Faith were to amass testimony from many epistemically virtuous Christians, there would, in all probability, be just as many (or more) honest and sincere individuals who could provide counter-testimony. And this sufficiently casts doubt on Faith's belief that her religious beliefs are epistemically better grounded than Victor's, at the very least it makes it likely that there exists epistemic parity between hers and Victor's beliefs.[4]

Should a rationality defeater of this sort arise, it must be dealt with adequately. If the rationality of Faith's religious beliefs depends, at least in part, on evidence for thinking that her religious experiences are epistemically better grounded than Victor's, then, in the absence of that evidence, Faith's religious beliefs would be subject to defeat and no longer (fully) rational. Thus, in this case, the continued rationality of Faith's religious belief depends on evidence (namely, her reasons for thinking that her religious experiences are generally epistemically better grounded than Victor's), even if she need not continually bring that evidence before her mind. In that case Faith's religious beliefs would be warranted but no longer (fully) properly basic. Strictly speaking, my position is consistent with the main thesis of Reformed Epistemology; I agree that one's religious belief *can* be justified or warranted apart from argumentation. And yet there are very many people whose religious beliefs won't in fact be justified or warranted apart from evidence and argumentation. How many people will be fully satisfied in thinking that their religious beliefs are warranted in a properly basic way, apart from all evidence and argumentation? It's hard to say. But for many who reflect on the problems I call attention to, the "can" of Reformed Epistemology expresses a kind of counterfactual possibility, and that this is so takes much steam out of the engine of Reformed Epistemology (at least for them).

By way of conclusion, I haven't argued that Plantinga's Proper Functionalism is wrong, but rather that it is incomplete and stands in need of modification and/or amendment. Specifically, I have argued that, sometimes, reasonable religious belief requires believing in accord with the meta-cognitive virtue of reasonableness. I also argued that reasonableness requires that one have and exercise intellectual virtues, which isn't something that happens automatically and just in case one's cognitive faculties are functioning properly, and so on. Moreover, sometimes, reasonableness requires that one have a defeater-defeater that depends on evidence. Thus, for many people, their reasonable religious beliefs won't be justified and/or warranted apart from at least some evidence and argumentation, especially in order for at least some of their defeater-defeaters success to be effective.

Notes

1. Baldwin, *Fully Informed Reasonable Disagreement and Tradition Based Perspectivalism*, 65.
2. Plantinga, *Warranted Christian Belief*, 111.

3. Robert C. Roberts and W. Jay Wood, *Intellectual Virtues: An Essay in Regulative Epistemology* (Oxford: Oxford University Press, 2007), 110–11.

4. Erik Baldwin and Michael Thune, "The Epistemological Limits of Experience-Based Exclusive Religious Belief," *Religious Studies* 44, no. 4 (2008): 452–53.

Proper Functionalism: Response to Critics

Tyler Dalton McNabb

Ad DePoe

DePoe questions the definition that I give for Reformed Epistemology. He states,

> It seems consistent with K. Scott Oliphint's Covenantal Epistemology and Erik Baldwin's Traditions Approach. Moreover, this characterization is compatible with the Phenomenal Conservative approach to epistemology given by Gage and McAllister who also describe their approach as justifying theistic belief without argumentation. In fact, my own view of Classical Evidentialism may even satisfy this broad statement of McNabb's depending on how rigidly one defines "argumentation."

Notice my definition is similar to Andrew Moon's definition which states, "*Reformed epistemology*, roughly, is the thesis that religious belief can be rational without argument."[1] Moon makes the same point DePoe does, in that the thesis of Reformed Epistemology is compatible with most contemporary epistemological theories. In some sense, not counting DePoe, I think the contributors in this volume do endorse the thesis of Reformed Epistemology. Gage and McCallister make this clear in their response to me and Baldwin seems to indicate as much as well. What is unique to my approach is the way I argue for it.

I care about knowledge more so than I care about justification. Hence, I primarily talk about warrant rather than justification. As for justification,

I agree with Gage and McAllister that justification comes cheap. What's really interesting is whether it is possible that a subject possesses knowledge. I have laid out conditions that I take to be necessary and jointly sufficient for warrant, and I have argued that religious belief could be warranted apart from argument if the aforementioned conditions are in place. While in some sense, it is easier to argue for the thesis of Reformed Epistemology on a theory like Phenomenal Conservatism (as Gage and McAllister point out), if what one is concerned about is knowledge, Phenomenal Conservatism will have significant limitations. So, whether one should utilize Proper Functionalism or Phenomenal Conservatism, it depends on the context.

DePoe also hints at externalists struggling to endorse any meaningful meta-level requirement. Elsewhere, I have suggested the following:

> Proper Functionalist MP: If it is in principle impossible to show S's belief that p is in part based on a successful argument, whenever it is such that the design plan requires p to be based on a successful argument, then S is not warranted in believing that p.[2]

Notice, that this meta-level principle requires that agents with respect to nonbasic beliefs exercise their rational faculties as reflective agents. Thus, DePoe's claim that Proper Functionalism entails that agents act purely mechanistically seems wrong.

DePoe of course, has other complaints:

> McNabb isn't opposed to people having evidence to support their religious beliefs, but they are superfluous to determining whether one's religious beliefs have positive epistemic standing. At best, a person's reasons for holding religious beliefs become relevant only when addressing defeaters for one's religious beliefs.

While I agree that some persons won't need arguments for the proper formation of religious beliefs, I think that there are some who will need such arguments to not only stave off defeat but also initially form their belief to begin with.

Finally, DePoe calls an old friend, the Great Pumpkin:

> When questioned about his devotion to the Great Pumpkin, Linus can respond like Plantinga—that if there is a Great Pumpkin, then very likely his belief has warrant. Similar responses are available to a number of different belief traditions ranging from the mainstream (Christianity, Hinduism, Islam, Mormonism, etc.) to the eccentric (the Church of Jimi Hendrix,

Westboro Baptist members, etc.) …. Consequently, religious disagreements can boil down to: "I'm right, if I'm right; and you're wrong, if you're wrong." This is hardly fertile ground for productive religious dialogue.

Of course, there are some important disanalogous points to consider between Christian belief and Great Pumpkin belief. For example, Great Pumpkin belief is extremely susceptible to defeat. One could merely go to a pumpkin patch during Halloween and see that he doesn't exist.[3] One couldn't just as easily go to Jesus's tomb and see the body of Jesus still in the grave. There is another point to be made, however. Plantinga argues that if theism is true, then belief in theism is probably warranted. His reasoning for endorsing the said conditional is that if there was a loving God, He'd likely want a relationship with humans, so, He would likely create a faculty in humans so that they would become aware of Him. But what justification would Great Pumpkinites have for endorsing their conditional that if Great Pumpkinism is true, then Great Pumpkin belief is probably warranted? Plantinga states it best:

> But why think it likely that if Great Pumpkinism is true, there will be a *sensus cucurbitatis*? Why think the Great Pumpkin has created us? Why think this pumpkin would care about whether human beings know anything about it? Why think it is conscious, capable of knowledge, and the like? All the story says is that there is this very large and scary-looking pumpkin that returns to Linus' pumpkin patch every Halloween. The argument for there being a *sensus cucurbitatis* if Great Pumpkinism is true, has very little going for it.[4]

If the Great Pumpkin thesis entails that the Great Pumpkin is this extremely powerful being, who, out of love, designed human faculties in such a way as to produce belief about his existence, then maybe what we are talking about isn't really so different than generic theism.[5] This doesn't in anyway make implausible the conditional that Plantinga defends.

With respect to diverse religions, Baldwin and I have argued in great detail that not all serious religious traditions can utilize Plantinga's religious epistemology.[6] In fact, ultimately, those religions that can utilize Plantinga's religious epistemology are those traditions that share much in common with the Judeo-Christian religion. Again, this isn't evidence against Plantinga's conditionals or AC models.

Finally, is DePoe right in that my approach leads to a stalemate of sorts where the two differing religious subjects have to agree to disagree? Not necessarily. Again, my religious epistemology isn't at odds with natural theology. While it would entail that the two subjects could lack arguments, and yet, one of the subjects still possesses warranted religious belief, it doesn't entail that there isn't fertile ground for productive religious dialogue. There is nothing here that prevents a subject from utilizing natural theology to try to convince his religious counterpart. But, let's be honest. There are very few arguments in philosophy that convince most truth-seeking persons of a controversial opinion. Not being able to do this is not a failure of Proper Functionalism or Reformed Epistemology.

Ad Gage and McAllister

Gage and McAllister give two objections to my view. First, while they don't question the necessity of the proper function conditions, they do question if such conditions are jointly sufficient for warrant. Specifically, they argue that in conjunction with the proper functionalist constraints, I need to endorse an internal rationality constraint. Second, they argue that even if Proper Functionalism is a plausible theory of warrant, Phenomenal Conservatism is a better theory to argue for the thesis of Reformed Epistemology. This is because on Phenomenal Conservatism, it is easier to argue that belief in God is properly basic for an individual, while on Proper Functionalism, at best, one can argue for the epistemic possibility that belief in God is properly basic. Since they take it that I am arguing for the truth of Reformed Epistemology, I need to recognize the superiority of their position.

Starting with the second objection, I'll take each objection in turn. First, to clarify, I argued "for the plausibility of the thesis of Reformed Epistemology." I don't take this to be exactly the same thing as arguing that the thesis is true. Second, mentioned in the DePoe discussion, the motivation of arguing for Proper Functionalism rather than Phenomenal Conservatism relates to my worries about knowledge. Perhaps our intuitions clash with respect to if we should focus on knowledge or justification, but I don't see a real need to be divided here. I, for one, am grateful for Gage and McAllister arguing for Reformed Epistemology in the way that they do.

As it pertains to the first question, Gage and McAllister give an example of Skyler. Skyler takes a drug that he knows can oftentimes cause random beliefs. From seeing a pink flamingo in the yard, Skyler, all of a sudden, finds himself believing that God exists. He reflects and reflects and, try as he might, he can't shake the belief. He sincerely believes that God exists. What are we to think of Skyler? Is proper function enough? Gage and McAllister argue that it is not enough. For starters, they state that, "there needs to be some intelligible connection between the content of her belief and that on which it is based."

Kenneth Boyce succinctly summarizes Michael Bergmann's work on there not needing to be a tight connection between what we experience and our beliefs:

> Bergmann notes, for example, that "the tactile sensations we experience when touching a hard surface seem to have no logical relation to (nor do they resemble) the content of the hardness beliefs they prompt." Because this is so, Bergmann argues that the evidential support relations that hold between various sensory experiences and the beliefs formed in response to them cannot be explained in terms of necessary connections. But this prompts the question as to what does explain these support relations.[7]

Boyce and Bergmann both suggest that the answer to this question is a proper functionalist account. So, why think Skyler doesn't know in this case? If Skyler's faculties are designed to produce the belief that God exists (designed to produce theistic belief even in light of being aware of taking said pill that is known for causing random beliefs) when he sees a plastic flamingo, and, if his faculties are aimed at truth, and there is a high objective probability of the belief being true under these conditions, it seems like his belief isn't sufficiently lucky in any relevant sense. We should consider Skyler's belief warranted.

Ad Baldwin

Baldwin largely agrees with my approach to epistemology. In fact, we have coauthored several papers and a book on the topic of religious epistemology. While I perceive myself as a card carrying or traditional Plantingian, Baldwin's epistemology combines elements from both Plantinga's and McIntyre's work. As it shouldn't be much of a surprise, where Baldwin and I differ is with respect to the McIntyre bit. Baldwin encourages me to consider Proper Functionalism as a tradition of inquiry rather than a theory that transcends traditions. Baldwin also disagrees with my view that the proper functionalist constraints are sufficient for warrant when it comes to a subject entertaining a defeater for one of her beliefs. I'll briefly respond to both of these concerns in turn.

I'm still not entirely sure I understand the motivation for considering Proper Functionalism as merely a tradition of inquiry, rather than a theory that transcends tradition. Baldwin, again, argues that the encyclopedia advocates were extremely naïve in thinking that all rational and nonbiased individuals would agree on objectively sound arguments. And, I can totally agree with him that those belonging to the encyclopedia tradition are in a self-defeating position. There are nonbiased people who disagree with the arguments endorsed by the encyclopedia advocates, and granting this, it would follow that we should consider their arguments unsound. But, I'm still not sure why it follows that, "there is no such thing as universal rationality or theoretical-rationality-as-such, but rather that there are numerous rival tradition-based standpoints each with their own particular standards of rational justification." I'm simply not familiar enough with McIntyre's philosophical position to speak more to this issue. As of what I have to go off of, I must kindly decline Baldwin's proposal to see Proper Functionalism as merely a tradition-based inquiry.

With respect to Baldwin's second point, there might not be a way to resolve our disagreement here outside of agreeing that we have an intuition clash. As long as subject S reflects on the potential defeater and still firmly believes that p, and her firmly believing that p is due to her truth-aimed faculties properly functioning, and there is a high objective probability that p is true, then S's belief that p is warranted. While I agree that the design plan could contingently be such that with respect to some of our beliefs (e.g., belief in the correct theory of warrant), in light of defeaters, we might need to meet access or virtue requirements, I don't have any reason to think that the human design plan is such that when it comes to religious beliefs, that such requirements exist.[8] At least, this doesn't fit well with how my religious beliefs seemed to be formed. And, while I don't think Proper Functionalism leads to a purely mechanistic view of all of our knowledge (see response to DePoe), surely there is a sense in which some of our beliefs come about in a nearly pure mechanistic way. In this case, if S's faculty correctly processes an experience or input of some kind, and it reliably leads to the true belief that p, there isn't anything else that is needed. I think religious beliefs are often formed in this way.

Ad Oliphint

Oliphint argues that Plantinga's interpretation of Calvin is wrong. Rather than thinking that the SD is a faculty, we should interpret the SD as actual knowledge that God exists. A consequence of this view is that if all humans have the SD, then all humans have knowledge that God exists. This is clearly Oliphint's view: "Paul's point is that, by virtue of all people being made in the image of God, all people inevitably know the God in whose image they are made."

Calvin's main justification for thinking that humans possess an SD is Rom. 1. How ought we understand this passage? A robust debate on how best to interpret Rom. 1 is beyond the limits and the scope of this reply. However, I do want to briefly mention two things. First, to be clear, there are esteemed biblical scholars who reject the view that Rom. 1 entails that all persons possess knowledge that God exists.[9] Second, to interpret Rom. 1 as suggesting that literally all human persons know that God exists would be to commit ourselves to the incredibly implausible view that embryos, newborns, and severely mentally challenged individuals know that God exists. It seems like we need to make some sort of allowance for Rom. 1 to not apply to every single person who has ever lived. Viewing the SD as a faculty, rather than as knowledge, fits better with making such allowance.

Lastly, while I won't debate whether Calvin's view of the SD is closer to Plantinga's or Oliphint's, I do think it is important to clarify that Plantinga's epistemology doesn't depend on whether his interpretation of Calvin is right or wrong. Plantinga primarily argues that warranted theistic and Christian belief is epistemically possible. While it is right to say that Plantinga's religious epistemology is at least inspired by Calvin, whether he has correctly interpreted Calvin makes little difference to the plausibility of his religious epistemology. Of course, for those following the Reformed tradition, the clear inspiration from Calvin in Plantinga's epistemology should be considered sufficient to count Plantinga's epistemology as broadly within the tradition.

Notes

1. Moon, "Recent Work in Reformed Epistemology," 879.
2. McNabb, "Proper Functionalism and the Metalevel: A Friendly Response to Timothy and Lydia McGrew."
3. Joseph Kim, *Reformed Epistemology and the Problem of Religious Diversity: Proper Function, Epistemic Disagreement, and Christian Exclusivism* (Cambridge: James Clarke, 2012), 77.
4. Alvin Plantinga, "Replies to My Commentators," in *Plantinga's Warranted Christian Belief: Critical Essays with a Reply by Alvin Plantinga*, ed. Dieter Schönecker (Berlin: De Gruyter, 2017), 248.

5. Ibid., 248.
6. See Baldwin and McNabb, *Plantingian Religious Epistemology and World Religions.*
7. Boyce, "Proper Functionalism."
8. For a detailed discussion on possible design plan requirements, especially requirements in light of potential defeaters, see chapter 11 of Baldwin and McNabb, *Plantingian Religious Epistemology and World Religions.*
9. For example, see Scott W. Hahn, *Romans* (Grand Rapids, MI: Baker, 2017); Also, see Douglas J. Moo, *The Epistle to the Romans* (Grand Rapids, MI: Eerdmans, 1996), 123.

4

Covenantal Epistemology

K. Scott Oliphint

The view of religious epistemology presented in this chapter will be decidedly and centrally Christian. Though some might want to argue that epistemology is underdetermined with respect to Christianity, the truth of the matter is that Scripture and the theology that flows from it give us significant and substantial *principia* that undergird and determine certain principles of epistemology. In that way, Christianity is a sure and certain guide to religious epistemology.

To put the matter in more common parlance, the guiding principle of a Covenantal approach to epistemology is *credo ut intelligam*—I believe in order to understand. In other words, the tenets of the Christian *faith* guide and direct a proper *understanding* of epistemology, generally, and of religious epistemology, more specifically. So determinative is Christian faith for epistemology that Scripture can say, "The fear of the LORD is the *beginning* of knowledge ..." (Prov. 1:7, ESV, my emphasis).

So, there is no way, properly, to discuss the philosophical aspects of religious epistemology without first recognizing the theological foundations that support and inform those aspects. Thus, a Covenantal Epistemology must be explicated, first of all, according to its theological tenets in order to recognize its philosophical implications and entailments. In that way, a Covenantal Epistemology rests on God's (covenantal) revelation, as that revelation finds its home in creation and in Scripture.

In order to properly grasp the main contours of a Covenantal Epistemology with respect to our knowledge of God, two central categories are in view. We must first clarify who this God is and then recognize who we are as covenant creatures before Him.

The central truth that grounds everything else is that this God whom we know is the Triune God who climactically reveals Himself in history in the

Lord Jesus Christ. This God is one God in three *hypostases*.[1] That is, the three *hypostases*—Father, Son, and Holy Spirit—are each identical in one essence, even as they remain distinct in their respective hypostases.

This great and majestic *truth* is, of course, a great and majestic *mystery*. Even as the church has been careful in its history to articulate this truth, this is a truth that the mind is unable wholly to grasp. For the Father to be *essentially* identical to the Son, for example, and yet remain the Father, and *not* the Son, is impossible for us completely to comprehend. We affirm it because Scripture requires it. And we strive to articulate it in ways that will enhance our understanding of it. But the fullness of its truth is beyond our intellectual grasp.

This "Triune" nature of God is the focus of everything else that we say about Him, including His incomprehensibility. The Athanasian Creed puts it this way:

> The Father incomprehensible: the Son incomprehensible: and the Holy Ghost incomprehensible. The Father eternal: the Son eternal: and the Holy Ghost eternal. And yet they are not three eternals: but one eternal. As also there are not three uncreated: nor three incomprehensibles, but one uncreated: and one incomprehensible.[2]

The distinct hypostases, in other words, are each the one essential God, even as they remain distinct. The eternity of the Father *just is* the eternity of the Son, and so on.

God's Triune incomprehensibility is the (metaphysical) foundation of a Covenantal Epistemology. When we confess that God is incomprehensible, we are acknowledging the fact that human beings are creatures and that the Triune God alone is not a creature. As Augustine put it, "if you comprehend him it is not God you comprehend."[3]

Instead, the Triune God, as the *Westminster Confession of Faith* puts it, is "infinite in being and perfection, a most pure spirit, invisible, without body, parts, or passions; immutable, immense, eternal, incomprehensible, almighty, most wise, most holy, most free, most absolute ...."

Once we recognize the *incomprehensibility* of the Triune God, we immediately ask how it could be that we could *know* this God. The fact of the matter is that in order to know God *He would first have to make Himself known*. And He would have to make Himself known in a way that limited, sinful, and dependent creatures could receive and understand. Of course, since the beginning, that is exactly what God has done.

Christianity maintains that this Triune God is the Creator of the universe (compare Gen. 1:1-2 and Jn 1:1-3). At the point of creation, God (centrally in the Son) condescends to His creation, and to His creatures, in order to relate to them on their level. This is called God's covenantal condescension. The *Westminster Confession of Faith*, chapter seven, section one, says it concisely and profoundly:

> The distance between God and the creature is so great, that although reasonable creatures do owe obedience unto Him as their Creator, yet they could never have any fruition of Him as their blessedness and reward, but by some voluntary condescension on God's part, which He hath been pleased to express by way of covenant.

The "distance" of which the Confession speaks is metaphorical. What "distance" means to say is that there is an ontological *distinction* between God and creation such that the latter can have no "fruition" of the former until and unless God "voluntarily" condescends by way of covenant.

Whatever its other particulars, and those are monumentally important, God's covenantal condescension entails that He establishes a perpetual, reciprocal relationship with all of His creatures, but most especially all of His human creatures.[4] Thus, Reformed theology maintains that God is our ultimate, ever-present, and immediate environment.

But what does it mean that God is our ultimate environment? Two emphases can be given here, the first dealing with who we are and the second, more directly relevant to our topic and depending on the first, with what we know.

When the Triune God condescends to His creation, He does so in order to relate to that creation, to be involved in it (all the while remaining who He essentially is). More specifically, He creates man (which, in biblical terminology, includes *both* male and female) *in His own image*. Without detailing just exactly what that image is, there can be no question that it constitutes our basic identity as human beings. It means that we are, originally, fundamentally, and eternally, image. This truth goes hand-in-hand with the fact that God is our ultimate environment (more on this below). As our environment, we all, as human beings, live our lives *coram deo*; we live our lives in the presence of Him in whose image we are.

It might help us to think of image here in terms of a mirror image. What has to be the case for a mirror image to be present? The first requirement is that the "original" be present, in front of the mirror. It is also true that the image, as image, while reflecting the original, depends at every second on the presence of the original for its very existence. If the original is no longer present, the image is gone. Image is, essentially, dependent for its existence and every one of its characteristics on the presence of the original whose image it is. So it is with God in relation to human beings.

The Lord God who made us as image gave us responsibilities with respect to His creation, responsibilities that presuppose our inextricable (universal) bond with creation. Given that He is Lord, we were meant to be "under-lords" over God's creation; He gave us dominion over what He had made. This dominion includes (though it does not exhaust) the fact that there is a "lordship" relationship between man, as male and female, and the rest of creation. In order to understand just what this lordship relationship is, we look, in the first place, to God who is the Lord. Two aspects of lordship should be highlighted here.

(1) As Lord, God has committed Himself, for eternity, to His creation. He has promised not to annihilate what He has made, but rather to keep it for Himself forever. As was alluded to above, we call this commitment a covenant; it is a commitment of God the Lord to tie himself so inextricably to what He has made that creation, being bound by God to God, will go on into and for eternity. (2) As Lord, the relationship that obtains is not one of equality. Because God has committed Himself to us it does not entail that He has become an equal partner in this relationship. He is and remains God and we are and will remain His creatures. He neither depends on us nor owes us anything (Rom. 11:33*ff*.). We owe him allegiance and worship, and we owe it to him for eternity. He rules over us—lovingly, sovereignly, wisely—and we submit to that rule (either now or in the future—cf. Phil. 2:9-11).

When God created man in His own image, He intended for us to be lords over everything else that He made. This lordship over creation carries the same two implications, noted above, of God's lordship over us. God has committed us to creation in such a way that we are inextricably linked to it.

For example, it is instructive to notice that, in creating the animal world, God used the same "dust" that He used in creating Adam. In creating Adam, notice, "the LORD God formed the man of dust from the ground" (compare Gen. 2:7 with Eccl. 3:20). This is intended to show us, at least, that we, like the beasts, are children of dust (Gen. 3:19). Adam (and, indirectly, Eve, since Eve came from Adam) came from the same "stuff" as the beasts (Gen. 2:19). Thus, we are linked with the creation of the world, in one sense, because we are taken from it; as human creatures we are also, quite literally, a part of the world that was created prior to us. God took the dust of the world and made Adam.

But there is a significant difference in the creation of Adam, a difference, we could say, that marks us off from everything else created: "... then the

LORD God formed the man of dust from the ground and breathed into his nostrils the breath of life, and the man became a living creature" (Gen. 2:7). Of course, the beasts of the earth were living as well when God created them. But our "living," that act of God that constituted man as a "living creature," was a result of God's own *inbreathing*. It was that inbreathing, the imparting of the very breath of God in us, that made us images of God.

The point to be made here is that, in creating us as image, God bound us together, not only with creation, but primarily with *Himself* as the Triune Lord. There is a covenantal bond of humanity with (the rest of) creation such that, since creation, one will not, and cannot, exist without the other.

It is for this reason that Paul, in speaking of the condition of creation after the fall, can say confidently that the whole creation groans and itself was subjected to futility (Rom. 8:19-20). It does not groan because of its own inherent deficiencies. It groans because, in our sinning, we subjected it to futility (cf. Gen. 3:16-19). Creation, in covenant with man, fell, *because we fell*.

It is this fall of man that brings into creation all of the discordance and depravity that we now face. The world is not now as it was in the beginning. In the beginning, it was all very good (see Gen. 1:4, 10, 12, 18, 25, 31). Once Adam determined to interpret reality on his own, rather than in dependence on God and what He had said, everything was spoiled, to the point of rottenness. So, we are spoiled and will rot, as will the rest of creation.

It is because we are spoiled from our original creation, and spoiled to the point of rottenness, that we have a problem of knowledge in the first place. Before sin entered the world, there was an immediate (i.e., noninferential) and natural coherence between God and human beings, between human beings, and between human beings and creation. The most natural thing for Adam and Eve was to know God in relation to themselves, and themselves in relation to God and to the rest of creation. For example, as soon as Eve was created, Adam immediately recognized her as one equal to himself— "Bone of my bone and flesh of my flesh" (Gen. 2:23). He knew, immediately, that another human being had been created, and she was created in order to be in an intimate relationship with Adam. So also, when God told Adam and Eve to have dominion over His creation (Gen. 1:28), there was no "problem of knowledge" with respect to that creation. There was no "problem of knowledge" prior to the fall because there were no problems in the Garden, when everything was very good, because everything was created "very good" by God who is the source of all goodness.

How, then, do we assess the problem of the knowledge of God, given the fall into sin?

The first thing we have to see is that sin is a deep, insidious, and pervasive problem for all of creation, and most especially for us. The condition of sin is a condition of spiritual *death* (Eph. 2:1), not simply of sickness. We are *enslaved* (Rom. 6:16-17) by and to sin. It is our master and we seek diligently to obey it.

In our resolute obedience to our master, sin, things that were originally not a problem have become deeply problematic. Once the "link" between close fellowship with our Creator and ourselves was broken by Adam's sin, we are detached as well from those initial and natural connections that our Creator embedded into his creation. We seek, after the fall and because of our sin, to interpret ourselves, other people, and the rest of creation without reference to the Triune God who made it all and who sustains it by His sovereign power. Worse, we insist that it can all be properly understood whether or not we refer it all to Him. The "link" that sin broke is a link that we, in our sin, pretend was never there in the first place.

This is all to say that the reason there is a problem with respect to knowledge of God is because *of us*. The problem is not God's and He bears no responsibility for it.

One way, perhaps the best way, to describe the sin problem with respect to our knowledge, generally, and our knowledge of God, more specifically, is to recognize that sin has rendered us *irrational* with respect to the things that we claim to know. We can take a fairly standard understanding of what is rational and what is irrational as our framework here:

> In its primary sense, rationality is a normative concept that philosophers have generally tried to characterize in such a way that, for any action, belief, or desire, if it is rational we ought to choose it.[5]

This notion of "ought-ness" opens up a plethora of problems, but we can leave them aside for our purposes here. Alternately,

> Irrationality seems to be the more fundamental normative category; for although there are conflicting substantive accounts of irrationality, all agree that to say of an action, belief, or desire that it is irrational is to claim that it should always be avoided.[6]

Clearly, attempting to understand ourselves, others, and the rest of creation *without reference to and in defiance of* the One who made it all and who sustains its every detail "should always be avoided." Instead of being avoided, however, such an attitude is embraced, even celebrated. That is, our own sin entices us and lures us into thinking that we ourselves and the world around us are all self-sufficient, able to be and to work quite apart from the One who created and sustains it all.

This way of understanding what is rational and what is irrational presupposes that we know what we *should* do. Surely we can't be deemed irrational for not avoiding something that we have no way of deeming harmful. We can't be faulted for believing in something which we could not know is to be avoided. This brings us to the first of two important and crucial aspects of a Covenantal Epistemology.

How, we could ask, is it possible to reconnect the link that sin has broken between the Triune God and us? How can the natural and initial connection, given at creation, between God, people and all of creation be restored to its proper and prominent place?

The Apostle Paul actually addresses questions like this as he writes his epistle to the Romans. In that epistle, Paul begins by considering the effects of sin on all of humanity. He does that because the bad news has to be understood and embraced in order for the good news of the righteousness of Christ in the gospel (Rom. 3:23ff.) to be seen for what it is. That is, for us to see our desperate need for the righteousness of Christ, we first have to recognize our own sin and utter unrighteousness.

We should first note what Paul says and then see how what he says is foundational for epistemology. We will focus our attention on ch. 1, vv. 18-23, 25, and 32:

> [18] For the wrath of God is revealed from heaven against all ungodliness and unrighteousness of men, who by their unrighteousness suppress the truth. [19] For what can be known about God is plain to them, because God has shown it to them. [20] For his invisible attributes, namely, his eternal power and divine nature, have been clearly perceived, ever since the creation of the world, in the things that have been made. So they are without excuse. [21] For although they knew God, they did not honor him as God or give thanks to him, but they became futile in their thinking, and their foolish hearts were darkened. [22] Claiming to be wise, they became fools, [23] and exchanged the glory of the immortal God for images resembling mortal man and birds and animals and creeping things. [25] ... they exchanged the truth about God for a lie and worshiped and served the creature rather than the Creator, who is blessed forever! Amen. [32] Though they know God's righteous decree that those who practice such things deserve to die, they not only do them but give approval to those who practice them.

In the latter half of Rom. 1 (and into Rom. 2), Paul has one overarching concern, that is, to explain just how the wrath of God is made manifest among those who are outside of Christ, those who remain in Adam. In order to make clear the effects of God's wrath, as it is now revealed, Paul directs us both backward, to the beginning of creation itself, and forward, to the outworking of God's wrath for those who are covenant-breakers in Adam.

As Paul begins his discussion of the revelation of God's wrath from heaven, he has two primary aspects of that wrath in view—the cause and the effects. He gives the universal scope of the cause itself in v. 18. God's wrath is revealed from heaven "against all ungodliness and unrighteousness of men, who by their unrighteousness suppress the truth." It is ungodliness and unrighteousness against which God's wrath is revealed. But Paul goes on to define, in a striking way, just what it is that motivates God's wrath toward all who are in Adam, all who are covenant-breakers. He introduces a specificity to this unrighteousness; it is an unrighteousness that is defined essentially as a "suppression of the truth."

Verse 18, then, is a general announcement of the fact that God's wrath is revealed, and the reason for that wrath. The cause of God's wrath toward us is our unrighteous suppression of the truth. In other words, God's wrath is revealed from heaven because, in our sinful wickedness and unrighteousness (in Adam), we hold down (in our souls) *that which we know to be the case*. In sum, our sin causes us to suppress what we know.

Within the context of this general announcement, however, Paul knows that he has introduced two concepts—suppression and truth—that will necessarily need clarification. In vv. 19-23, Paul develops and amplifies the notions of "suppression" and of "truth."

In this section, we can begin to see how Paul puts flesh on his (so far skeletal) notion of "the truth" as he reiterates what he means by truth in vv. 19, 20, 23, and 32. In each of these verses, Paul gives more specificity to the concept of truth mentioned in v. 18. We shall take these verses together in order to understand what Paul means by "the truth" that is suppressed.

In v. 19, Paul tells us that the truth that we sinfully suppress is "that which is known about God." The truth that is suppressed, therefore, is specifically truth about God. The way in which we come to know this truth is two-fold. We come to know it, in the first place, because it is evident among us. Paul will expand this idea in the next verse. Before that, however, he wants us to understand just how this truth, *this knowledge of God*, is evident, or clear, among us.

This is vitally important. It is vitally important, as we will see, both because Paul is concerned with God's activity in revealing Himself (more specifically, revealing His wrath) and, in tandem with that, because Paul wants to highlight the contrast between what God is doing in this revelation, on the one hand, and what we (in Adam) do with it, on the other.

So, Paul says immediately (even before he explains the sweeping scope of that which is evident among us) that the reason that God's revelation is known by us and evident among us is that *God has made it evident to us*.

We should be clear here about Paul's emphasis. What Paul is concerned to deny, in this context, is that we, in our sins, as covenant-breakers in Adam, would ever, or could ever, produce or properly infer this truth that we have, this knowledge of God, in and of ourselves. Paul wants to make sure that we are not tempted to think that the truth of God, as evident among us, is evident because we have marshaled the right arguments or have set our minds in the proper direction. (This has implications for natural theology, which we will address below.)

His point, at least in part, in this entire section, is to remind us of the devastating effects sin continues to have on our thinking (in Adam). The truth that we know, that we retain, possess, and suppress, therefore, is truth that is, fundamentally and essentially, *given by God to us*. God is the One who ensures that this truth will get through to us. It is his action, not ours, that guarantees our possession of this truth.[7]

And now the subject of our problem takes center stage. The truth which we all, as "image of God" creatures in Adam, know and suppress is a *truth about God*. Even more specifically (v. 20), it is a truth concerning the "invisible things" of God, that is, His eternal power and deity. What might Paul mean by this description? Had Paul wanted to limit his description by delineating only one or two characteristics of God, he would more likely have told us explicitly what those one or two characteristics are. Instead, he gives us two broad categories that are meant to contain "all the divine perfections."[8]

This truth that we all know, then, is the truth of God's existence, including His infinity, eternity, immutability, glory, wisdom, and so on. As Paul is developing this thought in v. 23, he speaks of this knowledge of the truth as "the glory of the incorruptible God." It is this that we all know in our capacity as creatures made in the image of God. It is this that God gives, and that we necessarily receive as knowledge, that comes to us by virtue of His revealing Himself to us in and through all of creation.

Given what Scripture tells us here, we should recognize that the so-called problem of divine hiddenness is, in reality, not a problem of *divine* hiddenness at all. Instead it is a problem of willful and stubborn human myopia. God is not hidden at all. His revelation is evident and manifest in and through all of creation, including in our own consciences (see Rom. 2:15). *The problem is ours, not His.* The problem is that our sin motivates us to suppress what is obvious, to hold down that truth given by God. To think that there is a problem of divine hiddenness is to assume that we all interpret and understand the world properly, at least at a basic level. But, because the "link" between God and the world is broken by our sin, we willfully misinterpret what God has made; we misunderstand it, assuming it to be sufficient unto itself.

There are two important aspects to this knowledge of God, which are crucial to see. First, we should be clear about the context for this knowledge. It is not knowledge in the abstract of which Paul speaks. He is speaking here of a knowledge that ensues on the basis of a real and reciprocal relationship. It is not the kind of knowledge we might get through reading about someone or something in a book or in the newspaper. This is relational, covenantal, knowledge. It is knowledge that comes to us because, as creatures in the image of God, we are, always and everywhere, confronted with the God we are meant to image. We are, even as we live in God's world every day, set squarely before the face of the God who made us, and in whom we live, and move and exist (Acts 17:28). This, then, is decidedly *personal* knowledge. It is knowledge of a person, of *the* Triune Personal God, whom we have come to know by virtue of His constant and consistent revealing of Himself to us. And this knowledge is meant to elicit worship and honor.

This personal aspect of the knowledge that we have is made all the more prominent in v. 32. This verse serves as a transition between Paul's exposition of God's wrath revealed in ch. 1, and the revelation, through creation, of God's law in ch. 2. Notice that Paul can affirm that those who are in Adam "know the righteous decree" of God. This knowledge of God's righteousness is coterminous with our knowledge of God. To know God, in the way that Paul is affirming here, is to know (at least something of) His requirements. Along with the knowledge of God, in other words, comes the knowledge "that those who practice such things [i.e., sin] deserve to die."

Instead of repenting (Rom. 2:4), however, we, in Adam, rejoice in our disobedience and attempt to gather together others who share in our rebellion. Therefore, because this knowledge is a relational knowledge, and because the relationship is between God and the sinner, God ensures that we all know that the violations of His law in which we willingly and happily participate are capital offenses; they place us under the penalty of death. Our knowledge of God is a responsible, covenantal, knowledge, which brings with it certain demands of obedience.

Second, Paul is emphatic about the fact that this knowledge of God that we have, as given, is abundantly clear, and is understood. There is no obscurity in God's revelation. It is not as though God masks Himself in order to keep Himself hidden from His human creatures. The problem with the revelation of God that He gives in and through all of creation, and on this we need to be as clear as possible, *is not from God's side*, but from ours.

In other words, what is clear in Rom. 1 is that all human beings have a true knowledge of God. Paul's point about our "suppression of the truth" would make no sense unless we actually *possessed* the truth. We cannot suppress what we do not have. And our culpability for that suppression presupposes that we act against what we know to be the case.

This knowledge of God is often described as the *sensus divinitatis*.[9] We need to be clear here that, for Paul and consequently for Calvin, the *sensus divinitatis* is not, in the first place, a mere function. It is not an empty *capacity* that may or may not be filled with *content*. For Paul, the *sensus* is *content*; it is the content of the knowledge of God's characteristics, which knowledge renders all human beings without excuse before Him (Rom. 1:20).

So, here is the situation with respect to knowledge of God after the fall. First, even though the image of God has been marred and distorted after the fall, human beings remain image of God. Because we remain image, and remain responsible to image the One who has made us, God has ensured that we will always *know* Him. There has never been, nor will there ever be, a time when those who are God's image will be outside of His presence, ignorant of His character.

Second, the *way* in which we know God is, initially, by way of *God's* activity, not ours. Historically, this knowledge that we all have has been dubbed *cognitio insita*; it is the *implanted* knowledge of God that God Himself plants within us, through and by the things He has made. In this way, we should recognize that, with respect to the knowledge of God, human beings are *first* knowers, even if they neglect to believe in God (in the biblical sense of "believe"). It is not the case, therefore, that the fairly standard formula of "justified true belief" can be applied when it comes to our knowledge of God. Because to be a self-conscious human being entails knowledge of God, we know Him even when or if we claim that we don't know Him. In that sense, true knowledge is prior to our belief or disbelief in God.

This is one reason why the account of knowledge must be, from the beginning, *covenantal*. As human beings made in God's image, we come into

His world, a world in which He is always and everywhere present, revealing Himself, both within and without us, in such a way that we *know* Him and His character (and His requirements, Rom. 1:32).

Perhaps Bertrand Russell can help us here. In his essay, "Knowledge by Acquaintance and Knowledge by Description," Russell explains the former in this way:

> I say that I am acquainted with an object when I have a direct cognitive relation to that object, i.e., when I am directly aware of the object itself. When I speak of a cognitive relation here, I do not mean the sort of relation which constitutes judgment, but the sort which constitutes presentation.[10]

This is not to say that Russell's entire epistemological structure is legitimate. It is only to say that, covenantally, there is truth in the fact that because God is present and revealing himself, we *know* Him, quite apart from the need for inference.[11]

And this leads to our third point. As we can see from Paul's affirmations above, if we remain apart from Christ, the knowledge of God that is ours by nature is suppressed. That suppression includes exchanging the truth of God for a lie, it includes substituting an idol—another created image—for the worship of the true God.

With respect to Covenantal Epistemology and the reality of peer disagreement, we should recognize that our "natural" tendency, which itself is a product of our sinfulness, is to disagree with what God has said. This was the genesis of the first sin in the Garden. When Satan, through the serpent, approached Eve, his question, subtle but devious, was this: "Did God actually say …?" (Gen. 3:1). His subtle but determined attempt to get Adam and Eve to disagree with what God had said was successful, and creation has been fighting against God ever since. Since a Covenantal Epistemology has its source, not in what *we* say, but in what *God* has said in Scripture, any disagreement with respect to it must be measured by the plumb-line of Scripture, which is God's Word. So, a Covenantal Epistemological approach is, at its root, more a *gift* than a *task*. It requires, as we said above, the *gift* of faith—*credo ut intelligam*. No one comes by this epistemological approach "naturally"; we are all centrally opposed to it, until and unless we trust in Christ. Apart from that trust, we convince ourselves to believe that which we know to be false.

This is where the irrationality which we referenced above comes into focus. Instead of choosing what we ought to choose with respect to our knowledge of God—choosing to honor Him and give thanks, choosing to worship Him and Him alone (rational)—we choose those things that should always be avoided—a lie instead of the truth, serving created images instead of the One whose image we are meant to maintain (irrational).[12]

In other words, if God, and not something in creation, is the standard for what is rational and what is irrational, it will never do simply to ascribe warrant to various beliefs with respect to creation, until and unless those beliefs have their foundation and their ultimate reference in God and what He has said (in creation and in Scripture).

We need to make clear here a distinction that is crucial to maintain between natural revelation and natural theology. Generally speaking, natural revelation is what *God* does; natural theology is what *human beings* do. So, Paul's discussion above concerns natural revelation. Even so, it is God's revelation in and through creation that always and everywhere gets through to us, so that the very *sensus divinitatis* itself is a product, not of natural theology, but of natural revelation. Our knowledge of God through creation is itself *implanted* by God—not possessed by our inferring—so that it is God's doing, not ours.

What Rom. 1 teaches us is that we will not, if we remain in our sins, move from creation to a proper understanding of God. Instead, we will take the knowledge of God that we have and pervert it. This is only one of the reasons why some of the standard ways of attempting to prove God's existence fail.[13] Put all too simply, it is not possible, given a purely creaturely foundation, to move from this world to the eternal, infinite, immutable, and Triune God. In order properly to ascribe those characteristics to God, another, transcendent, foundation is necessary.

So far, though, we have affirmed a covenantal, universal, and clear knowledge of God that all people have. But, someone may protest, this looks too much like a sleight of hand. What good is knowledge that is suppressed and not acknowledged? How can this knowledge of God be affirmed when our response to it is to suppress and exchange it for a lie?

In order to answer that question, we move to the second, and primary, aspect of a Covenantal Epistemology. As we have already seen, when God created Adam and Eve, He spoke to them. He told them what they were to do under Him, and He told them what they must refrain from doing. Had they listened to God and obeyed His Word, then there would have been no fall. There would have been, eventually, the opportunity for them to eat from the tree of life. Instead, when they fell, they were forever barred from that tree. Death ensued, both spiritual and physical.

But God continued to speak. There has not been a time in history when God's Word has been absent. Not only does God speak clearly in and through all that He has made, but He speaks, verbally, throughout redemptive history (see Heb. 1:1-4). That speech of God reaches its climax in the appearance of God-in-the-flesh, the Messiah, Jesus Christ.

As God has spoken in history, He also determined that His speaking would be committed to writing. It is in the Holy Scripture—the Old Testament and the New Testament—that has been revealed to us, by the Triune God Himself, both God's character and what He, as God, requires of those of us who are in His image. God tells us who He is in various ways in Scripture, including the names that He gives Himself. For example, He calls Himself the "I Am"—Yahweh—that we might recognize that He alone is who He is, and that He needs nothing and no one in order to be who He is or to accomplish His sovereign purposes (see Exod. 3:1-16). In the New Testament, the name that He gives reaches its historical climax, as He identifies Himself in the one name of the Father, Son, and Holy Spirit (Mt. 28:18).

But a problem remains for us. As we have seen, our reaction to God's revelation in creation is to suppress and exchange it. So also with what God has spoken. We learn from Scripture that

> The natural person does not accept the things of the Spirit of God, for they are folly to him, and he is not able to understand them because they are spiritually discerned. (1 Cor. 2:14, ESV)

In other words, those things that are revealed to us in the Holy Scripture are beyond our ability to acknowledge if we remain in our sins. In order to acknowledge both natural revelation and the special revelation that is found in Scripture there must be "spiritual discernment." That discernment can only come by way of a change of heart. And a change of heart is a work of the Holy Spirit that moves us to believe in the Lord Jesus Christ. It is incumbent on all of God's human creatures to repent and believe in the Lord Jesus Christ (see Acts 17:30). When we repent and believe we submit ourselves to what God says both in creation and in His Word. It is through faith that we have and acknowledge the true knowledge of God, which He alone gives in His revelation.

This revelation of God highlights for us the importance of testimony in a Covenantal Epistemology. If we take "testimony" to be that which we believe because someone has told us, then God's revelation is testimony *par excellence*. When God says *p*, it is incumbent upon us to believe *p* and to take *p* as true.

The problem, as we have said, is that, since the fall into sin, none of us has the "natural" ability to take God at His Word. We have set ourselves against Him and against His truth. So, in that sense, there is a "double testimony" that is necessary for us properly to know. The Westminster Confession puts it this way, "… our full persuasion and assurance of the infallible truth and divine authority thereof, is from the inward work of the Holy Spirit bearing witness by and with the Word in our hearts" (1.5). In other words, what is needed for a *credo ut intelligam*, Covenantal Epistemology is the *testimony* of the Scriptures, together with a *testimony* of the Spirit "by and with the Word" testifying "in our hearts" that the testimony in Scripture is, in fact, the Word of God.

So, all told, a Covenantal Epistemology recognizes that the true knowledge of God is a necessary constituent of what it means to be human. Once God freely chooses to make man—male and female—in His image, He thereby establishes a covenant relation with them. From that point into eternity we are and remain responsible to God to image Him. Once we plunge ourselves into the dark depths of sin, however, that responsibility is beyond our ability unilaterally to accept. We remain covenantally bound to God, but we cannot do, in and of ourselves, what we were created to do.

As Paul declared to the philosophers (and others) at Athens, God "now commands *all people everywhere* to repent" (Acts 17:30). When we repent of our enslaving sin and submit ourselves to our Creator by putting our trust in, *believing in*, Christ, the truth that we have in and through creation, as well as the truth that is written for us in Holy Scripture, is acknowledged by us as the truth of God Himself. Only then can we properly affirm the true knowledge of God that God Himself has provided. When we trust Christ, the covenant that God established in the Garden reaches its *telos* and *terminus* as we begin to be renewed into the image of Christ. Covenantal Epistemology is Christian epistemology. Without Christ, who is the substance of the covenant (see *Westminster Confession of Faith*, chapter 7, section 6) we will not, because we cannot, acknowledge the true knowledge of God, which comes to us, first, in and through creation, and then primarily and foundationally, in His Word.

Notes

1. We use the Greek technical term hypostasis here in order to avoid problems that might surround the notion of "person." Hypostasis is equivalent to the

Latin term subsistentia and is defined thus: "indicating a particular being or existent, an individual instance of a given essence ." Richard A. Muller, *Dictionary of Latin and Greek Theological Terms: Drawn Principally from Protestant Scholastic Theology* (Grand Rapids, MI: Baker, 1985), 290.

2. Æternus Pater: æternus Filius: æternus [et] Spiritus Sanctus. Et tamen non tres œterni: sed unus æternus. Sicut non tres increati: nec tres immensi: sed unus increatus: et unus immensus. Philip Schaff, *The Creeds of Christendom: With a History and Critical Notes* (New York: Harper, 1890), 2: 66–7. We should note here that, according to Schaff, "incomprehensible" is a poor translation of immensus. Rather, it should be translated as "infinite" or something similar.

3. Quoted in Herman Bavinck, John Bolt, and John Vriend, *Reformed Dogmatics: God and Creation*, vol. 2 (Grand Rapids, MI: Baker, 2004), 37.

4. A "reciprocal" relationship in no way implies that the ones relating are in any way equal. What it implies is that God condescended *as God* to reveal Himself and to relate to us on a human level, so that His human creatures might know Him.

5. Robert Audi, *The Cambridge Dictionary of Philosophy*, 2nd ed. (Cambridge: Cambridge University Press, 1999), 772.

6. Ibid.

7. The late South African philosopher, Hendrik Stoker, argues for what he calls a phanerotic (revelational) investigation of reality. This, it seems to me, is fundamental to a Covenantal Epistemology. See Stoker, "Reconnoitering the Theory of Knowledge of Prof. Dr. Cornelius van Til," esp. 26–34.

8. Charles Hodge, *Romans* (Wheaton, IL: Crossway, 1994), 37.

9. Calvin, *Institutes of the Christian Religion*, sec. 1.3.

10. Bertrand Russell, *Mysticism and Logic and Other Essays* (London: George Allen & Unwin, 1917), 209–10.

11. To be clear, knowledge of God *can* be had by way of inference, but that inference depends on the breaking of the noetic effects of sin.

12. For more on this irrationality, see Oliphint, "The Irrationality of Unbelief."

13. For a more extended treatment of the failure of Thomistic proofs for God's existence, see K. Scott Oliphint, *Thomas Aquinas: Philosopher Theologian* (Phillipsburg, NJ: Presbyterian & Reformed, 2017), 54–120.

A Classical Evidentialist Response to Covenantal Epistemology

John M. DePoe

K. Scott Oliphint's "Covenantal Epistemology" places theology prior to epistemology. In his view, theology provides foundational *principia* that support and shape epistemic principles. Therefore, he claims, it is of central importance to understand who God is and the covenantal relationship we bear to Him in order to know and practice sound epistemology. Although I am a Christian and often find myself agreeing with Oliphint's general theological views, I think the covenantal approach is misguided as an epistemic theory. In what follows, I shall organize my critical response to Covenantal Epistemology around two themes. First, I shall argue that it isn't possible for theology to provide *principia* to all epistemic principles since some epistemic principles must be exercised in the acquisition of sound theology. Second, I shall recommend an alternative way to understand the relationship between faith and reason.

First Things First

At the outset Oliphint states that sound theology must precede epistemology. He writes, "that Scripture, and the theology that flows from it, give us significant and substantial *principia* that undergird and determine certain principles of epistemology," and "Christianity is a sure and certain guide to religious epistemology." What epistemic principles does he have in mind?

Perhaps the most important one is Augustine's maxim, *credo ut intelligam*, "I believe in order to understand." He takes this to mean (among other things) that the doctrines and holy writings of the Christian faith "guide and direct a proper *understanding* of epistemology, generally, and of religious epistemology, more specifically."

Taken strictly, Oliphint's view is untenable because it cannot account for the proper exercise of epistemic principles in the procurement of sound theology. General epistemic principles, like those that prescribe when justified beliefs or knowledge follows from a reliance on different doxastic sources such as sense perception, memory, testimony, and rational intuition, are utilized in the discovery of theological truths. When reading the Bible, for instance, to learn theological truths about humans' covenantal relationship to God, one must exercise epistemic principles regarding sense perception, memory, textual testimony, and rational intuition. With bad epistemic principles, a person's theological investigations will almost certainly go astray. Thus, if theology is supposed to provide bedrock *principia* for all epistemic principles without qualification, then there is no noncircular way to begin. For one must have sound theology to discover sound epistemology, but without sound epistemic principles one cannot discover sound theology.

Starting with theology is problematic also because there are many different and incompatible theological traditions vying for our allegiance. Why adopt Reformed Christian theology rather than Shi'ite Muslim theology or Theravada Buddhism or scientistic atheology? Without good epistemic principles to evaluate the truthful integrity of religious worldviews, intellectual judgments about which theology (or atheology) are justified must be decided by nonrational factors. To the contrary, I believe that it is important to apply sound epistemic principles logically prior to theology precisely because decisions of this importance ought to be decided by truth-indicative standards. If the knowledge and application of these standards are unavailable until one has already accepted correct theology and extrapolated epistemic principles from it, then acquiring both true theology and epistemic principles is at best a product of luck.

I am not so pessimistic about humans' access to correct epistemic principles to think that only an elect few are in a position to know them. Indeed, humanity as a whole does not appear to be completely clueless when it comes to finding good epistemic principles. We tend to distrust habitual liars, we take corroboration of multiple independent sources as an indicator of truth, a certain degree of proven reliability and accuracy is required before accepting the information reported by an instrument, and so on. The principles of logic have found widespread recognition from reflective people across all cultures and religions. I am curious, then, as to why Oliphint does not place the knowledge of epistemic principles in the class of knowledge known to Reformed theologians as "common grace." The doctrine of common grace is the view that God has granted to all humanity certain unmerited endowments regardless of each person's relationship to God. Oliphint appears to classify an awareness of proper epistemic principles as "special grace," a theological category reserved for God's gifts that are given only to a select few. As a matter of common grace, I maintain that good epistemic principles can be discovered and followed to a large degree apart from a correct theology.

Faith and Reason

One potential objection to my approach that might be raised with those who are sympathetic to Oliphint's view is that it places reason over faith, but the proper order is for faith to guide and instruct reason. On my view, how is it possible for one's faith justifiably to inform and guide one's epistemic principles and practices?

The view I take on faith and reason follows general epistemic principles about the acceptance of an external epistemic authority (hereafter, "authority"). An authority is a source outside of oneself that one trusts for epistemic goods (by immediately endorsing beliefs based on that source) and practices (by refining one's epistemic principles to accommodate beliefs based on that source). Authorities play a valuable epistemic role because they are avenues for justified beliefs and knowledge that are inaccessible to us without them, or they make the procurement of epistemic goods more convenient.

For example, I may take a geometry textbook written by a highly qualified mathematician that has been issued by a reputable publisher as an authority on geometry. As I read sections of the book, I immediately endorse the beliefs about geometry that I acquire from the source. Moreover, I revise my epistemic principles to accord with the beliefs that I am gaining. For instance, I may have previously accepted the principle that whenever I sum the interior angles of a triangle and the sum does not equal two right angles, then I must be mistaken. However, in light of learning about curved geometry, I revise my principle to take into account this new and unusual set of beliefs that I accept on the basis of authority. Importantly, however, for me to embrace this authority justifiably, I must have good reasons to trust the source as an authority in the domains where I regard it as an authority. You don't need me to tell you that trusting an authority without good reason can quickly wreak havoc on one's noetic structure.

Believing by authority, then, is not necessarily a bad epistemic practice. At the crux of the matter is whether one is *justified* in accepting the authority. Adopting an authority without good reason, however, is too risky to constitute a justified epistemic practice. We would not sanction unsubstantiated trust in authorities to justify specialized beliefs in medicine, bridge engineering, or the history of Japan. For authorities in these domains to justify one's beliefs about them requires some justified basis for accepting their authority. The same goes for religious beliefs. They are too important to entrust to an authority without good reason.

I believe that it is possible for religious texts, traditions, institutions, and leaders to be authorities. Using epistemic principles commonly available, one can acquire sufficiently good reasons to trust a religious source as an authority. From there, one will endorse beliefs that follow from that source and revise his epistemic principles to accommodate the beliefs acquired from that source. Moreover, if the religious authority is an authentic source of true beliefs, a person who accepts its authority is in a position to discover more truths and integrated understanding about reality than he would without this source.

My approach to faith and reason follows C. S. Lewis who wrote, "I believe in Christianity as I believe that the sun has risen: not only because I see it, but because by it I see everything else."[1] Lewis accepts his Christian faith on the basis of evidence ("I see it"), and upon accepting its authority he integrates his knowledge of Christianity into the rest of his beliefs that consequently enjoys greater explanatory coherence ("by it I see everything else"). This is exactly what we would expect from an authentic religious authority. In the tradition of the Abrahamic religions, God is the author not only of divine revelation but also the Creator of all things. The truths from these two areas should compose a beautiful integrated system of beliefs about reality (cf. Psalm 19).

Faith seeking understanding, then, is not at odds with my view. Oliphint's approach that affirms that special revelation should shape our beliefs and epistemic principles is admissible on my view as well. Placing theology categorically before epistemology may sound pious; however, it is not feasible. Fortunately, I believe that God has granted sufficient common grace to humanity that allows the possibility of justifiably accepting religious authorities that can subsequently guide and shape one's epistemic practices.

Note

1. C. S. Lewis, "Is Theology Poetry?," in *The Weight of Glory*, reprint ed. (New York: Harper, 2001), 140.

A Phenomenal Conservatist Response to Covenantal Epistemology

Logan Paul Gage and Blake McAllister

Oliphint's version of Covenantal Epistemology includes theses in both of the following areas:

I.   The general relationship between epistemological theorizing and Christian revelation (particularly as embodied in scripture).

II. Specific epistemic principles gleaned from Christian revelation.

First, we will challenge Oliphint's reading of scripture. This is not a critique of the Covenantal approach *per se* but rather Oliphint's particular outworking of it. Afterward, we will challenge Oliphint's understanding of the general relationship between scripture and epistemology.

§1 What Does Scripture Teach Us about Knowledge of God?

There is a conceptual distinction between what scripture says and what Oliphint interprets scripture as saying. No doubt Oliphint is striving to make his interpretation match that which is revealed through scripture, but God does not guarantee that our personal attempts to interpret scripture be infallible and free from error, as Oliphint surely agrees. It follows that to critique Oliphint's view is not to critique scripture, but only his interpretation of it.

As far as we can tell, Oliphint maintains that all of the following can be gleaned from a proper reading of the Bible:

II.a. God, if he is to be known by us at all, must make Himself known through a special act of revelation. (By a "special act" we mean one that goes beyond God's mere creation of humans and the bestowal upon them of standard rational faculties capable of gathering knowledge.)

II.b. All our knowledge of God is implanted in us by God through a special act.

II.c. We are wholly passive in the reception of this knowledge. Our rational faculties play no role in the acquisition of this knowledge or any part of it.

II.d. Our knowledge of God is not an ordinary kind of knowledge involving justified belief in a proposition, but is a special, personal kind of knowledge.[1]

Oliphint offers several lines of support for these theses, none of which have us convinced.

First, Oliphint appeals to God's incomprehensibility to us creatures. Oliphint seems to think that God's incomprehensibility provides support for II.a. We disagree. Notice that the traditional doctrine of God's incomprehensibility does not maintain that we creatures can know *nothing* about God, but only that we cannot know *everything* about God. There is a full and complete comprehension of God that is beyond our grasp (even after we have received the beatific vision, in fact). Regarding those aspects of God that *can* be known to us, however, the doctrine says nothing about which methods God must use to reveal these things.

The doctrine of incomprehensibility aside, it is generally accepted that there are some aspects of God which can, in principle, be known by us that cannot be accessed through our God-given rational faculties alone. But again, it does not follow that *everything* knowable about God is inaccessible to our rational faculties. Why can't it be that some aspects of God can be known by us through our God-given rational faculties and others must be made known through a special act of revelation? Consider the traditional distinction, exampled by Aquinas, between general revelation and special revelation.[2] Aquinas maintains that God's existence and basic attributes are accessible to humans through reason alone, but that such knowledge is insufficient for knowledge of some important divine attributes, such as God being triune, let alone for salvation. Thus, God acts in a special way to reveal that which is lacking. Such an alternative position acknowledges that much of God is inaccessible to our unaided rational powers (especially after the Fall) while avoiding the extreme position that we are unable to know anything at all about God apart from His special intervention. It is surprising that Oliphint does not consider such a position, especially given its prominence in the Christian tradition. Regardless, the crucial point is that this alternative has as good a claim to being the scriptural view as II.a., if not better.

Oliphint's second line of support comes from Rom. 1, especially v. 19: "For what can be known about God is plain to them, because God has shown it to them." This verse states that God provides knowledge of Himself to humans. But what are the specific *means* by which God reveals Himself to humanity? Remarkably, Oliphint thinks that II.b. and II.c. are both established by this verse. That is, he concludes from the phrase "because God has shown it to them" that our knowledge of God is implanted in us by a special act of revelation and that our rational faculties play no active role whatsoever in the reception of this knowledge. We think it clear that informed and faithful readers of scripture can disagree with Oliphint's specific interpretation of this verse. For instance, why can't God show Himself to humans simply by creating them with rational faculties capable of readily grasping His existence? Indeed, that view fits better with the next verse, which states, "For his invisible attributes, namely, his eternal power and divine nature, have been clearly perceived, ever since the creation of the world, in the things that have been made." On Oliphint's view, in what way are God's attributes perceived "in the things that have been made?" Our knowledge is directly implanted by God; the perception of nature plays no substantive role in it. Whereas on the alternative we're proposing, reason acting on observations of nature can lead us to knowledge of God. Our point is not to defend this alternative interpretation as much as to show that there *are* plausible alternatives to Oliphint's reading. Thus, he has failed to established II.b. and II.c. as the position of scripture.

The same critique can be lodged against Oliphint's defense of II.d., which he also claims to find in Rom. 1. Putting aside the fact that Oliphint gives us little idea what this personal kind of knowledge is supposed to be, where exactly does he find this specific sort of knowledge being talked about by Paul? Oliphint doesn't tell us. No doubt Oliphint could say more were he given the opportunity to further defend his interpretation, but looking only at what he does say, he has not shown that II.d. is implied by Rom. 1 or any other part of scripture.

§2 Epistemology and Scripture

It is not entirely clear to us what exactly the Covenantal approach maintains about the relationship between epistemology and scripture. At times, some of what Oliphint says sounds like he's endorsing the following:

I.a. In our fallen state, we are only capable of discerning epistemological truths with the aid of scripture.

We think this view is mistaken. (If this is not Oliphint's view, then consider this an opportunity for Oliphint to clarify his position.)

Let us begin by affirming that scripture can give us insight into epistemology. We would contest only that epistemological insight is *exclusively* gained through the aid of scripture. As a comparison, it is sensible to think that scripture can teach us something about history, psychology, medicine, science, or even mathematics; but it is false to think that our only access to these areas is through scripture. We do not tell the archeologist to stop digging or the scientist to stop experimenting. This is because God gave us rational faculties capable of gaining insight into such areas apart from special revelation. Note, the claim here is not that we can *fully* understand creation without understanding God's role in it. We are making the more moderate claim that God gave us rational faculties capable of grasping *some* truths about the world without requiring an intricate system of theology to be operating in the background. If this is true in all the aforementioned disciplines, why would we expect matters to be different in epistemology? Sin affects our minds, to be sure. But the effects of sin do not prevent the mathematician from obtaining at least some mathematical truth. The matter is no different for epistemologists. Our cognitive faculties are damaged, but this does not render them entirely useless.[3]

It is good that this is so, for while scripture can provide some insight into epistemology, it doesn't address every important question we have. The same is true in any of the aforementioned disciplines. Scripture gives us great insight into history, but there's lots about history that scripture doesn't tell us. In the same way, there is much we would like to know in epistemology that scripture does not address, or does not address in sufficient detail. It would seem that the Covenantal approach has little to say about such issues. If we want answers, we must be willing to use other resources in addition to scripture—in particular, our God-given rational faculties.

When we acknowledge that non-scriptural resources are available to us and are capable of leading us to truth, it becomes implausible to maintain that we cannot do epistemology without our conclusions being firmly rooted in scripture or right relationship with God. That's not true in history or science or mathematics, and it's not true in epistemology.

Notes

1. At least, we think this is what Oliphint maintains. It's not altogether clear.
2. See, for instance, the first question of the *Summa Theologica* where Aquinas argues, "It was therefore necessary that besides philosophical science built up by reason, there should be a sacred science learned through revelation."
3. This has been the view of many great Christian theologians. In his *Confessions* (V.III), for example, Augustine holds that while the secular astronomers/ astrologers of his day use their God-given faculties to discover many true things about the universe, this learning doesn't reach its true *telos*. That is, while they have genuine knowledge, these secular scientists do not offer up their lives and work as worship and sacrifice to God. Citing Romans 1, Augustine holds that their learning doesn't go far enough, doesn't reflect back up on the author of nature. Secular learning can be genuine learning— without being grounded in scripture and even without a right relationship with God. But, Augustine emphasizes, it is spiritually (and ultimately) fruitless if it leads to pride rather than humility before God.

A Proper Functionalist Response to Covenantal Epistemology

Tyler Dalton McNabb

Scott Oliphint argues for what he calls Covenantal Epistemology. Roughly, the idea is that every human person, because they are made in God's image, possesses knowledge that the God of the Christian Scriptures exists. Though this isn't merely reducible to propositional knowledge, Oliphint argues that this knowledge is "relational" and "personal." We are bound to God by a covenant to know Him and obey Him. The basis for much of his religious epistemology, or so he argues, is Rom. 1:

> For what can be known about God is plain to them, because God has shown it to them. For his invisible attributes, namely, his eternal power and divine nature, have been clearly perceived, ever since the creation of the world, in the things that have been made. So they are without excuse. For although they knew God, they did not honor him as God or give thanks to him, but they became futile in their thinking, and their foolish hearts were darkened.

Oliphint thinks that God has gifted human beings with the *sensus divinitatis* (SD). Oliphint calls the SD, "content." Specifically, it is content of the knowledge of God and his characteristics. Oliphint rejects that the SD is a faculty that has the ability to produce the said content. Rather, he thinks that being made in God's image entails that all humans do, in fact, possess the relevant content. Thus, humans are all accountable to God in how they honor Him and respond to His commands. And it's because of all of this that Oliphint argues that there is no problem of divine hiddenness. The existence of God is clear to everyone. But, because of humanity's sinfulness, humans have suppressed that knowledge of God and have exchanged it for a lie. In order to no longer suppress this knowledge, humans need to enter into union with Christ. Humans need the Spirit to come and regenerate their hearts. Upon this work of the Spirit, one would be enabled to acknowledge the truth of the testimony of Scripture, and no longer have suppressed knowledge.

There is much that I agree with in Oliphint's essay. For example, I think that humans possess an SD. And, while I might disagree that the SD is functioning properly in every human person, I agree that God is not hidden and that the existence of religious diversity can primarily be explained by way of sin. I also commend Oliphint on how important Scripture is to formulating his epistemology.

However, I'm still not without my concerns. Primarily, my main concern relates to how best to convey one's epistemology. I don't see how Covenantal Epistemology, at least as it was articulated, avoids circular reasoning. Notice that my epistemology was largely glossed in conditionals. If God exists and if our belief that God exists was produced from the proper function conditions, then belief that God exists would be warranted. Of course, I do think that I have something like an SD and I do think that God exists, but I need to be careful in merely assuming these beliefs when I construct an epistemological framework if I am to avoid informal fallacies.

Perhaps Oliphint thinks that there are times when circular reasoning is permissible. For example, I think meta-level circularity is permissible with respect to certain beliefs. However, the question becomes what makes it such that circularity with respect to belief that p is permissible, but circularity with respect to belief that p^* is not? As a Proper Functionalist, I believe that it is the design plan of our cognitive faculties that designates when circularity is permissible and when it is not. Perhaps Oliphint will want to argue that God makes the decisions on these matters. I'd welcome this response for it wouldn't be far off from my own. For how does God make it such that some types of circularity are permissible and that other types of circularity are not? The Proper Fantunctionalist would argue that the answer lies in how God has created our faculties. I'd like to invite Oliphint to clarify his views on these matters.

A Tradition-Based Perspectival Response to Covenantal Epistemology

Erik Baldwin

Oliphint defends a specifically Christian religious epistemology inspired by Reformed Theology. It seems to me that his view satisfies the necessary conditions for any adequate first-order religious epistemological theory, at least as I understand things. I agree with a great deal of what he says. However, I take issue with his philosophical methodology. He writes that *credo ut intelligam* is "the guiding principle of a Covenantal approach to epistemology," and maintains that Rom. 1 and Prov. 1:7 support that approach. As these claims appear foundational to his project, I focus my attention on them, and so from the perspective of Thomas Aquinas, whose philosophy is, according to MacIntyre, a paradigmatic exemplar of the rationality of traditions approach to philosophical inquiry.[1]

Anslem writes, "I do not seek to understand in order to believe; I believe in order to understand."[2] He echoes Augustine, who writes, "Do you wish to understand? Believe. For God has said by the prophet: Unless you believe, you shall not understand. Isaiah 7:9"[3] *Credo ut intelligam* has as its complement *intelligo ut credam*—I understand so that I may believe:

> As the right order requires us to believe the deep things of Christian faith before we undertake to discuss them by reason; so to my mind it appears a neglect if, after we are established in the faith, we do not seek to understand what we believe.[4]

In affirming that Christians should use reason to understand the Christian faith, Anselm again follows Augustine. For example, on the failure of the religious teaching of the Manicheans, Augustine writes,

> I used to recall many true observations made by [the natural philosophers] made about the creation itself. I noted particularly the rational, mathematical order of things, the order of the seasons, the visible evidence of the stars. I compared these with the sayings of Mani who wrote much on these matters very copiously and foolishly. I did not notice any rational account of solstices and equinoxes or eclipses of luminaries nor anything resembling what I had learned in books of secular wisdom. Yet I was ordered to believe Mani. But he was not in agreement with the rational explanations which I had verified by calculation and had observed with my own eyes. His account was very different.[5] [For instance, Manicheans believed that "eclipses occurred when the sun or the moon wished to veil their eyes from the terrible cosmic battles between light and darkness."[6]]

While Augustine and Anselm maintain that Christians should understand all truth in a rational manner, they didn't clearly distinguish theology and philosophy. In contrast, Aquinas maintains:

> We must bear in mind that there are two kinds of sciences. There are some which proceed from a principle known by the natural light of the intelligence, such as arithmetic and geometry and the like. There are some which proceed from principles known by the light of a higher science: thus the science of perspective proceeds from principles established by geometry, and music from principles established by arithmetic. So it is that sacred doctrine is a science, because it proceeds from principles established by the light of a higher science, namely, the science of God and the blessed.[7]

Apparently, Oliphint's view on the nature of relationship between theology and philosophy is rather Augustinian/Anselmian, whereas I count myself as Aquinian. I see Aquinas as an improvement on both Augustine and Anselm, who both failed to clearly distinguish two distinct modes of inquiry. As such, I think that some of his positions belong to the province of theology. Having said that, I don't mean to affirm that there is no overlap between philosophy and theology. Aquinas's overall intellectual project is motivated by theological concerns; philosophy isn't autonomous, and it certainly isn't set above theology in order of importance. He maintains that "scripture inspired of being God, is no part of philosophical science, which has been built up by human reason" and that "it was necessary for man's salvation that there should be a knowledge revealed by God, besides philosophical science built up by human reason."[8] This is reminiscent of some of what Oliphint says. For instance, it seems that Aquinas would agree with Oliphint on the incomprehensibility of God. Using philosophical reasoning, Aquinas argued that it is impossible for any created intellect to intellectually see the essence of God by its own natural power, for things are known by the mode of the knower, in accord with its own nature. And since to God alone belongs self-subsistent being, knowledge of God's essence belongs to God alone.[9] Because we cannot comprehend God's essence, we cannot prove ie exists *a priori*, but it can be demonstrated by reasoning from causes and effects.[10]

My second main disagreement with Oliphint pertains to how best to interpret the relevant passages in Romans and Proverbs. On the point that the Gentiles are without excuse, having suppressed truths about God that have been shown to them by God, in his *Commentary on Romans*, Aquinas writes:

> rightly do I say that they have suppressed the truth about God. For they did possess some true knowledge of God, *because that which is known of God*, i.e., what can be known about God by men through reason, *is manifest in them*, i.e., is manifest to them from something in them, i.e., from an inner light. Therefore, it should be noted that some things about God are entirely unknown to man in this life, namely, what God is.[11]

He continues:

> when he says *God has manifested it unto them*, he shows by what author such knowledge was manifested to them and says that it was God .... Here it should be noted that one man manifests something to another by unfolding his own thought by means of such external signs as vocal sounds or writing. But God manifests something to man in two ways: first, by endowing him with an inner light through which he knows: *send out your light and your truth* (Ps. 43:3); second, by proposing external signs of his wisdom, namely, sensible creatures: *he poured her out*, namely, wisdom, *over all his works* (Sir. 1:9). Thus God manifested it to them either from within by endowing them with a light or from without by presenting visible creatures, in which, as in a book, the knowledge of God may be read.[12]

In sum, Aquinas notes that the Gentiles had knowledge of the created order sufficient for them to know God as creator. However, failing to give God proper glory and honor, they suppressed the truth in unrighteousness, making themselves culpably ignorant of the knowledge of God that was available to them by means of reasoning on the created order and rendering ineffectual the "the inner light" God gave them. Having broken the law, they stand in need of grace, which God provides to all humanity, both Jews and Gentiles. Of note is how Aquinas reads Romans in light of the distinction between theology and philosophy, and the fact that he takes Rom. 1:20 as justification for the projects of natural law and natural theology.[13]

While there are substantial overlaps between Aquinas's reading of Romans and Oliphint's, there are significant divergences, too. While I am not a theologian, I don't see how what Paul says in Rom. 1 is foundational to epistemology *per se*. Rather, it seems to me that the entire thrust of the book is Christological:

> Chapter 1 of the Romans Commentary tells us among other things how injustice and ingratitude reduced the character of the natural law—like nature itself – from strength to weakness and left in need of mercy … it is a radically theological story … Aquinas characterized the whole epistle from 1:16b to 12:1 as "show[ing] forth the power of the gospel of grace." His Commentary reveals that the purpose of the natural knowledge of God's will or law, as of the natural knowledge of God's existence, is to show forth the power of the gospel grace of Christ.[14]

Lastly, it seems to me that the purpose of Prov. 1 is to call attention to how reflection on the proverbs of Solomon enables people to acquire wisdom, justice, judgment, equity, prudence, discretion, and understanding, virtues that accompany or are necessary prerequisites for having a proper "fear of the Lord." Lacking these, one is in no position to properly appreciate or respond to wisdom and instruction from God. Fools, despising wisdom and instruction, and having no fear of God, therefore, aren't able to begin to receive or acquire knowledge. The primary epistemological upshot of this seems to be that knowledge (particularly knowledge of the things of God) requires or involves the cultivation of various moral, intellectual, and spiritual virtues and that these virtues can be acquired only if one is open to instruction from God, having the fear of Lord. For what it's worth, read in its overall context, I don't see grounds for thinking that Prov. 1:7 entails or strongly suggests Covenantal Epistemology as such.

Notes

1. Christopher Lutz writes, "Thomas Aquinas, who lived in a boundary condition between Aristotelianism and Augustinianism, who understood

the conceptual schemes of both traditions from within, who had become, 'so to speak, a native speaker of two first languages,' stands for MacIntyre as a paradigmatic practitioner of tradition-constituted and tradition-constitutive enquiry." Christopher Stephen Lutz, *Tradition in the Ethics of Alasdair MacIntyre: Relativism, Thomism, and Philosophy* (Lanham, MD: Lexington Books, 2004), 127.

2. Anselm, *Monologion and Proslogion: With the Replies of Gaunilo and Anselm*, trans. Thomas Williams (Indianapolis, IN: Hackett, 1995), 95.

3. In Augustine, *Nicene and Post-Nicene Fathers, First Series*, ed. Philip Schaff and Kevin Knight, trans. John Gibb, reprint ed. (Buffalo, NY: Christian Literature, 1888), http://www.newadvent.org/fathers/1701.htm. Note that Augustine makes use of the Septuagint translation of Isaiah. Accessed December 24, 2018.

4. Anselm, *Cur Deus Homo*, trans. Sydney Norton Deane, reprint ed. (Chicago: Open Court, 1903) book 1, chapter 2, 178.

5. Augustine, *The Confessions*, trans. Henry Chadwick, reprint ed. (Oxford: Oxford University Press, 1992), 75.

6. Ibid., n. 6.

7. Thomas Aquinas, *Summa Theologica*, 1, q. 1, a. 2.

8. Ibid., 1, q. 1, a. 1.

9. Ibid., 1, q. 12, a. 4.

10. Ibid., 1, q. 2, a. 2.

11. Thomas Aquinas, "Commentary on Romans," sec. 114, accessed December 24, 2018, https://aquinas.cc/196/198/~1.

12. Ibid., 116.

13. Thomas Aquinas, *Summa Theologica*, 1, a. 93, q. 2; and Thomas Aquinas, "Commentary on Romans," 117–25.

14. Eugene F. Rogers Jr, "The Narrative of Natural Law in Aquinas's Commentary on Romans 1," *Theological Studies* 59, no. 2 (1998): 260–1.

Covenantal Epistemology: Response to Critics

K. Scott Oliphint

I am grateful to all of the respondents to my essay on Covenantal Epistemology. It is always helpful to observe how others read and assess an essay like this. Overall, there seemed to me to be a clear understanding of what I was attempting to argue.

There were, however, a couple of assessments that were significantly wide of the mark. This could be due to my own lack of clarity, or perhaps a "reading into," that skewed the point(s) I was attempting to make. It would be best to clear those away first, I think.

First, Gage/McAllister (GM) misunderstood my view on the knowledge of God and thus their responses were not directed at my position. They say:

> God, if he is to be known by us at all, must make Himself known through a special act of revelation. (By a "special act" we mean one that goes beyond God's mere creation of humans and the bestowal upon them of standard rational faculties capable of gathering knowledge.)

It's not clear to me what GM mean by "a special act of revelation." The simple point I argue is that for God to be known He must reveal Himself to us. The creation of Adam and his standard rational faculties is necessary for knowledge of God, but not sufficient. Not only so, but embedded in the Christian tradition, both Catholic and Protestant, is the fact that God is so qualitatively different from us that it is necessary for Him to condescend to us and reveal Himself if we are going to know Him properly. In the words of the *Westminster Confession of Faith*, chapter seven, section one, for example, it says:

The distance between God and the creature is so great that although reasonable creatures do owe obedience unto him, they could never have any fruition of him as their blessedness and reward but by some voluntary condescension on God's part which he has been pleased to express by way of covenant.

It is the "distance" between God and us, together with our (prefall) desire for blessedness that requires, on God's part, His condescension. That condescension is replete throughout Scripture, but includes His speaking to Adam, and others after the fall, revealing Himself in and through all that has been made (Rom. 1:20), making Himself known through various created media (e.g., fire in Exod. 3:2ff., human form in Josh. 5:13-15). So, in order to know God, He must "come down" to tell us who He is.

The second point to address from GM is their II.d.:

Our knowledge of God is not an ordinary kind of knowledge involving justified belief in a proposition, but is a special, personal kind of knowledge.

They say, in light of this, that I think that "Our knowledge is directly implanted by God; the perception of nature plays no substantive role in it." As a matter of fact, the perception of nature (assuming "nature" means "creation") is the primary (though not only) means by which the knowledge of God is implanted. In agreement with the Reformed tradition since Calvin, the means that God uses to implant true knowledge of Him in us is His creation, and the works of the law that are implanted in our hearts (Rom. 2:14-16). So, God's "special act" of revelation just is God revealing Himself in and through all of creation, in His Word, and supremely in His Son. So much for the misunderstandings.

Baldwin counts himself a Thomist, so he and I will necessarily disagree on most epistemological and metaphysical matters. Thomism remains the best Romanist option, but it is difficult to see how Thomas's system is in any way foundational to a Protestant approach to epistemology or metaphysics.[1] Thomas badly mangles Paul's discussion in Rom. 1:18ff. even though he had at his disposal the more accurate interpretation of John of Damascus, an interpretation that he explicitly rejects. Thus, his read of Rom. 1 is tainted by his philosophical interests and is, therefore, concessive to the supposed neutrality of human reason, a neutrality that is, in actual fact, a fantasy.[2]

Baldwin can't see how Rom. 1 "is foundational to epistemology *per se.*" I am not quite sure how epistemology differs from "epistemology *per se,*" but the thesis is this: if it is the case that the Scriptures teach us that all people everywhere, from the beginning of creation forward, due to their creation in the image of God, are always and everywhere people who truly *know* the true God, this seems to be directly relevant, even *foundational*, to epistemology, whether *per se* or not *per se*. In developing a theory of knowledge, therefore, especially in the context of philosophy of religion, necessarily included in that theory would be that people are, by virtue of God's implanting and revealing activity, knowers of God. And they are knowers of God *because* God reveals Himself in and through that which He has made. Entailed in a knowledge of God, therefore, which is itself universal, is the knowledge of creation itself. With respect to *how* we know, then, we ought necessarily to include that we know by virtue of God's activity in and through the things He has made. The "link" between the subject and object is provided by the One who transcends both. Our environment is wholly personalistic, not impersonal. It is infused with the active, dynamic presence of the God who is revealing Himself. That revelation includes within it the knowledge of creation.

This does not mean that because we know God truly in and through creation we necessarily and always know everything in and about creation truly. While Paul is not concerned to delineate for us the link between our knowledge of God, given in and through creation, and our knowledge of creation as the media through which God is known, we can at least recognize that God ensures that our knowledge of creation is sufficient unto our knowledge of God. We know God truly by knowing what He has made. Unfortunately, the knowledge that we have, and for which we will be held accountable (Rom. 1:20), is also constantly suppressed in unrighteousness. And what does that suppression look like?

Minimally, it looks like theories of knowledge exclude God and his activity. It looks like an assumption that reality is fundamentally *impersonal*. It looks like a strictly horizontal perspective on knowledge, without recognizing the necessarily vertical dimension that grounds the entire horizontal in the first place.

McNabb has concerns about the problem of circular reasoning. This concern comes up repeatedly in various discussions, especially in discussions among Christians who deal with epistemology. McNabb is not as dismissive of circularity as most are, and that is a refreshing advance in epistemology. He thinks meta-level circularity is permissible, and he wants to argue that the criterion for circularity lies, somehow, in God's creation of our cognitive faculties. Overall, this is a helpful way to begin to think about this issue, I think.

It is not, however, sufficient. More, and substantially more, has to be said about circularity, in this context, than simply referring it to our cognitive faculties (I think McNabb would agree with this point).

Since a Covenantal Epistemology is, by definition, Reformed, it has its ground and foundation in the theology that was clarified and set forth during the Reformation, over against the Roman Catholic view.

The utilization of circular reasoning is not unique to Covenantal, or Reformed, apologetics, but it goes back, at least, to the Reformation itself. The reason the notion of circular reasoning came to the fore during the Reformation was because of the so-called "formal cause" of the Reformation—*Sola Scriptura*. For the Reformers, and thus for *Protestants* generally, when the matter of a *principium cognoscendi* (foundation of knowledge) was at issue, there were only two options. Either one will stand on the self-attesting authority of God's revelation, or one will attempt to stand somewhere outside of that revelation.[3] In the latter case, it is the "outside" authority that concludes for Scripture's authority, so the "outside" authority is, by definition, the *principium*; for Romanists, the church is the *principium* since it supposes itself to establish the authority of its Bible. For the Reformers, one either opts for Scripture (and God's general revelation) as *principium*, or one opts for man (which would include the church) as *principium*. There is no third alternative.

When the Reformed theologian Gisbertus Voetius (1589–1676) argued for Scripture as our foundation for knowledge (*principium*), he received a response (as we might expect) from a Romanist theologian, Martin Becanus, entitled *The Calvinistic Circle*.[4] In one of his disputations on the relationship of faith and reason, Voetius considers the fact of Scripture's foundational (*principial*) status in light of the function of reason. He concludes:

> No other principle or external means whatsoever that is distinct from Scripture and prior, superior (either in itself or with respect to us), more certain and better known, exists or can be invented that is suitable to certainly and infallibly demonstrate to us the authenticity and trustworthiness of Scripture, or to radiate by a clearer light than Scripture itself radiates.[5]

Voetius goes on to reject the notion that anything else could provide credibility to the Bible as our basic foundation, primarily because anything else would assign ultimate credibility to "the testimony of man."

In light of his assertion of the foundational status of Scripture, Voetius was accused of circular reasoning. The Romanist objection to Voetius was this:

> The circle of Calvinist theology ... consists in first proving the Divine authority of the Bible by referring to the subjective testimony given by the Holy Spirit, and then attempting to prove that this inner acknowledgement comes indeed from the Spirit of God by referring to the Bible.[6]

Voetius made a distinction between the objective *principium* of Scripture and the subjective *principium* of the testimony of the Holy Spirit. In that way, God's own revelation must be the foundation (*principium*) for anything else that we rightly believe or know, and for anything else that we argue.[7]

Another Reformed theologian, John Owen (1616–1683), engaged in a similar discussion. In speaking of the reason why men must believe the Scriptures to be the Word of God, Owen refers us to the formal object of Scripture.[8] For Owen, there is a distinction between the formal object and the material object of our faith. Whereas the formal object of our faith deals with the *reason* why we believe, the material object deals with *what* we believe, that is, the actual things that are revealed to us.

In dealing, for example, with the *reason* for Christian faith, Owen concentrates on the formal object. The sole reason why, the ground whereon, we are to believe the things revealed by God (which, remember, is the material object) is by the evidence of Scripture alone. Owen is never afraid to give a reason for this most basic belief. He is quick to show that there is indeed evidence for the authority of Scripture, but such evidence is in the Scripture itself.

Owen makes a further distinction under the rubric of the formal object of faith. He does not simply state that Scripture is what it is because of what it is, but he goes on to affirm that Scripture is what it is because of who *God* is. Here he begins to broaden his circle. Owen says that the reason we must believe the Bible to be the Word of God is because of the authority and veracity of God Himself.

Owen has at least two formal reasons for believing Scripture to be God's Word. He speaks of the authority and veracity of God as the ultimate reason or the ultimate formal object of our faith, whereas the Scripture itself is the first, immediate formal object of our faith. (Here Owen shows the inextricable link between what is called the *principium essendi*—the foundation of existence—and the *principium cognoscendi*—the foundation of knowledge. This is why any proper discussion of epistemology must include, as well, the (metaphysical) affirmation of God and His character.)

The relevance of this to our discussion of the supposed problem of circularity is that Owen, too, was charged (by the "Papists") with circular reasoning. His response to the charge was ingenious:

"We cannot," say the Papists …, "know the Scripture to be the word of God by the testimony of the Spirit. For either it is public testimony, which is that of the church" (and if this be granted they have enough); "or it is private testimony. But then," they say, "it will follow, 1.that our faith in the Scripture is enthusiasm. 2.That if the private testimony of the Spirit be questioned; it cannot be proved but by the Scripture; and so the Scripture being proved by the Spirit, and the Spirit again by the Scripture, we shall run in a round, which is no lawful way of arguing."[9]

Is it the case that this Reformed view of revelation consigns one to "run in a round?" Owen had an answer to such a charge. First of all, the Scriptures are testified to publicly and not just internally. Such a public testimony is given, not by the church, nor by man, but by the Holy Spirit. Owen will readily admit that men will only concede the authority of Scripture when the Holy Spirit applies that which is *public testimony* to the hearts of men. Owen then makes another helpful and biblical distinction:

For if I be asked, how I know the Scripture to be the Word of God; this question may have a double sense: for either it is meant of the power and virtue whereby I believe; and then I answer, By the power and efficiency of the Spirit of God, opening the eyes of my understanding, and enabling me to believe;—or it is meant of the medium or *argument made use of*, and by which, as a motive, I am drawn to believe; and then I answer, Those impressions of divinity the Spirit hath left on the word, and by which he witnesseth it to be of God, are the *argument or motive persuading me* to believe.[10]

Here Owen makes a distinction between that which enables the Christian to believe, and that which is the objective cause or argument causing the Christian to believe. It is the latter, according to Owen, the motive of belief, that cannot be attributed to the internal work of God the Holy Spirit. The motive of our faith must be, not the Spirit's internal testimony as the Romanists assume, *but the "evidences of divinity" that we see in Scripture itself, through the Spirit's enlightening us.*

In other words, Owen believes his argument to be more reasonable and "evidential" than the argument of the Romanists. As a matter of fact, Owen goes on to argue that it is the Romanist who reasons in a circle and that the circle is in fact a noose. He argues that Rome is caught between two different motives of faith, neither of which can prove the other without at the same time contradicting itself as the motive of faith:

And, indeed, they do plainly run into a circle, in their proving the Scripture by the authority of the church and the authority of the church again by the Scripture; for with them the authority of the church is the motive or argument, whereby they prove the divine authority of the Scripture, and that again is the motive or argument, by which they prove the authority of the church. And so both the church and the Scripture are more known than each other, and yet less, too: more known, because they prove each other; and less known, because they are proved by each other.[11]

This circular "noose" would hold not simply for Romanists, but for anyone who joins Romanism in its rejection of circular reasoning with respect to our *principia*.[12] Cognitive faculties and their design are necessary, but they cannot be a sufficient condition for circularity until we recognize the self-attesting character of God's revelation, as the necessary content of those faculties.

I can only briefly respond to DePoe's article. The material above should be sufficient to respond to his suggestion of circularity. With respect to "First Things First," I have attempted to argue that the *first thing* that human beings know truly and infallibly is the true God. Such knowledge grounds God's own judgment of people, should they not repent (Rom. 1:20) so it is imperative that it obtain. This does not, of course, eliminate or otherwise deny the realities of various *modes* of knowledge acquisition—memory, sense, testimony, and so on. Those modes and faculties are necessary for knowledge to be had. But by themselves they are no help. Once they are seen as avenues by which God reveals Himself—given that they are all a part of God's creation—then they themselves will be used by God to implant in us the true knowledge of His character. In other words, and this is true both historically and theologically, modes and faculties are not, in the strict sense, *principia*. They cannot be foundational because they are not the *source* of what we know, only the avenues by which we gain the content that we do know or believe.

Secondly, DePoe thinks that starting with a theology is problematic because there are so many of them. He asks, "Why adopt reformed Christian theology rather than Shi'ite Muslim theology or Theravada Buddhism or scientistic atheology?" The answer to this can be put simply, though it has its own complexities. Reformed Christianity is adopted because it is true, and the others opposing it are not. Its truth, however, does not sit in a vacuum. It is true because it comports with God's revelation in and through creation, which all human beings receive and by which they know God. In Reformed

Christianity we also believe that "adopting" these principles requires a change of heart and mind, which can only be accomplished in and by the Holy Spirit speaking in Scripture. Apart from that, any other theology is, by definition, false.[13]

This is one reason why a Covenantal Epistemology cannot be simply *adopted*. It must be *received*, and its reception depends on a merger between the truth of God as it is given in creation and Scripture, and a work of the Spirit, who speaks in and by that truth. Covenantal Epistemology, therefore, just is *Christian* epistemology in all of its fullness. It has its focus in Jesus Christ, our covenant head, to whom Christians are united by faith alone.

Notes

1. With apologies to the reader, I will note a few works in the footnotes where I am able to expand on what I am only able briefly to point out in this essay. On this topic, see Oliphint, *Thomas Aquinas*, and K. Scott Oliphint, "Review of Evangelical Exodus: Evangelical Seminarians and Their Paths to Rome," *Themelios* 41, no. 2 (2016): 360–3.
2. For an exegetical discussion of this passage, see Oliphint, "The Irrationality of Unbelief."
3. See, for example, the *Westminster Confession of Faith*, 1.4.
4. Aza Goudriaan, *Reformed Orthodoxy and Philosophy, 1625–1750: Gisbertus Voetius, Petrus Van Mastricht, and Anthonius Driessen* (Leiden: Brill, 2006), 47.
5. Ibid., 45–6.
6. Ibid., 46. Notice that this kind of circular reasoning is embedded in the Protestant theology that opposes Roman Catholicism.
7. As Richard Muller notes, "The classical philosophical language of principia was appropriated by the Reformed orthodox at a time and in a context where … [it] served the needs both of the Reformation sense of the priority of Scripture and the Reformation assumptions concerning the ancillary status of philosophy and the weakness of human reason. By defining both Scripture and God as principial in the strictest sense—namely as true, immediate, necessary, and knowable …—the early orthodox asserted the priority of Scripture over tradition and reason and gave conceptual status to the notion of its self-authenticating character in response to both Roman polemicists and philosophical skeptics of the era." Richard A. Muller, *Post-Reformation Reformed Dogmatics: Prolegomena to Theology*, 2nd ed., vol. 1 (Grand Rapids, MI: Baker, 2003), 432.

8. John Owen, *The Works of John Owen*, ed. William H. Goold (London: T&T. Clark, 1862), 4: 16–20.
9. Ibid., 8:524.
10. Ibid., 8: 526.
11. Ibid., 8:527.
12. Some of this material on circularity is taken from K. Scott Oliphint, "Gauch's 'Gotchas': Principia and the Problem of Public Presuppositions," *Philosophia Christi* 17, no. 2 (2015): 443–56. See that article for a fuller development of this point.
13. For more on this point, see K. Scott Oliphint, *Covenantal Apologetics: Principles and Practice in Defense of Our Faith* (Wheaton, IL: Crossway, 2013), esp. chapter 7.

5

Tradition-Based Perspectivalism

Erik Baldwin

Traditions of Inquiry and Tradition-Based Perspectivalism

Clearly, people of various religious traditions engage in belief-forming practices and there are various rival tradition-based approaches to the rational evaluation of religious practices and beliefs. According to Alasdair MacIntyre's rationality of traditions approach to philosophical inquiry, efforts to formulate theories about whether and if so how religious beliefs and practices have something going for them epistemically take place within and are guided by historically conditioned traditions of inquiry. On this view, there is no tradition-independent way to evaluate the epistemic merits of our religious beliefs and practice, no such thing as tradition-independent rationality, and no such thing as religious-epistemology-as-such that applies universally across all religious traditions. For example, divine revelation must be given to people who are situated within a social–historical context, and the rational appropriateness of their religious beliefs and practices can only be interpreted in accord with the substantive standards of rationality of some tradition of inquiry or other. As MacIntyre writes, "There is no standing ground, no place for enquiry, no way to engage in the practices of advancing, evaluating, accepting, and rejecting reasoned argument apart from that which is provided by some tradition or other."[1] In this chapter, inspired by MacIntyre's rationality of traditions, I articulate and defend a MacIntyrean approach to religious epistemology.

According to Edward Shils, tradition, broadly construed, is "anything that is transmitted or handed down from the past to the present."[2] While traditions of inquiry aren't literally handed down, through practices of education and instruction, experts present novice members with patterns of action, norms, and modes of behavior; accounts of belief; interpretations and methods of interpretation; as well as conceptions of justification and knowledge. Following Jennifer Herdt's characterization, by traditions of inquiry, I mean "groups of people engaged in a common conversation on a set of topics over an extended period of time, groups that may overlap and have fuzzy edges and whose set of topics is constantly evolving."[3] MacIntyre defines a practice as,

> any coherent and complex form of socially established cooperative human activity through which goods internal to that form of activity are realized in the course of trying to achieve those standards of excellence which are appropriate to, and partially definitive of, that form of activity, with the result that human powers to achieve excellence, and human conceptions of the ends and goods involved, are systematically extended.[4]

These days, analytic philosophers of religion typically take it that among the aims of religious epistemology is to provide an analysis in terms of necessary and sufficient conditions of what is it for S to know P and put it to work to determine what we can know or be rationally justified in believing about some divine or ultimate reality. My project is more in keeping with the aims of second order, or metaepistemology, which are somewhat nebulous. Richard Fumerton writes, "in metaepistemology one is primarily concerned with analyzing the concepts fundamental to epistemological discourse."[5] Kourken Michaelian writes that metaepistemology "is concerned with epistemological phenomena, with, that is, epistemological theories, theorists, and theorizing."[6] And Christos Kyriacou writes, "Metaepistemology is, roughly, the branch of epistemology that asks questions about first-order epistemological questions. It inquires into fundamental aspects of epistemic theorizing like metaphysics, epistemology, semantics, agency, psychology, responsibility, reasons for belief, and beyond. So, if as traditionally conceived, epistemology is the theory of knowledge, metaepistemology is the theory of the theory of knowledge."[7] Along these lines, Tradition-Based Perspectivalism is a second-order, metaepistemological theory that articulates necessary conditions that any adequate first-order religious epistemological theory must satisfy. Tradition-Based Perspectivalism is the conjunction of the following three theses:

- *The Tradition-Source Thesis*: Starting points for dialectical argument, including foundational beliefs about what is reasonable to believe and why (*endoxa*), have their origins in and are passed down by particular traditions of inquiry.
- *The Tradition-Based Thesis*: Rational standards that guide human enquiry are appropriately grounded in belief-forming practices that are historically situated and tradition-based.
- *The Perspectival Thesis*: There is no perspective-free starting point or epistemic point of view for human inquiry.

The meaning of these theses will become clearer as we proceed.

In providing a metaepistemological theory, I aim to transcend the limitations of my own or indeed any other particular tradition of inquiry, but what I say remains tradition-dependent. That is to say, I maintain that while philosophical inquiry aims at tradition-transcendent truths, we can't discover them without relying on the resources of some tradition(s) of inquiry or other. This is because epistemological theorizing about religious matters relies on conceptual resources, tools, and methods that are products of traditions of inquiry. While inquiries into truth rely on tradition, truth itself is tradition-independent. The MacIntyrean epistemological approach endorses Thomas Aquinas's realist view that truth is the conformity of the intellect to things (*adaequatio intellectus ad rem*) in a world that exists independent of human cognition.[8]

I maintain that there are and that we can know some tradition-transcendent truths, including basic logical principles and laws, such as "two is more than one," "every whole is greater than its parts," and The Laws of Identity and Noncontradiction. These truths set in place necessary constraints or limits on what is coherent and meaningful to say and think. However, these truths can't by themselves provide us with suitable starting points for inquiry; we must add to these formal logical truths substantive principles that are rooted in traditions of inquiry.[9]

The Case for Tradition-Based Perspectivalism

In this section, I provide three arguments in favor of Tradition-Based Perspectivalism, each rooted in the thinking of Alasdair MacIntyre.

First Argument: The Necessity of Tradition-Based Inquiry

According to Aristotle, "the end [*telos*] of theoretical inquiry is truth" (*Metaphysics*, 993^b20–21).[10] He maintains that philosophical enquiries must begin with *endoxa*, for example, with reputable opinions "which are accepted by everyone or by the majority or by the wise—i.e., by all, or by the majority, or by the most notable and reputable of them" (*Topics*, 100^b21–23). Regarding our search for better, more credible opinions, he writes:

> As in our other discussions, we must first set out the way things appear to people [*phainomena*], and then, having gone through the puzzles, proceed to prove the received opinions [*endoxa*] about these ways of being affected—at best, all of them, or, failing that, most, and the most authoritative. For if the problems are resolved, and received opinions remain, we shall have offered sufficient proof.[11]

Elsewhere, in *Topics* 100b21–3, Aristotle maintains that endoxa – propositions that are "esteemed (endoxos) by everyone or by most people; or by the wise" – supply us with good starting points for arguments[12] In the terminology of contemporary epistemology, we may characterize *endoxa* as epistemically basic beliefs that play a foundational role in subsequent determinations about what counts as a good or bad reason, ground, or bit of evidence to believe some proposition or other is true or probably true.

Aristotle's metaphysical writings have a narrative structure and are presented in the context of his historical predecessors, beginning with Thales, Anaximander, and Anaximenes, continuing with Heraclitus and Parmenides, and culminating with his immediate predecessors, Socrates and Plato. Thomas Aquinas's philosophy is heavily influenced by Aristotle and the Neo-Platonist philosophers Philo and Pseudo-Dionysius the Areopagite.[13] He both critically engages with and draws from various Arabic and Jewish philosophers, including Ibn Sina, Ibn Rushd, and Maimonides.[14] His thinking is also shaped by Christian philosophers and theologians, including Augustine and Boethius, among others. Following Aristotle and Aquinas, the MacIntyrean rationality of traditions approach involves paying attention to the philosophical conversations and inquiries of our predecessors and understanding the nature of their problems, for our problems stem from those of our predecessors and as such can only be fully adequately solved if we attend to them in their historical context. We make progress by recognizing the mistakes of competing theories and proposing theories that correct and explain the nature of those errors.

I take it that the denial of *The Tradition-Source Thesis* is tantamount to the position that paying attention to the history of ideas and to philosophical traditions isn't necessary for doing good philosophy and can even be an obstacle to it. Descartes, who, in his attempt to secure a certain foundation for scientific knowledge, set out to treat as false anything that could not be known with absolute certainty, illustrates this attitude. Similarly, Immanuel Kant maintained that overcoming tradition is necessary for philosophical enlightenment, which, briefly, involves one becoming an autonomous, mature thinker. Kant writes,

> *Enlightenment is man's emergence from his self-incurred immaturity. Immaturity* is the inability to use one's understanding without guidance from another. This immaturity is *self-imposed* when its cause is not lack of understanding, but in lack of resolve and courage to use it without guidance from another. *Sapere Aude!* "Have courage to use your own understanding!"—that is the motto of the enlightenment.[15]

Descartes explicitly rejects the Aristotelian view that our inquiries do and ought to start with *endoxa*. He writes,

> Reason now leads me to think that I should hold back my assent from opinions which are not completely certain and indubitable just as carefully as I do from those which are patently false. So, for the purpose of rejecting all my opinions, it will be enough if I find in each of them at least some reason for doubt.[16]

Regarding Descartes's skepticism, MacIntyre writes,

> Descartes's doubt is intended to lack any [background of rightly held and well-founded beliefs]. It is to be contextless doubt. Hence also that tradition of philosophical teaching arises which presupposes that Cartesian doubts can be entertained by anyone at any place or time. But of course someone who really believed that he knew nothing would not even know how to begin on a course of radical doubt; for he would have no conception of what his task might be, of what it would be to settle his doubts and to acquire well-founded beliefs. Conversely, anyone who knows enough to know that does indeed possess a set of extensive epistemological beliefs which he is not putting in doubt at all.[17]

MacIntyre notes that Descartes didn't doubt his ability to use the French and Latin languages, nor did he doubt what he inherited along with his ability to speak and write in them, namely, "a way of ordering both thought and the world expressed in a set of meanings."[18] Descartes overlooked the fact that the meanings of the Latin words he used had a history. The seventeenth-century Latin Descartes used in *Mediations on First Philosophy* bears the marks of the languages of Scholastic Philosophers, which itself bears the marks of twelfth- and thirteenth-century Latin. As such, Descartes failed to realize the fact that "much of what he took to be the spontaneous reflections of his own mind was in fact a repetition of sentences and phrases from his school textbooks."[19]

Descartes's attempt to overcome tradition by employing his method of doubt was possible only because he was a beneficiary of conceptual resources and modes of theoretical and practical reasoning passed down to him by traditions of inquiry, including the meanings of words and basic conceptual schemes. As Ludwig Wittgenstein has shown, there are limits to that which can be intelligibly doubted. For example, English speakers use the words "hand" and "tree" to refer to hands and trees. That these words have those meanings is a contingent, empirical fact. As such, Descartes's method would have us doubt their meanings. But we can't intelligibly express substantive doubts (such as "I don't know that this is a hand" or "I don't know that that is tree") without presupposing the meanings of the words used to express them. One's having genuine doubt about such things would seem to require a robust kind of insanity or some other serious cognitive malfunction. Descartes's method of universal doubt, therefore, is rationally self-defeating and his attempt to overcome tradition could only end in abject failure.[20]

Basically, the problem with Kant's Enlightenment Ideal, according to the MacIntyrean, is that it is an unobtainable pipe dream. Apparently, Kant failed to appreciate that no individual can possibly achieve the goods of maturity and autonomy unless he or she is situated within a social context. Even our ability to reason about and autonomously determine our ends is dependent on the help and assistance we receive from others, particularly when we are young, elderly, or infirm. We are rarely, if ever, fully able to use our own understanding without any guidance or help from others, at least not for very long.[21] Moreover, Kant overlooks the fact that there are different philosophical and religious traditions of inquiry, and different and incompatible conceptions about the nature of reason and what it requires. Commenting on the Enlightenment philosophers' conception of rationality, MacIntyre writes,

> Rationality itself, whether theoretical or practical, is a concept with a history: indeed, since there are diverse traditions of enquiry, with histories,

there are, so it will turn out, rationalities other than [Enlightenment] rationality.[22]

If these arguments are sound, no attempt to get at truth in a completely tradition-independent manner can possibly succeed. We are thereby led to accept the view that rational standards that guide human inquiry can't be appropriately epistemically grounded unless we rely on resources we've inherited from traditions of inquiry. That this is so supports both *The Tradition Source* and *Tradition-Based Theses*.

Second Argument: Against Modern Liberalism

Another expression of the view that philosophical inquiry can dispense with the rationality of traditions is modern political liberalism (liberalism for short), which affirms, briefly, that the state can provide a fully objective and value-neutral framework within which citizens are free to pursue their own conceptions of the good. According to Michael J. White, contemporary political liberalism is defined by its search for a way to justify a view of liberty that doesn't rely on "comprehensive doctrines" or some particular "comprehensive conception of the good," adopting instead "a stance of neutrality with respect to competing conceptions of the human good or *telos*."[23] Liberals endorse substantive norms of action, moral principles, including views about what is rational to believe and why, that are (or are intended) to be implemented in social orders and societies. For these ideals to have traction, they must be embodied in institutions that are made up of persons. But institutions and their practices are products of tradition and cannot survive apart from the activity of the members who embody them. Thus, liberalism, too, fails to overcome tradition but has rather turned into yet another tradition-dependent mode of inquiry. MacIntyre writes,

> Liberal theory is best understood ... as itself the articulation of an historically developed and developing set of social institutions and forms of activity, that is, as the voice of a tradition. Like other traditions, liberalism has its set of authoritative texts and its disputes over their interpretation. Like other traditions, liberalism expresses itself socially through a particular kind of hierarchy.[24]

It follows that liberalism can't provide a neutral or tradition-independent starting point for inquiry. As MacIntyre notes, this line of argument is inductive and doesn't conclusively refute the views, ideals, and goals of liberalism *a priori*. But liberalism is the best defense of the view that inquiry can be tradition-independent and neutral. The fact that liberalism fails to overcome tradition, therefore, provides compelling reasons for thinking that there can't be any neutral starting points for philosophical inquiry.[25]

Given the unity of theory and practice, what MacIntyre says about principles of practical rationality applies, *mutatis mutandis*, to principles of theoretical rationality. Philosophers ask and answer questions about the nature of the good (or goods) specific to humans. According to MacIntyre, true theoretical answers to these questions must be "translatable into true answers that can be given to their practical questions by ordinary individuals." True answers to practical questions that individuals raise about their own good "presuppose some particular type of answer to the philosopher's question." MacIntyre concludes, "There is no form of philosophical enquiry—at least as envisaged from an Aristotelian, Augustinian, or Thomistic point of view—which is not practical in its implications, just as there is no practical enquiry which is not philosophical in its presuppositions."[26]

By way of further support for this view, note that all theory presupposes and is based on practice, for going about formulating theories can't get started unless one first engages in belief-forming practices. Insofar as belief-forming practices are social practices, embodied in social–political institutions with complex forms of cooperative activity, they, too, are among the resources that traditions of inquiry provide to us. For example, a great deal of what we take ourselves to know relies on testimony. Testimonial knowledge is inherently anti-individualist, for S knows that p by means of testimony from R only if R knows that p. For individuals to receive testimonial knowledge from others, there must be socially established modes of communication by which knowledge is transmitted person-to-person, including shared languages and shared linguistic conventions, and people must be able to trust that others are generally trustworthy.[27]

To reject the rationality of traditions approach to religious epistemology is tantamount to presupposing something close to the view that the resources of traditions of inquiry can be set aside and that our inquiries into whether our religious beliefs are true, or justified, or warranted, or what have you, can proceed in a completely tradition-independent manner. However, we cannot engage in philosophical inquiry without entering into critical dialogue with others who have asked and proposed answers to specific philosophical questions. All such dialogue takes place within a social context that has a narrative history in which centrally important figures either affirm and defend or alternatively criticize and reject or otherwise cast doubt on particular points of view that are recorded in and passed down in texts. Participating in this dialogue requires that we learn various methods of interpretation so as to see to it that texts are interpreted properly. Philosophical inquiry so understood is a social practice or activity that requires cultivating and exercising moral and intellectual virtues, or skills, which are learned from competent teachers and mentors and are in turn passed down to others. This line of argument supports all three theses of Tradition-Based Perspectivalism.

Third Argument: Tradition vs. Both Encyclopedia and Genealogy

The MacIntyrean rationality of traditions approach is opposed to any mode of inquiry according to which the resources of tradition are considered unnecessary or superfluous. Contemporary philosophers who think otherwise typically suppose that there is a unique, universally applicable conception of rationality in accordance with which we can formulate epistemological principles that ought to be recognized by anyone who is fully reasonable and fully informed of the evidence and the relevant facts. In accepting this view, philosophers endorse, at least implicitly, the Enlightenment ideal of pure objectivity. A paradigmatic expression of this view is found in the ninth edition of the *Encyclopedia Britannica* (1875–89), produced by members and associates of the Scottish Enlightenment as a conservative reaction to *Encyclopédie, ou dictionnaire raisonné des sciences, des arts et des métiers* (*Encyclopaedia, or Classified Dictionary of Sciences, Arts, and Trades*, 1751–72), spearheaded by French philosophers Denis Diderot and Jean le Rond d'Alembert. The encyclopedists, namely, the editors of and contributors to *The Encyclopedia Britannica*, understood their project to be a compilation and systematization of facts that would eventually take the form of a comprehensive synthesis codifying all human knowledge.[28] At the heart of this approach is the rejection of traditional authorities and the acceptance of the notion that philosophical progress can and should be advanced by modes of rational argumentation that ignore anthropological and sociological factors.[29] MacIntyre writes that the encyclopedists, "took it for granted that not only all rational persons conceptualize data in one and the same way and that therefore any attentive and honest observer, unblinded and undistracted by the prejudices of prior commitment to belief would report the same data, the same facts, but also that it is data thus reported and characterized that provide enquiry with its subject matter."[30] They maintained that, "All rational people … could agree with objectively sound arguments. Traditions [are] superfluous, and their pronouncements irrational unless they [can] be backed up by arguments that Enlightenment thinkers could accept."[31] Their guiding principle was "that substantive rationality was unitary, that there is a single if perhaps complex, conception of what the standards and achievements of rationality are, one which every educated person can without too much difficulty be brought to agree in acknowledging."[32] In sum, encyclopedists believed that all fully rational and fully informed people will agree that the same body of reasons and evidence is compelling and that the standards of substantive rationality hold everywhere equally and universally.[33] But, as we've seen in the arguments in the previous sections, this view is implausible.

Essentially, genealogists agree with the MacIntyrean's critique of the encyclopedists but also reject the rationality of traditions. Paradigmatic representatives of genealogy include Friedrich Nietzsche and Michel Foucault. Nietzsche, for instance, took both rationality and truth to be intellectual artifacts. For Nietzsche, there is no truth-as-such but only "a multiplicity of perspectives within each of which truth-from-a-point-of-view may be asserted" and there are no rational constraints or rules of rationality to appeal to but rather only "strategies of insight and of subversion."[34] Because genealogy frames its project with reference to the rejection of both the rationality of traditions and of encyclopedia, its goals and projects conceptually depend on and make sense only insofar as they are understood in terms of what it aims to reject. Moreover, genealogical research is possible only if those doing the research have the kind of metaphysical identity that the genealogy rejects, it the genealogical narrative is incoherent.[35] For instance, Nietzsche wrote books and in doing so presupposed the ability to record and communicate his thoughts to others, which involves making a host of metaphysical assumptions, including that there are texts, readers, and modes of interpreting and understanding them. Insofar as he thought that overcoming the resources of tradition was possible, Nietzsche's enquiries must have had an intellectual end or goal. Having told us in his books that he has given up on the idea that the goal of inquiry is truth, Nietzsche proclaims that truth is merely rhetoric, poetry, and metaphorical illusion.[36] If the goal of genealogical inquiry isn't truth, then what is it? Genealogists may propose that the goal of inquiry is nonathletic, that it is a means to power, an aesthetic, or perhaps a way to multiply possibilities. But if the genealogical method is construed in any of these ways, it is something other than an intellectual research project. Thus, the goals of genealogy, *qua* intellectual research project, are unintelligible and rationality incoherent.

In sum, encyclopedia and genealogy, the main rivals to the rationality of traditions, both fail. That leaves us with the rationality of traditions. If my arguments are sound, then we should accept that substantive standards of theoretical rationality are tradition-dependent. We should also accept that there is no such thing as universal rationality or theoretical-rationality-as-such, but rather that there are numerous rival tradition-based standpoints each with their own particular standards of rational justification. Compared to its rivals, the rationality of traditions approach offers a better way of framing and solving the problem of epistemological diversity with respect to religious belief and offers a better solution to the problem of how to go about comparatively evaluating the epistemological merits of the central claims of the world's great religions. That this is so gives us reason to accept that it is true. This line of argument supports all three theses of Tradition-Based Perspectivalism.

Tradition-Based Perspectivalism and Issues in Contemporary Religious Epistemology

In this concluding section, I briefly consider some the ramifications of the rationality of traditions approach to religious epistemology.

As a metaepistemological theory, Tradition-Based Perspectivalism leaves the evaluation of the prospects of traditional natural theology (used to show that there is a God) and ramified natural theology (used to support particular detailed doctrinal claims) to be answered by the members of particular traditions of inquiry.[37] There are no general or tradition-independent substantive answers as to whether this or that theistic argument for the existence of God or this or that proposed solution to the problem of evil or divine hiddenness is successful. For example, those in or aligned with the Humean philosophical tradition broadly construed take a dim view of the prospects of both traditional and ramified natural theology. Typically, evidentialists explicitly affirm that religious beliefs ought to be held in proportion to one's evidence, a view paradigmatically represented by John Locke and William Clifford. Plantingians and Reformed Epistemologists maintain that rational belief in the existence of God and in particular religious doctrines doesn't require evidence or argumentation. As a MacIntyrean, I think that the general framework of the nature of philosophical inquiry presented by Thomas Aquinas is, by and large and for the most part, correct.

I think there are convincing arguments that support the existence of God and various specific Christian doctrines.[38] However, parting company with popular interpretations, it is anachronistic to read Aquinas as a religious evidentialist in the contemporary sense. Aquinas's views on demonstration are not as stringent as contemporary philosophers generally take them to be and he maintains that articles of faith, such as the doctrines of the trinity and creation *ex nihilo*, are known to us only on the basis of divine revelation, which is inconsistent with religious evidentialism.[39] Moreover, in *Summa Contra Gentiles* 1.4, Aquinas maintains that if inquiries into truths about God were limited to that which can be demonstrated by means of human reason, "three awkward consequences would follow." First, very few people would possess knowledge of God, for demonstration requires having and exercising mental capacities that many people lack. Others who have the requisite mental capacities, due to the daily grind of life and having more pressing obligations, lack time and opportunity to devote themselves to the task. Others with both ability and sufficient time lack the desire to do so. Second, those who are fully dedicated to the cause have their work cut out for them, for knowledge of God acquired solely by means of human reason is difficult to obtain and can take a lifetime. Third, the human intellect is comparatively weak and reliant on images, making even the most diligent and careful scholar prone to error. Aquinas concludes that it's a great good for humanity that God reveals things to us that we could discover using human reason, for it is one way He shows us mercy. These views are hardly in keeping with the spirit of contemporary religious evidentialism. Having said that, however, the tradition of inquiry founded by Aquinas and furthered by MacIntyre (and others) is a very wide umbrella, with room enough for a wide variety of specific traditions of inquiry and specific views on traditional and ramified natural theology. Just which of these narrower traditions of inquiry is most empirically adequate, all things considered, is an extremely vexing question, which I can't address here given my present purposes.

Another important question is who has the burden of proof concerning major religious claims and why. A fully satisfactory answer to this question requires addressing what makes for a good or acceptable proof. We must bracket that question and assume we have an intuitive understanding what makes for a good or bad argument. Following Plantinga and the Reformed Tradition more generally (and, as argued above, Aquinas too!), rational belief in God as well as particular doctrines about God does not require good arguments, as such beliefs can be appropriately grounded, for instance, on faith or on testimony.[40]

It is important to note that by their own lights, a person of faith can take himself or herself to have sufficient reason or justification to believe in God or to accept some particular religion-specific doctrine regardless of whether others take those reasons or justifications to be acceptable. To generalize, one can rationally believe something without demonstrating it to the satisfaction of others and no one always has the burden of proof. Rather, the burden of proof regarding matters of faith and practice contingently rests on those who would go about convincing others to agree with them about such things. Voluntarily taking up that burden, it is incumbent on one to present and defend one's views to others in ways that are explicable and intelligible to them. One must approach others where they are, not where one would like them to be, and one must be open to correction from others as well. The MacIntyrean maintains that we can do this by exposing our views to radical external critique, which has the added benefit of enabling to see our blind spots and to discover hidden faults and errors in our own ways of thinking about things. Cross-traditional and cross-cultural modes of understanding and philosophizing are in this way indispensable for the members of traditions of inquiry to make progress and get closer to the truth of things. There are, to be sure, other ramifications of MacIntyre's rationality of traditions approach to religious epistemology to be worked out.

Notes

1. Alasdair MacIntyre, *Three Rival Versions of Moral Enquiry: Encyclopaedia, Genealogy, and Tradition* (Notre Dame, IN: University of Notre Dame Press, 1990), 350.
2. Edward Shils, *Tradition* (Chicago: University of Chicago Press, 1981), 12.
3. Jennifer A. Herdt, "Alasdair MacIntyre's" Rationality of Traditions "and Tradition-Transcendental Standards of Justification," *The Journal of Religion* 78, no. 4 (1998): 544.
4. Alasdair MacIntyre, *After Virtue* (Notre Dame, IN: University of Notre Dame Press, 2013), 187.
5. Fumerton, *Metaepistemology and Skepticism*, 1.

6. Kourken Michaelian, *Mental Time Travel: Episodic Memory and Our Knowledge of the Personal Past* (Cambridge, MA: MIT Press, 2016), 37.

7. Christos Kyriacou, "Metaepistemology," ed. James Fieser and Bradley Dowden, *Internet Encyclopedia of Philosophy*, n.d., accessed June 27, 2019, http://www.iep.utm.edu/meta-epi/.

8. MacIntyre writes, "One of the great originating insights of tradition-constituted enquiries is that false beliefs and false judgments represent a failure of the mind, not of its objects. It is mind which stands in need of correction. Those realities which mind encounters reveal themselves as they are, the presented, the manifest, the unbidden. So the most primitive conception of truth is of the manifestness of the objects which present themselves to mind; and it is when mind fails to represent that manifestness that falsity, the inadequacy of mind to its objects, appears." MacIntyre, "First Principles, Final Ends, and Contemporary Issues," 162; Also see Thomas Aquinas, who writes, "... truth resides, in its primary aspect, in the intellect. Now since everything is true according as it has the form proper to its nature, the intellect, in so far as it is knowing, must be true, so far as it has the likeness of the thing known, this being its form, as knowing. For this reason truth is defined by the conformity of intellect and thing; and hence to know this conformity is to know truth." Thomas Aquinas, *Summa Theologica*, 1, 2, a.

9. As MacIntyre puts it, "[the] observance of the laws of logic is only a necessary and not a sufficient condition for rationality, whether theoretical or practical." Alasdair MacIntyre, *Whose Justice? Which Rationality?* (London: Duckworth, 1988), 4.

10. Unless noted otherwise, quotations from Aristotle's works are taken from Aristotle, *The Complete Works of Aristotle*, trans. Jonathan Barnes, reprint ed., 2 vols. (Princeton, NJ: Princeton University Press, 1988).

11. Aristotle, *Nicomachean Ethics*, trans. Roger Crisp, reprint ed. (Cambridge: Cambridge University Press, 2004), 120.

12. Christopher Shields writes, "Endoxa play a special role in Aristotelian philosophy in part because they form a significant sub-class of phainomena (EN 1154b3–8): because they are the privileged opinions we find ourselves unreflectively endorsing and reaffirming after some reflection, they themselves come to qualify as appearances to be preserved where possible." Christopher Shields, "Aristotle," ed. Edward N. Zalta, *The Stanford Encyclopedia of Philosophy* (Metaphysics Research Lab, Stanford University, 2016), accessed December 25, 2018, https://plato.stanford.edu/archives/win2016/entries/aristotle/.

13. For a discussion of the influence of the Neo-Platonists on Aquinas's philosophy, see Wayne J. Hankey, "Aquinas, Plato, and Neoplatonism," in *The Oxford Handbook of Aquinas*, ed. Brian Davies and Eleonore Stump (Oxford: Oxford University Press, 2012), 55–64.

14. On this point, see, for instance, David B. Burrell, "Thomas Aquinas and Islam," *Modern Theology* 20, no. 1 (2004): 71–89; and Neil A. Stubbens, "Naming God: Moses Maimonides and Thomas Aquinas," *The Thomist: A Speculative Quarterly Review* 54, no. 2 (1990): 229–67.

15. Immanuel Kant, "An Answer to the Question: What Is Enlightenment?," in *Perpetual Peace and Other Essays*, trans. Ted Humphrey, reprint ed. (Indianapolis, IN: Hackett, 1983), 41.

16. René Descartes, *The Philosophical Writings of Descartes*, trans. John Cottingham, Robert Stoothoff, and Dugald Murdoch, vol. 1 (Cambridge: Cambridge University Press, 1985), 12.

17. MacIntyre, "Epistemological Crises, Dramatic Narrative and the Philosophy of Science," 8–9.

18. Ibid., 9.

19. Ibid.

20. This argument draws on Ludwig Wittgenstein's book Ludwig Wittgenstein, *On Certainty*, ed. G. E. M. Anscombe and G. H. von Wright, trans. Paul Denis and G. E. M. Anscombe (New York: Harper & Row, 1969), particularly passages 114, 307, 456, 486. One might object that Descartes's method of doubt is intelligible as a form of metacognitive doubt that presents us with a skeptical hypothesis which if true would entail the falsity of all of our first-order beliefs. But metacognitive doubt is ultimately self-undermining, too, for we can't entertain metacognitive doubts without presupposing and trusting the meanings of our words either.

21. For more on this line of argument, see Alasdair C. MacIntyre, *Dependent Rational Animals: Why Human Beings Need the Virtues* (Chicago: Open Court, 1999), chaps. 7–10.

22. MacIntyre, *Whose Justice?*, 9.

23. Michael J. White, *Partisan or Neutral?: The Futility of Public Political Theory* (Lanham, MD: Rowman & Littlefield, 1997), 1.

24. MacIntyre, *Whose Justice?*, 345.

25. MacIntyre writes, "Liberalism does not provide a neutral tradition-independent ground from which a verdict may be passed upon the rival claims of conflicting traditions in respect of practical rationality and justice, but turns out itself to be just one more such tradition with its own highly contestable conceptions of practical rationality and of justice" … "That liberalism fails in this respect, therefore, provides the strongest reason that we can actually have for asserting that there is no neutral ground, that there is no place for appeals to a practical-rationality-as-such or a justice-as-such to which all rational persons would by their very rationality be compelled to give their allegiance. There is instead the practical-rationality-of-this-or-that-tradition and the justice-of-this-or-that-tradition." Ibid., 346.

26. MacIntyre, *Three Rival Versions of Moral Enquiry*, 128. Note that while the unity of theory and practice view is associated with Marxism and Nietzsche, MacIntyre argues that there is commonality between Marx and Christianity. See also Alasdair MacIntyre, "Marxists and Christians," *The Twentieth Century* 170 (1961): 28–37; Alasdair MacIntyre, *Marxism and Christianity* (Notre Dame, IN: University of Notre Dame Press, 1968); Kelvin Knight, *Aristotelian Philosophy: Ethics and Politics from Aristotle to MacIntyre* (Malden, MA: Polity, 2007).

27. Moreover, while S's testimonial knowledge that p is typically transmitted by R to S immediately and non-inferentially, S knows p only if there is some nontestimonial ground for R's belief that p, such as perception, memory, or rational insight. Robert Audi writes, "Surely if no one knew anything in a non-testimonial mode, no one would know anything on the basis of testimony either. More specifically, testimony-based knowledge seems ultimately to depend on knowledge grounded in [another knowledge source, such as perception, memory, consciousness, or reason]. To enable others to know by attesting to it, I must know it myself; and my knowledge must ultimately depend at least in part on someone's non-testimony-based knowledge ...." Robert Audi, *Epistemology : A Contemporary Introduction to the Theory of Knowledge*, 3rd ed. (New York: Routledge, 2010), 160.

28. MacIntyre, *Three Rival Versions of Moral Enquiry*, 18–23.

29. Lutz, *Tradition in the Ethics of Alasdair MacIntyre*, 52.

30. Ibid., 53.

31. Ibid.

32. MacIntyre, *Three Rival Versions of Moral Enquiry*, 14.

33. Lutz, *Tradition in the Ethics of Alasdair MacIntyre*, 54.

34. MacIntyre, *Three Rival Versions of Moral Enquiry*, 42.

35. See Lutz, *Tradition in the Ethics of Alasdair MacIntyre*, 54.

36. Nietzsche writes, "What then is truth? A movable host of metaphors, metonymies, and anthropomorphisms: in short, a sum of human relations which have been poetically and rhetorically intensified, transferred, and embellished, and which, after long usage, seem to a people to be fixed, canonical, and binding. Truths are illusions which we have forgotten are illusions—they are metaphors that have become worn out and have been drained of sensuous force, coins which have lost their embossing and are now considered as metal and no longer as coins." Friedrich Nietzsche, *The Portable Nietzsche*, ed. Walter Kaufmann, trans. Walter Kaufmann, reprint ed. (New York: Penguin, 1976), 46–7.

37. These definitions of natural theology and ramified theology are proposed by Richard Swinburne. See Richard Swinburne, "Natural Theology, Its 'Dwindling Probabilities' and 'Lack of Rapport,'" *Faith and Philosophy* 21, no. 4 (2004): 533.

38. For instance, I think William Craig's presentation of the Kalam Cosmological Argument has a lot of force and that Aquinas's argument for the existence of God in On Being and Essence is sound. William L. Craig, *The Kalām Cosmological Argument*, reprint ed. (Eugene, OR: Wipf and Stock, 2000); and Craig and Sinclair, "The Kalam Cosmological Argument." For Aquinas' argument in On Being and Essence, Thomas Aquinas, *On Being and Essence*, trans. Armand A. Maurer, 2nd ed. (Ontario: Pontifical Institute of Mediaeval Studies, 1968). For a recent formulation of the argument, Edward Feser, *Five Proofs for the Existence of God* (San Francisco, CA: Ignatius Press, 2017). For strong philosophical defenses of the Christian doctrines of the Trinity, the Incarnation, the Resurrection, and the Atonement, see Richard Swinburne, *The Christian God* (Oxford: Clarendon Press, 1994); Richard Swinburne, *The Resurrection of God Incarnate* (Oxford: Oxford University Press, 2003); and Richard Swinburne, *Responsibility and Atonement* (Oxford: Oxford University Press, 1989).

39. For more in defense of these claims, see, for instance, Arvin Vos, *Aquinas, Calvin, and Contemporary Protestant Thought: A Critique of Protestant Views on the Thought of Thomas Aquinas* (Exeter: Paternoster Press, 1985).

40. For instance, in *De Veritate* Q14 A4, Aquinas writes, "The act of faith consists essentially in knowledge, and there we find its formal or specific perfection. This is clear from its object, as has been said. But, with reference to its end, faith is perfected in the affections, because it is by reason of charity that it can merit its end. The beginning of faith, too, is in the affections, in so far as the will determines the intellect to assent to matters of faith." In *Summa Theologica* II-II q.4 a.1, he defines faith as "a habit of the mind, whereby eternal life is begun in us, making the intellect assent to what is non-apparent." And in *Scriptum Super Libros Sententiarum* d.23, q.2, a.2, qc.2, he writes, "The reason why the will is inclined to assent to what it does not see is because God says it, just as a human being concerning things he does not see believes the testimony of a good man who sees what he himself does not see." The translation of the last passage is taken from Bruno Niederbacher, "The Relation of Reason to Faith," in *The Oxford Handbook of Aquinas*, ed. Brian Davies and Eleonore Stump (Oxford: Oxford University Press, 2011), 337–47.

A Classical Evidentialist Response to Tradition-Based Perspectivalism

John M. DePoe

The tradition-based approach of religious epistemology given in Erik Baldwin's contribution takes its starting point with the admission that there is no approach to religious epistemology that originates independently of some tradition. From here, he concludes that likewise there are no standards of rationality that apply universally to the religious beliefs of all peoples and times. I believe that this inferential leap is dubious and undermines an essential element of the tradition-based epistemology. In the brief space I am allotted, I shall sketch how it is possible to admit that all epistemologies are traditions-dependent without conceding that it follows that there are no universal standards of rationality or necessarily true epistemic principles.

Do Traditions Lead to Relative Standards?

It is obvious that every person is a product of one's own culture. Every person who has formulated a view of religious epistemology has done so from the traditions of his particular circumstances. Take even the trivial point that religious epistemologies must be put into a language in order to be communicated to others, and that language itself is a by-product of the culture in which one has been raised. In articulating an idea, one must draw upon a body of knowledge, languages, and practices that have been acquired through the idiosyncratic circumstances of culture and time. At least in this sense, I agree with Baldwin that views of religious epistemology are tradition-based.

But what exactly should follow from this observation? Does it follow, therefore, that no accessible standards exist that transcend culture? Ought we to conclude that there is no hope of finding universal standards of rationality? Here, Baldwin and I part ways. The inference from the premise that (in some sense) all religious epistemologies are tradition-based to the conclusion that therefore there are no universal, culturally independent standards of rationality appears to be a *non-sequitur*. Let's consider this point with some examples.

All theories of mathematics are grounded in the traditions of the mathematicians who produce them. It is undeniable that the background knowledge, practices, language, culture, and other circumstances of a mathematician's tradition cannot be ignored as crucial influences on how he formulated his views on mathematics. Yet, this does not prevent mathematicians from arriving at necessary universal truths that transcend culture, such as $2+3=5$. Likewise, good plant biology, though formed within a tradition, will never produce an account that prescribes withholding water from your rose bushes in order for them to yield their beautiful blooms. Even with man-made artifacts, like airplanes, we do not think that there are significantly different, yet equally justified, tradition-based standards on how to land an aircraft.

Perhaps the tradition-based view recognizes exceptions to cases like mathematics, basic plant biology, and landing airplanes. No tradition, they might argue, could maintain different views from the universally accepted ones as a matter of survival or coherence with basic readily available observations. Baldwin himself concedes some knowledge of principles that transcend culture, such as that every whole is greater than its parts, two is more than one, and fundamental laws of logic. Yet, for reasons that are not clear to me, he claims that we are incapable of accessing epistemic principles that transcend one's tradition. If we are capable of discovering universal truths that apply to all traditions in some cases, what makes this task impossible in religious epistemology?

Are There Universal Standards of Rationality?

Baldwin's arguments against universal standards of rationality are based on examples from the history of philosophy, like Aristotle's *endoxa* and pointing out that the epistemic ideals of Descartes and Kant are traditions-dependent. These claims, however, seem no different to me than the examples given above for mathematics, plant biology, and landing airplanes as well as his own examples of mereological, logical, and quantitative truths. All of these bodies of knowledge follow from discoveries acquired through a tradition, yet their universality is not jeopardized by recognizing their unavoidable genesis within a tradition. I fail to see essential differences in the principles of religious epistemology from mathematics or logic that make the one inescapably traditions-bound and the others capable of arriving at truths that transcend tradition.

Yet, Baldwin is forced to admit that some metaepistemic principles transcend traditions or else he will be saddled with complete subjectivism in religion (a position that I am assuming he wishes to avoid). The critical interaction in this book among different epistemologists about the proper epistemic principles presupposes a significant amount of common ground that transcends traditions about the methods of adjudicating metaepistemic principles. But how is this possible when religious epistemology has no universal standards of rationality? At best, we could hope that we happen to share some of the same principles (perhaps by membership in the same traditions). At worst, we would have to "agree to disagree" about every issue in religious epistemology, resulting in a disappointing exchange for our readers. In essence, without some principles that transcend traditions, we are in no position to tell whether any theory in religious epistemology is employing principles that are more likely to yield true beliefs or not. Indeed, Baldwin undoubtedly thinks that many of my views in religious epistemology are wrong, which relies on the presumption that there are universal standards for judging religious epistemologies accessible to both of us. If we can know these principles that transcend traditions, why not others?

One of the virtues of my approach is that it proposes epistemic principles that are applied equally to all religious beliefs. A person is justified in holding his religious beliefs, in my view, insofar as he possesses an awareness of good grounds for believing them. The standards I propose, such as having an awareness of one's beliefs following deductively or probabilistically from one's evidence, are not peculiar to my tradition. These are universal standards that apply to all traditions. It is precisely when traditions have departed from these standards that bizarre beliefs and brutal practices are admitted into a religion. Without epistemic standards that transcend one's traditions, on what grounds can we argue that worship of the Great

Pumpkin, following a Jonestown cult, embracing Westboro doctrines, and Roman Emperor worship, is epistemically unjustified? Since these beliefs and practices are unjustified (even if the traditions that underwrite them say otherwise), it follows that there must be some universal standards for religious epistemology.

No doubt, those in sympathy with Baldwin will point out that I am espousing a view in epistemology rooted in my own tradition. Like Descartes and Kant, they might claim that I am asserting an unwarranted position of authority. My defense, put briefly, is that the traditions of language, culture, education, and the like provide the tools by which I am able to discover universal truths that transcend traditions. Like teaching a child addition using apples, the particular tools of learning provide a way to see beyond them or through them to universal truths. Children who learn addition through a tradition using apples are not inescapably bound to think that addition only applies to apples. Through the exercise of the imaginative and rational faculties, it is possible to go beyond the particular truths of one's own tradition to universal truths that transcend them all.

Circular Reasoning

My final critical point on Baldwin's tradition-based religious epistemology is that it makes epistemic practices for religious claims circular. In his exposition of the role of natural and ramified theology, Baldwin states that their proper use is to be prescribed by the particular members of each tradition. Consequently, on the MacIntyrean view, every tradition sets its own epistemic standards, and then draws its own conclusions from these standards. For example, suppose a religious tradition states that religious beliefs can be justified when their religious authorities say so. These authorities, in turn, claim to be infallible messengers delivering the teachings of God. By its own standards, then, it can say its authorities tell the truth since they affirm their own authority. Similarly, a scientistic materialist might claim as a matter of his tradition that methodological naturalism ought to be followed in all matters of evidential reasoning. Thus, restricting all epistemic principles to admit only beliefs that adhere to naturalism, the epistemology of his tradition overwhelmingly confirms scientistic materialism as true.

But isn't this circular reasoning? If the traditions that set these standards already have certain religious (or antireligious) beliefs built into them and the traditions are used to determine what religious beliefs are justified, then the outcome has already been loaded into the starting point. The conclusion is assumed in the premise. By taking the standards of rationality from religiously laden traditions to judge the rationality of its own religious beliefs, it makes the whole enterprise of religious epistemology circular on the tradition-based view. Ultimately, meaningful religious epistemology requires standards that transcend tradition, a way to judge which practices within traditions are conducive to truth.

A Phenomenal Conservatist Response to Tradition-Based Perspectivalism

Logan Paul Gage and Blake McAllister

MacIntyrean metaepistemology, as Baldwin presents it, is a second-order (or meta-level) reflection of our epistemic practices, standards, and systems. As such, it is related but also orthogonal to first-order theories of warrant and justification such as Phenomenal Conservatism (PC), Proper Functionalism, and Classical Evidentialism. Thus, the MacIntyrean approach is not necessarily an alternative to these first-order theories.[1] In what follows, we aim to show how PC incorporates many of the insights of MacIntyrean metaepistemology while addressing some concerns.

Notice first that there are moderate as well as extreme readings of nearly all of MacIntyre's key theses. Take Baldwin's claim that "there is no tradition-independent way to evaluate the epistemic merits of our religious beliefs and practice, no such thing as tradition-independent rationality, and no such thing as religious-epistemology-as-such that applies universally across all religious traditions." Such statements might be taken in a moderate way, claiming only that our inquiry into the rational standards governing religious belief will be heavily influenced by our various traditions and, as a result, different individuals operating in different traditions might reasonably come to different conclusions about which rational standards are correct. Or such statements can be taken in an extreme, relativistic way, claiming that there is no objective truth as to who is right about the rational standards governing our beliefs.

Taken straightforwardly, many of Baldwin's statements strongly suggest the extreme reading. He asserts, "there is no such thing as universal rationality or theoretical-rationality-as-such, but rather that there are numerous rival tradition-based standpoints each with their own particular standards of rational justification." For comparison, what would we make of an ethicist who asserted, "there is no such thing as universal morality or morality-as-such, but rather that there are numerous rival tradition-based standpoints each with their own particular standards of morality?" We would interpret them as a moral relativist—someone who denied the existence of tradition-transcendent moral truths. At best, this would be a particularly misleading way to express the more moderate claim that, though there *are* objective moral truths, people coming from different traditions will often come to different conclusions about those truths.

Despite such statements, it appears to us that both MacIntyre and Baldwin proffer these theses in their more moderate senses. That is, they stress the importance of traditions in guiding our inquiries, beliefs, concepts, practices, and so on, but maintain that there are tradition-transcendent truths and that these are at least sometimes accessible to us. At times, Baldwin seems to assert this plainly: "I maintain that there are and that we can know some tradition-transcendent truths."[2] He mentions in particular necessary truths, such as those of logic. We will assume, then, that Baldwin does not deny that there are universal, tradition-transcendent standards of rationality, but is merely pointing out how profoundly our investigations into such truths are guided by the tradition in which we find ourselves.

It is important to emphasize, then, that if we have correctly identified PC as a necessary truth about the nature of justification, then PC is such a tradition-transcendent truth. (For the record, PC states that if it seems to S that p, then S thereby has some degree of justification for believing p, absent defeaters.) Baldwin's point is just that our ability to recognize PC as true depends on the tradition in which we are located, and that people operating in different traditions may not have the resources needed to appreciate its truth or might even be reasonable in dismissing it. We would agree with this point.[3] What is reasonable to believe ultimately depends on how things seem to a person, and things may seem different to people from different traditions.

On a more general level, we also agree with Baldwin and MacIntyre that traditions and communities play a much larger role in epistemology than Enlightenment rationalists supposed. However, we do not think that this is a straightforward *epistemic* role, but rather largely a *causal* role. Many of

Baldwin's arguments point to traditions as necessary conditions for organizing our language, concepts, and beliefs. We agree. But in what sense does this make tradition necessary? It is necessary causally, not epistemically. For example, oxygen is also necessary (in some sense) for our beliefs to be justified—for without oxygen, there would be no beliefs at all. But that is not to say that oxygen plays an *epistemic* role as part of what makes a belief justified or unjustified. Similarly, a community's beliefs or standards do not themselves make a belief justified or unjustified, at least not in any straightforward way. Rather, having a community of thought is a necessary causal condition for formulating your own seemings, thoughts, and beliefs,[4] and it is these things that play the epistemic role in the justification of one's beliefs.

The position we are taking here is complicated, so allow us to explain it in another way. We agree that one's tradition has a profound influence on what one is justified in believing; we just want to stress that this influence is indirect—it exerts this influence by causally altering experience. The story goes like this: One's tradition affects one's conceptual frameworks, linguistic practices, and background beliefs. These affect one's experiences of the world. And how one experiences the world ultimately determines, in accordance with tradition-transcendent rational standards, what one is justified in believing. Importantly, communal beliefs and standards do not automatically become normative for an individual operating within that tradition (otherwise one would be justified in believing whatever one's community accepts, regardless of how these beliefs fit with one's own experiences).

To its credit, PC allows us to accept what is true here—namely, that our communities and traditions greatly affect our seemings and therefore what beliefs are justified for us—without accepting that the standards of rationality differ from tradition to tradition or that it is rational to accept all and only the beliefs and standards of one's own initial tradition. In this way, PC captures what is true about MacIntyrean metaepistemology while avoiding potential pitfalls.

Another big advantage of PC highlighted by Baldwin's discussion is that PC can make sense of why one is justified in accepting one's tradition-dependent starting points. In order to help establish the tradition-bound nature of our epistemic starting points, Baldwin looks to Aristotle, whose philosophical methodology held that philosophy should start with the common opinions of one's community (*endoxa*) and attempt to clarify and elaborate upon them, only rejecting them as a last resort.[5] Notice, though, that *endoxa* are not rock bottom. These *endoxa*, as Aristotle himself recognizes, are based upon the way things appear to people (*phainomena*).[6] Even our communal beliefs and standards are based on the way things seem, thus confirming the claim of PC that experiences form the evidence on which our justification depends.

Lastly, we think that PC fits nicely into MacIntyre and Baldwin's tripartite schema: tradition-based perspectivalism, Enlightenment hyper-rationalism (represented by the encyclopedists), and postmodern deniers of truth (such as Nietzsche). PC fits best with perspectivalism, allowing for enough objectivity to avoid postmodernism and enough subjectivity to avoid hyperrationalism. Postmodernism says, *if it seems true then it is true* (for that person). PC counters, *if it seems true then it is reasonable to believe* (for that person), but the truth of the belief remains an entirely objective matter. On the other side, PC avoids the hyperrationalist position that reasonable inquirers will all reach the exact same conclusions. PC allows for a perspectival view of rationality, where what is reasonable to believe depends on the information available from one's subjective point of view.[7] Since the available information can differ greatly from subject to subject, rational inquirers can come to vastly different conclusions. In short, PC gives us the best of both worlds: it affirms objective truth and tradition-transcendent standards of rationality so as to avoid postmodernism; and it also incorporates a humane, perspectival, and even tradition-dependent account of evidence so as to avoid hyperrationalism.

A Proper Functionalist Response to Tradition-Based Perspectivalism

Tyler Dalton McNabb

Erik Baldwin argues for a MacIntyrean epistemology. Roughly, the view can be summarized in the follow theses:

> *The Tradition-Source Thesis*: Starting points for dialectical argument, including foundational beliefs about what is reasonable to believe and why (*endoxa*), have their origins in and are passed down by particular traditions of inquiry.
>
> *The Tradition-Based Thesis*: Rational standards that guide human enquiry are appropriately grounded in belief forming practices that are historically situated and tradition-based.
>
> *The Perspectival Thesis*: There is no perspective free starting point or epistemic point of view for human inquiry.

A MacIntyrean epistemologist recognizes that, "there is no tradition-independent way to evaluate the epistemic merits of our religious beliefs and practice, no such thing as tradition-independent rationality, and no such thing as religious-epistemology-as-such that applies universally across all religious traditions." Instead, epistemic evaluation is wholly tradition dependent. The Buddhist, the Christian, and the naturalist will all have different evaluative methods and considerations. Thus, rationality is subjective and dependent upon the community of the subject in question.

Baldwin attempts to make plausible his epistemology by way of giving three different arguments. First, Baldwin argues that it is impossible to escape tradition. For example, Baldwin mentions that even Descartes attempted to escape tradition, assumed tradition. Second, Baldwin argues that the failure of modern liberalism makes plausible his epistemology. And third, Baldwin argued the Tradition-Dependent View is better than its encyclopedia and genealogy counterparts.

As a Catholic, I think there is a lot to appreciate in a MacIntyrean epistemology. In fact, I'm extremely sympathetic with the idea that both Descartes's project is unsuccessful and that liberalism became a self-defeating position. Moreover, I agree with Baldwin in that the advocates of the encyclopedia framework were extremely naïve in thinking that all rational and nonbiased individuals would agree on objectively sound arguments. But I'm not sure why it follows that "we should accept that substantive standards of theoretical rationality are tradition-dependent" or that "there is no such thing as universal rationality or theoretical-rationality-as-such, but rather that there are numerous rival tradition-based standpoints each with their own particular standards of rational justification." Just because we can't escape tradition and we must assume it as we analyze epistemic concepts, why think we can't make universal inferences as to what it means to be rational?

As a proper functionalist, I could see how tradition-based criteria could help us determine whether a subject is rational in a specific instance. For example, we would want to take into account the subject's background beliefs and the access of information that the subject possesses. But, again, why think that it follows that there is no such thing as a way to define rationality in all cultures?

Imagine that there is a culture that collectively endorses that humans should mutilate young infants for fun. According to this culture, the belief that humans should mutilate young infants for fun is a rational belief to have. However, I have a strong seeming (and I imagine most will too) that this is not a rational belief to have. In fact, I think that it's plausible that this belief can be deemed irrational by way of an objective analysis. On a pure MacIntyrean view, I'm not sure how that is possible.

This is where I think Proper Functionalism can help supplement the MacIntyrean. Perhaps we should consider Proper Functionalism as a transcendent truth. That is, while for the most part, rationality isn't universalized and is tradition dependent, we can endorse that independent of which tradition a subject belongs to, in order for her belief to be warranted, her faculties must function properly. I imagine that on this view, cognitive science would play a big role in figuring out what we should expect rational agents to believe; for cognitive science can help us identify what beliefs humans are hardwired to produce.

But of course, this approach might prevent Humeans or Marxists from utilizing their traditions to evaluate rationality claims with respect to theistic belief. For if Plantinga is right, and humans possess something like a *Sensus Divnitatis*, it would be probable that theistic belief is the result of properly functioning faculties. A Humean or Marxist then wouldn't likely be rational in her belief that God doesn't exist. This seems like a very un-MacIntyrean thing to say. So, I am aware that making the above addendum does have a significant consequence. However, I'm not sure how the view can be made plausible without it.

A Covenantal Epistemology Response to Tradition-Based Perspectivalism

K. Scott Oliphint

Tradition-Based Perspectivalism (TBP) has a good bit of insight in its favor. It rightly recognizes that all of us are situated in a particular context. As situated, it is impossible for us to come up with an acceptable epistemological theory that transcends our experience and our historical situation. As (TBP) affirms, "For individuals to receive testimonial knowledge from others, there must be socially established modes of communication by which knowledge is transmitted person-to-person, including shared languages and shared linguistic conventions, and people must be able to trust that others are generally trustworthy."

A Covenantal Epistemology will immediately recognize certain affinities with (TBP). A Covenantal Epistemology will agree with the critique of the enlightenment, for example, "At the heart of this [enlightenment] approach is the rejection of traditional authorities and the acceptance of the notion that philosophical progress can and should be advanced by modes of rational argumentation that ignore anthropological and sociological factors." Ignoring anthropological and sociological factors is a grave mistake; its appeal to objectivity is only pretense.

(TBP) affirms that "... divine revelation must be given to people who are situated within a social-historical context ...." Since it is the case, and has been from the beginning, that all people are who they are, essentially, by virtue of their covenant relationship to God, it will necessarily be the case that *how* people relate to God in history will inform how we understand "the theory of the theory of knowledge."

For example, Heb. 1:1-2 says,

> Long ago, at many times and in many ways, God spoke to our fathers by the prophets, but in these last days he has spoken to us by his Son, whom he appointed the heir of all things, through whom also he created the world.

Here the author of Hebrews recognizes that God's speaking has come by way of various social and personal contexts. In the past, God spoke "by the prophets," and the entire Old Testament fills out more precisely what that speaking entails, over a few millennia. But now, "in these last days," God's speaking has come "by his Son." There is, therefore, continuity with respect to what is known—in each case it is God speaking—but there is also discontinuity by virtue of the *ways*, or *modes*, or *vehicles* God has used to speak to His people in history.

In this respect, those who are designated as the covenant people of God are those who hear God's revelation and who are to take that revelation as the foundation for everything else that they know, and do, in history. Those who are the recipients of God's speech, His Word, and who affirm that speech as epistemologically foundational will interpret themselves and their environment in accordance with that speech. They will recognize their utter dependence on God for their knowledge of anything, preeminently of Him, and will see all that they see through the lenses of what God has said.

There are others, however, in history and presently, who are not the recipients of this special "speaking" of God. What, specifically, is their social context and historical situation? As we have been at pains to show, their primary, foundational and universal context and situation is that they are, at root, those who have and suppress the knowledge of God (Rom. 1:18-25). That is, their historical context is covenantal as well; it has its roots in the revelation that God gives in and through creation, a revelation that gets through to every self-conscious person, such that, as image of God, each person is one who knows the God he is meant to image. And since the knowledge of God entails that one know (certain aspects of) the facts of creation, knowledge of our context and situation has underneath it the revelation and knowledge of God that all people have. Covenantally, therefore, it is the responsibility of all who know God to interpret themselves and their situation in light of that knowledge. Because of the influence of sin on us all, however, we work diligently to hold down that knowledge of

God, even as we attempt to interpret all things apart from our knowledge of Him.

We can see, therefore, another aspect of (TBP) that is useful here:

> One of the great originating insights of tradition-constituted enquiries is that false beliefs and false judgments represent a failure of the mind, not of its objects. It is mind which stands in need of correction. Those realities which mind encounters reveal themselves as they are, the presented, the manifest, the unbidden. So the most primitive conception of truth is of the manifestness of the objects which present themselves to mind; and it is when mind fails to represent that manifestness that falsity, the inadequacy of mind to its objects, appears.

Since, for (TBP), "truth is the conformity of the intellect to things (*adaequatio intellectus ad rem*) in a world that exists independent of human cognition," a proper "conformity of the intellect to things" would require that "things" be understood, in the first place, as that in and through which God makes Himself known to us. To see "things" as independent of that revelation of God is fundamentally to misconstrue it. Thus, as (TBP) states, the problem is with the mind, not with the things. Because of sin, there is, in all of us, a "failure of the mind" with respect to our knowledge of the world (since it must include an acknowledgement of God, of ourselves as His creatures, of the world as governed and controlled by Him, etc.).

It is at this point that a Covenantal Epistemology cannot follow (TBP) when it asserts the following:

> Contemporary philosophers ... typically suppose that there is a unique, universally applicable conception of rationality in accordance with which we can formulate epistemological principles that ought to be recognized by anyone who is fully reasonable and fully informed of the evidence and the relevant facts. In accepting this view, philosophers endorse, at least implicitly, the Enlightenment ideal of pure objectivity.

As a matter of fact, there is a "universally applicable conception of rationality in accordance with which we can formulate epistemological principles that ought to be recognized by anyone who is fully reasonable and fully informed of the evidence and the relevant facts." That "universally applicable conception of rationality" is the knowledge of God that all people, everywhere and throughout history (i.e., "since the creation of the world," Rom. 1:20) have, and by which they ought to interpret everything else. To be "fully reasonable and fully informed of the evidence and relevant facts" in this case is to "conform the intellect" to "things" in the world (i.e., *adaequatio intellectus ad rem*) such that the person acknowledges what he knows and then conforms his beliefs to that knowledge (which is his by way of God's revealing activity). In this sense, and contra (TBP), there *is* "such thing as religious-epistemology-as-such that applies universally across all religious traditions." It is a religious epistemology, a true knowledge of God, that all people have, and that forms the foundation for evaluating true and false beliefs.

It is the speech of God—both "by the prophets and by the Son," as well as in and through all of creation (cf. Ps. 19:1-5)—that "sets in place necessary constraints or limits on what is coherent and meaningful to say and think." For this reason, the special and natural "speech of God" must be the foundation for knowledge for all of God's covenant creatures, and all creatures are covenantal by definition, since all are in a relationship to the One that created and sustains them.

Notes

1. Note that, for this very reason, Baldwin still has to defend his own first-order view of key concepts like knowledge, justification, and warrant.
2. Even these statements, however, can be given a relativistic reading. For Baldwin could just be saying that certain rational standards are intersubjective and, thus, "tradition-transcendent" in the sense that they will be present in all traditions. We don't think this is what he means, but in light of other statements he makes baldly denying universal rationality, his meaning is not as clear as it could be.
3. It is worth pointing out, however, that conservative principles like Phenomenal Conservatism have a long history across many times and places from ancients like Epictetus, to medievals like Augustine, to Enlightenment figures like Thomas Reid, to contemporary analytic philosophers like Michael Huemer. See Gage, "Objectivity and Subjectivity in Epistemology," 4.
4. To clarify, we do not think that a tradition is logically or metaphysically necessary for the formation of these things. God could create a human from scratch and in isolation—a Robinson Crusoe of sorts—that has thoughts, seemings, and beliefs absent any historical tradition. But this isn't the case of any actual human being. Thus, there is a lesser sense in which, for actual humans, a historical tradition plays an indispensable role in the formation of their experiences, thoughts, and beliefs. That is all we mean when we say that a tradition is "necessary."

5. See *Nicomachean Ethics*, 1145b, *Topics* 100b, and the beginning of *Categories* where Aristotle starts with, but clarifies and expands upon, what is "said" of things.

6. Nicomachean Ethics, 1145b. Reflect back, now, upon Baldwin's quotation from Christopher Shields, who claims that Aristotle treats endoxa as "a significant sub-class of phainomena … because they are the privileged opinions we find ourselves unreflectively endorsing and reaffirming after some reflection, they themselves come to qualify as appearances …." Shields, "Aristotle." That is, what those around us say and think represents our initial seemings and hence our starting points for reflection.

7. This is only "subjective" in the nonrelativistic sense that it takes into consideration the subject's point of view.

Tradition-Based Perspectivalism: Response to Critics

Erik Baldwin

I'd like to thank my fellow contributors. I've learned a great deal articulating my views and replying to criticisms. While I can't provide exhaustive or complete replies, I respond to criticisms I deem most important as best I can.

Invalid Inferences?

My main argument is logically valid, an argument by elimination. There are three jointly exhaustive and mutually exclusive options, the Rationality of Traditions, genealogy, and encyclopedia. (To affirm some of the views associated with TBP but reject others, being fundamentally at odds with both genealogy and encyclopedia is to fall in with TBP. Agnosticism isn't a genuine alternative, for inquiries into truth presuppose the truth or falsity of TBP.) I've provided, I think, good all-things considered reasons to reject genealogy and encyclopedia. My supporting arguments for TBP, being broadly inductive and dialectical, aren't formally valid. But tradition-based inquiry is and must be dialectical.

Is TBP a Tradition-Transcendent Truth?

All truth is tradition-transcendent, not for epistemic reasons, but because the objects of human knowledge are mind-independent realities. If true,

TBP is a tradition-transcendent truth. We can transcend the limitations of our tradition-based starting points only if we depend on tradition-based resources, which can't be completely overcome. While one may see how the substantive standards of rationality of their tradition of inquiry transcend the limitations of rival traditions, one can't see how they transcend the limitations of *all* tradition-based inquiry. TBP maintains that the rational acceptability of even tradition-transcendent truths is tradition-dependent.

Relative Standards, Science, and Math

TBP advocates maintain that no substantive standards of rationality are epistemically well-grounded independent of the tradition-based resources of particular traditions of inquiry. There are diverse substantive standards of rationality that members of different traditions of inquiry employ to get at truth, but not all of them are equally well-suited for the task. A TBP defender maintains that the standards of their tradition of inquiry are more empirically adequate and hence better than (in terms of getting at truth) those of rival traditions of inquiry. In short, TBP affirms *relativity* (that all judgments about what is rational to believe and why are made from within the perspective of some tradition of inquiry or other) but denies *relativism* (that truth is mind-dependent or relative to some conceptual scheme or framework).[1]

DePoe supposes that TBP allows for "equally justified, tradition-based standards on how to land an aircraft." However, TBP is consistent with the view that the objects of scientific knowledge are mind-independent realities and that by engaging in scientific inquiry we may discover tradition-transcendent truths. (Just how successful our endeavors are is another matter.) According to TBP, scientific beliefs aren't justified independently of the resources of traditions of inquiry for, at some level, we make use of tradition-based resources inherited from traditions inquiry when doing science. Why can't TBP defenders accept the most empirically adequate principles of aeronautics articulated thus far? Engineers take the laws of aerodynamics into consideration when designing aircraft. To those in the know, it's evident that helicopters ought to be flown and landed differently than cargo and fighter planes. What's to stop TBP defenders from accepting basic empirical facts about plants? It's evident that they need water to produce flowers. Any "biological science" that prescribes withholding water from plants to help flowers bloom is fatally flawed and woefully empirically inadequate.

A TBP defender might classify mathematical propositions as expressing tradition-independent truths, insofar as they are formally or logically true. Since knowledge of geometrical truths involves imagination or abstraction, perhaps it's better classified as self-evident, pertaining to the natures of abstract entities like triangles.

TBP and Logical Circularity

Traditions of inquiry begin with groups of people already engaged in belief-forming practices. William Alston has argued convincingly that while there are no noncircular arguments for the reliability of sense perception it's not irrational or arbitrary to believe things on its basis.[2] Arguments for the reliability of religious doxastic practices (e.g., prayer and meditation) are ultimately circular, too, but can be reasonable to engage in all the same. Members of traditions of inquiry, concerned about truth, rigorously subject their substantive standards of rationality to critical tests. Only some withstand sustained scrutiny. If a priest purports to deliver an infallible message from God but its content is evidently inconsistent with obvious empirical and historical facts, inquirers have good reason to dismiss that claim to authority.

DePoe supposes that TBP would permit the founders of traditions of inquiry to concoct a list of epistemic rules and principles and then explicitly appeal to it with the aim of justifying some predecided set of religious beliefs. The general worry appears to be how particular traditions of inquiry arise and how they should go about grounding their substantive standards of rationality in nonarbitrary ways. Here's a truncated account of such things.

First-century Jews and Gentiles converted to Christianity. Coming from their respective backgrounds, they inherited certain views, an accounting of which would require a separate discussion. Ultimately, however, all inquiry starts somewhere. People have no choice but to begin within the cultural settings they find themselves, having already absorbed various background assumptions. Beginning to inquire into things, people can do no better than start with *endoxa*, the opinions of the wise.

Early Christians asked questions, among them, how best to understand and defend their central truth-claims. Some early Church Fathers were philosophically inclined. Some were Platonists, others were Aristotelians, and so on. The conceptual resources of Greek philosophical traditions were employed in creative ways to address questions of orthodoxy and orthopraxy. For instance, the Church employed metaphysical concepts and technical terms inherited from Greek philosophy to articulate its central doctrines, including the doctrine of the Trinity. Philosophers such as Augustine, Boethius, and Anselm made contributions here, and to other points of doctrine. New generations had to consider and make sense of what was passed down to them. New doctrinal conflicts arose. Conflicts about how to resolve these and other conflicts arose. Determining which from among several competing views were acceptable and why became increasingly difficult, especially as the tradition entered into dialogue with Jewish and Islamic philosophers, such as Philo, Maimonides, Avicenna, and Averroes. How was the Church to go about rendering intelligible this conglomeration of ideas? Eventually, Aquinas, the paradigmatic representative of tradition-based inquiry, hit upon the proper way for the members of a tradition of inquiry to proceed:

> Aquinas ... engaged in a long series of constructive debates through whose arguments and conclusions he constructed and reconstructed a representation of the hierarchical order of the universe. What justifies his fundamental theses in ontology and in the theory of truth is their indispensability for the work of representation. What justifies his representation of the order of things over against its Averroist, Neoplatonist, and Augustinian rivals is its ability to identify, to explain, and to transcend their limitations and defects, while preserving from them everything that survives dialectical questioning in a way which those rivals are unable from their philosophical resources to provide any counterpart.[3]

Of course, there is much more to say, but space is short.[4]

A society that collectively endorses that humans should mutilate infant humans for fun?

Such a society wouldn't survive long, let alone thrive, given basic facts about humans and their way of being in the world. Thomists think that such actions are self-evidently wrong, being contrary to the first principle of practical reason, that "good is to be done and pursued, and evil is to be avoided."[5] With reference to that principle, we see that those actions are contrary to both the individual and to the common good. Aquinas writes, "the last end of human life is bliss or happiness [*felicitas vel beatitude*] ... Consequently the law [including the natural, or moral, law] must needs regard principally the relation to happiness [*beatitude*] .... Therefore every law is ordained to the common good."[6] All this is embedded in a metaphysics of Theism, of course. The community McNabb imagines has seriously empirically inadequate and flawed substantive standards of practical rationality. A Thomist is in a good position to defend that claim given the tradition-based resources at their disposal. MacIntyreans may argue in a similar fashion against substantive standards advocated by Humeans and Marxists.

Cognitive Science and Hard-Wired Beliefs

A MacIntyrean can use cognitive science to discover which sorts of beliefs humans are "hard-wired" to produce. However, due to deep-seated disagreement about human nature and the nature of ultimate reality, just which, if any, *specific* beliefs are we hard-wired to hold? Theists disagree about the specifics of the human design plan, too. Cognitive science doesn't float free of metaphysical and epistemological commitments. According to TBP, whatever reasons we have for thinking that we are hard-wired to accept *these* beliefs rather than *those* are rooted and grounded in tradition-based resources.

Necessity, Morality, and Causality

Gage and McAllister maintain that if they "have correctly identified Phenomenal Conservatism (PC) as a necessary truth about the nature of justification, then PC is such a tradition-transcendent truth." PC makes substantive claims about what epistemic seemings are, what epistemic work they do, and the like. The TBP defender maintains that when we look carefully, we find no concept of epistemic justification-as-such. Rather, we find various substantive accounts of justification in conflict, with people using the term "justified" to pick out beliefs with a wide range of properties. At best, PC articulates a necessary truth about one particular conception of epistemic justification. Alston, surveying the last 50 years or so of the literature on epistemic justification, comes to similar conclusions. He writes "there isn't any unique, epistemically crucial property of beliefs picked out by 'justified' ... all we have is the plurality of features of belief that are of positive value for the cognitive enterprise."[7] Regarding widespread disagreement between defenders of different theories, he writes,

> the most reasonable judgment [to make] is that the parties to at least the most radical of the disputes about epistemic justification are using "justified" to pick out different properties of beliefs, different epistemic desiderata or collections thereof. Instead of having persistent disagreements about a common target, they are arguing past each other.[8]

For the TBP defender, a major task of epistemological inquiry is which of these different conceptions of "epistemic justification" and the epistemic desiderata associated with them are most empirically adequate.

MacIntyreans maintain that there are rival and contested claims about what sorts of actions are just or unjust, the nature of moral rights, and so on. For instance, Humeans, Kantians, Aristotelians, and Thomists radically disagree about the nature of practical rationality, the range of goods that are available to us and which from among them is our highest good, the role that virtues play in ethical theory, and so on. The TBP advocate denies that we can make well-grounded normative and meta-ethical judgments if we eschew or set aside that which can be known only by relying on the resources of particular traditions of inquiry. This is consistent with moral realism and doesn't somehow support moral relativism.

Gage and McAllister maintain that tradition-based resources don't play a "straightforward *epistemic* role, but rather largely a *causal* role." They claim that historical traditions are "necessary" in the sense that they play an "indispensable role in the formation of [our] experiences, thoughts, and beliefs," in the actual environment that we find ourselves in. According to TBP, however, we can go about epistemically justifying our beliefs only by using tradition-based resources. Their role isn't merely causal or indirect. As MacIntyre puts it, "standards of rational justification themselves emerge from and are part of a history" and they are vindicated "by the way in which they transcend the limitations of and provide remedies for the defects of their predecessors within the history of that same tradition."[9] TBP maintains that tradition-based resources must be relied on in order for us to go about having reasonable beliefs about what to believe and why. Members of different traditions of inquiry disagree about which epistemic principles are applicable, in part because they disagree about human nature and the nature of ultimate reality, but also because they come at things from within the perspectives of different traditions of inquiry.

Covenantal Epistemology and TBP

According to TBP, formulating epistemic principles is a "bottom-up" activity aimed at producing substantive principles that capture, more or less accurately, how we get at and how we ought to get at truth. Members of philosophical-religious traditions pass down a vast mixed multitude of intellectual artifacts, including normative conceptions of rational belief, justification, reasonableness, evidence, and so on. Surveying *this* morass, there's no set of substantive standards of rationality that all people who are fully reasonable and fully informed of the evidence and the relevant facts agree on. All the more so given that people disagree about what reasonability is and requires, what counts as evidence, and what the facts are.

Consider an analogy. A large group of athletes is on the field. Some use their hands and feet, while others use exclusively one or the other. Some use bats, sticks, rackets, and so on. Some accept that it's permissible to tackle players. Each group of like-minded athletes thinks that their respective activities are fully rational given the rules they accept. Each thinks that the other groups are making serious mistakes. Watching the spectacle, we might suppose that we've got radical disagreement about the rules of "the game." But it'd be much more accurate to think that we have various subgroups attempting to play distinct games and that there is no one set of rules that makes rational sense of the activities of the group as a whole. Scoring is like getting at truth. The various incompatible rules pertaining to moving the ball around are analogous to reasoning well in accord with different sets of substantive standards of theoretical rationality all of which are truth-aimed. Of course, the analogy breaks down. It's fine to play different games, and so on. But there is only one truth, only some sets of substantive standards of theoretical rationality have a high degree of empirical adequacy, and only one set could be fully empirically adequate and correct, and so on. Nevertheless, the analogy illustrates an important fact: when it comes to inquiry, we aren't in agreement about the basic rules and methods. We don't find competing theories about "rationality" or "rationality-as-such," but rather various incompatible rationalities in fierce competition.

Philosophers, looking "bottom-up" at things, aim to articulate principles that everyone will or should find agreeable, at least in principle. We make claims about which substantive standards are correct, but we don't have a fully adequate perspective of things. While first-order epistemology is exceedingly difficult, the really tough questions are metaepistemological.

How are we to determine which theory of epistemic rationality is most adequate and which epistemological principles are most accurate? How are we supposed to determine what is epistemically appropriate to believe and why? My first-order views are broadly Aquinian and fully compatible with TBP. Whatever degree of empirical adequacy they have depends on facts about human nature and the world we inhabit. Viewed "top-down," from a God's-eye perspective, things are very different. God doesn't inquire, He knows.

I think *The Bible* is divine revelation. We must properly read and understand it. To that end, we engage in theological inquiry. We ask how to get at and what counts as a proper understanding and interpretation of the texts. While God leads His Church to understanding, our theological inquiries are steeped in the resources of multiple traditions of inquiry. Even if Covenantal Epistemology is correct, our coming to recognize that would involve employing tradition-based resources. Many of the passages Oliphint cites have broad philosophical implications, but I don't find them to strongly imply or suggest Covenantal Epistemology. Perhaps I'm wrong about that. Apparently, Oliphint and I don't disagree about whether TBP is true, but rather about which particular tradition of inquiry has the most going for it, all things considered. (After all, Oliphint gleans much from Calvin and the *Westminster Confession*, and in so doing, approaches theological and philosophical inquiry from a particular tradition-based perspective.)

By way of closing, I summarize major points of agreement and disagreement between myself and other contributors. I think God made us in accord with a design plan, but what is that plan? He didn't reveal the details to us. Just which of our religious beliefs are properly basic is hotly disputed. We can make progress toward the truth of things only by making use of tradition-based resources. To do that, we need to cultivate moral and intellectual virtues, something that doesn't happen just in case our cognitive faculties are functioning properly, and so on. Generally, I think that we have and that it is reasonable for us to rely on epistemic seemings, at least at certain stages of inquiry. However, judgments about their normative status are rooted and grounded in the resources of traditions of inquiry, even if we come to hold some of them by design. Further, we know that object-level epistemic seemings are sometimes misleading. Concerned about truth, we subject them to rigorous scrutiny and radical internal and external critique. Sorting things out requires higher-order reflection, including dialectal, tradition-based inquiry into what is most reasonable to believe and why. Epistemic seemings aren't the sorts of things that can provide ultimate justification for beliefs. I think that some divine revelation is genuine and fully reliable, at least in its original form. Setting aside difficulties associated with correctly discerning genuine revelation, properly interrupting and understanding it can be extremely difficult. To make progress, we must make use of tradition-based resources. And we must make use of them in our inquiries into metaphysical, scientific, and even mathematical and logical truths. For instance, it took centuries for the West to accept the concept of zero, which first took root in the East. Early Greeks recoiled at the notion of nonbeing and denied that it had any applicability to mathematics. They rejected irrational numbers, too.[10] Claims that sequences of mathematical symbols have cognitive significance can't be substantiated using only those symbols, for the meanings of "mathematical sentences must be embedded in a narrative in some natural language."[11]

Notes

1. See Lutz, *Tradition in the Ethics of Alasdair MacIntyre*, chap. 4.
2. William P. Alston, *The Reliability of Sense Perception* (Ithaca, NY: Cornell University Press, 1993).
3. MacIntyre, *Whose Justice?*, 172.
4. For more, see Alasdair MacIntyre, *God, Philosophy, Universities: A Selective History of the Catholic Philosophical Tradition* (Lanham, MD: Rowman & Littlefield, 2009). For those who would dig deeper, I recommend MacIntyre's major works MacIntyre, *After Virtue*; MacIntyre, *Whose Justice?*; MacIntyre, *Three Rival Versions of Moral Enquiry*.
5. Thomas Aquinas, *Summa Theologica* I-II, q. 94.
6. Ibid., I-II, q. 90, a. 2.
7. William P. Alston, *Beyond "Justification": Dimensions of Epistemic Evaluation* (Ithaca, NY: Cornell University Press, 2005), 22.
8. Ibid., 26.
9. MacIntyre, *Whose Justice?*, 7.
10. Charles Seife, *Zero: The Biography of a Dangerous Idea* (London: Penguin, 2000).
11. Philip J. Davis, "Review of Circles Disturbed: The Interplay of Mathematics and Narrative," ed. Apostolos Doxiadis and Barry Mazur, *The Society for Industrial and Applied Mathematics* 45, no. 5 (2012): 2.

Works Cited

Alston, William P. *Beyond "Justification": Dimensions of Epistemic Evaluation*. Ithaca, NY: Cornell University Press, 2005.

Alston, William P. "Referring to God." *International Journal for Philosophy of Religion* 24, no. 3 (1988): 113–28.

Alston, William P. *The Reliability of Sense Perception*. Ithaca, NY: Cornell University Press, 1993.

Anselm. *Cur Deus Homo*. Translated by Sydney Norton Deane. Reprint ed. Chicago: Open Court, 1903.

Anselm. *Monologion and Proslogion: With the Replies of Gaunilo and Anselm*. Translated by Thomas Williams. Indianapolis, IN: Hackett, 1995.

Aquinas, Thomas. "Commentary on Romans." Accessed December 24, 2018. https://aquinas.cc/196/198/~1.

Aquinas, Thomas. *On Being and Essence*. Translated by Armand A. Maurer. 2nd ed. Ontario: Pontifical Institute of Mediaeval Studies, 1968.

Aquinas, Thomas. *Questiones Disputatae De Veritate*. Translated by Robert Mulligan. Reprint ed. Indianapolis, IN: Hackett, 1994.

Aquinas, Thomas. *Summa Contra Gentiles: Book One: God*. Translated by Anton C. Pegis. Notre Dame, IN: University of Notre Dame Press, 1991.

Aquinas, Thomas. *Summa Theologica*. Translated by Fathers of the English Dominican Province, 2nd ed., 1920. Accessed December 24, 2018. http://www.newadvent.org/summa/.

Aristotle. *Nicomachean Ethics*. Translated by Roger Crisp. Reprint ed. Cambridge: Cambridge University Press, 2004.

Aristotle. *The Complete Works of Aristotle*. Translated by Jonathan Barnes. Reprint ed. 2 vols. Princeton, NJ: Princeton University Press, 1988.

Audi, Robert. "Contemporary Modest Foundationalism." In *The Theory of Knowledge: Classical and Contemporary Readings*, 3rd ed., edited by Louis Pojman, 174–82. Belmont, CA: Wadsworth, 2003.

Audi, Robert. *Epistemology : A Contemporary Introduction to the Theory of Knowledge*, 3rd ed. New York: Routledge, 2010.

Audi, Robert. *The Cambridge Dictionary of Philosophy*, 2nd ed. Cambridge: Cambridge University Press, 1999.

Augustine. *Against the Academicians and the Teacher*. Translated by Peter King. Reprint ed. Indianapolis, IN: Hackett, 1995.

Augustine. *Nicene and Post-Nicene Fathers, First Series*. Edited by Philip Schaff and Kevin Knight. Translated by John Gibb. Reprint ed. Buffalo, NY: Christian Literature, 1888. Accessed December 24, 2018. http://www.newadvent.org/fathers/1701.htm.

Augustine. *The City of God*. Translated by Marcus Dods. Reprint ed. Peabody, MA: Hendrickson, 2008.

Augustine. *The Confessions*. Translated by Henry Chadwick. Reprint ed. Oxford: Oxford University Press, 1992.

Austin, J. L. *Sense and Sensibilia*. Oxford: Oxford University Press, 1962.

Baldwin, Erik. *Fully Informed Reasonable Disagreement and Tradition Based Perspectivalism*. Leuven: Peeters, 2016.

Baldwin, Erik, and Tyler Dalton McNabb. *Plantingian Religious Epistemology and World Religions: Prospects and Problems*. Lanham, MD: Lexington Books, 2018.

Baldwin, Erik, and Michael Thune. "The Epistemological Limits of Experience-Based Exclusive Religious Belief." *Religious Studies* 44, no. 4 (2008): 445–55.

Barrett, Justin L. *Why Would Anyone Believe in God?* Lanham, MD: Altamira, 2004.

Barrett, Justin L. *Cognitive Science, Religion, and Theology: From Human Minds to Divine Minds*. West Conshohocken, PA: Templeton Press, 2011.

Bavinck, Herman, John Bolt, and John Vriend. *Reformed Dogmatics: God and Creation*, vol. 2. Grand Rapids, MI: Baker, 2004.

Bergmann, Michael. "Defeaters and Higher-Level Requirements." *The Philosophical Quarterly* 55, no. 220 (2005): 419–36.

Bergmann, Michael. *Justification without Awareness: A Defense of Epistemic Externalism*. Oxford: Oxford University Press, 2006.

BonJour, Laurence. "A Version of Internalist Strong Foundationalism." In *Epistemic Justification: Internalism vs. Externalism, Foundations vs. Virtues*, edited by Ernest Sosa and Laurence BonJour, 3–96. Malden, MA: Blackwell, 2003.

BonJour, Laurence. *The Structure of Empirical Knowledge*. Cambridge, MA: Harvard University Press, 1985.

Boyce, Kenneth. "Proper Functionalism." Edited by James Fieser and Bradley Dowden. *Internet Encyclopedia of Philosophy*, n.d. Accessed August 26, 2016. https://www.iep.utm.edu/prop-fun/.

Boyce, Kenny, and Andrew Moon. "In Defense of Proper Functionalism: Cognitive Science Takes on Swampman." *Synthese* 193, no. 9 (2016): 2987–3001.

Boyce, Kenny, and Alvin Plantinga. "Proper Functionalism." In *The Continuum Companion to Epistemology*, edited by Andrew Cullison, 124–40. London: Continuum, 2012.

Bruce, Frederick Fyvie. *The Letter of Paul to the Romans: An Introduction and Commentary*, 2nd ed. Grand Rapids, MI: Eerdmans, 1985.

Burge, Tyler. "Individualism and the Mental." *Midwest Studies in Philosophy* 4, no. 1 (1979): 73–121.

Burrell, David B. "Thomas Aquinas and Islam." *Modern Theology* 20, no. 1 (2004): 71–89.

Butchvarov, Panayot. *The Concept of Knowledge*. Evanston, IL: Northwest University Press, 1970.

Calvin, John. *Institutes of the Christian Religion*. Translated by Henry Beveridge. Reprint ed. Grand Rapids, MI: Eerdmans, 1990.

Chisholm, Roderick M. *Perceiving: A Philosophical Study*. Ithaca, NY: Cornell University Press, 1957.

Chisholm, Roderick M. *The Foundations of Knowing*. Minneapolis: University of Minnesota Press, 1982.

Chisholm, Roderick M. *Theory of Knowledge,* 1st ed. Englewood Cliffs, NJ: Prentice Hall, 1966.

Christensen, David. "Epistemology of Disagreement: The Good News." *The Philosophical Review* 116, no. 2 (2007): 187–217.

Christensen, David, and Jennifer Lackey. *The Epistemology of Disagreement: New Essays*. Oxford: Oxford University Press, 2013.

Christian, Rose Ann. "Plantinga, Epistemic Permissiveness, and Metaphysical Pluralism." *Religious Studies* 28, no. 4 (1992): 553–73.

Clark, Kelly James. *Return to Reason: A Critique of Enlightenment Evidentialism and a Defense of Reason and Belief in God*. Grand Rapids, MI: Eerdmans, 1990.

Clark, Michael. "Knowledge and Grounds: A Comment on Mr. Gettier's Paper." *Analysis* 24, no. 2 (1963): 46–8.

Cohen, Stewart. "Justification and Truth." *Philosophical Studies* 46, no. 3 (1984): 279–95.

Conee, Earl, and Richard Feldman. *Evidentialism: Essays in Epistemology*. Oxford: Oxford University Press, 2004.

Craig, William Lane. *The Kalām Cosmological Argument*. Reprint ed. Eugene, OR: Wipf and Stock, 2000.

Craig, William Lane. *Reasonable Faith: Christian Truth and Apologetics*, 3rd ed. Wheaton, IL: Crossway, 2008.

Craig, William Lane, and James Porter Moreland, eds. *The Blackwell Companion to Natural Theology*. Malden, MA: Blackwell, 2009.

Craig, William Lane, and James D. Sinclair. "The Kalam Cosmological Argument." In *The Blackwell Companion to Natural Theology*, edited by William Lane Craig and J. P. Moreland, 101–201. Malden, MA: Blackwell, 2009.

Cullison, Andrew. "What Are Seemings?" *Ratio* 23, no. 3 (2010): 260–74.

Davidson, Donald. "A Coherence Theory of Truth and Knowledge." In *Truth and Interpretation: Perspectives on the Philosophy of Donald Davidson*, 423–38. Malden, MA: Blackwell, 1986.

Davidson, Donald. "Knowing One's Own Mind." *Proceedings and Addresses of the American Philosophical Association* 60 (1987): 441–58.

Davies, Brian. *Thomas Aquinas's Summa Theologiae: A Guide and Commentary*. Oxford: Oxford University Press, 2014.

Davis, Philip J. "Review of Circles Disturbed: The Interplay of Mathematics and Narrative." Edited by Apostolos Doxiadis and Barry Mazur. *The Society for Industrial and Applied Mathematics* 45, no. 5 (2012).

DePaul, Michael R., ed. *Resurrecting Old-Fashioned Foundationalism*. Lanham, MD: Rowman & Littlefield, 2001.

DePoe, John M. "Bergmann's Dilemma and Internalism's Escape." *Acta Analytica* 27, no. 4 (2012): 409–23.

DePoe, John M. "Gettier's Argument against the Traditional Account of Knowledge." In *Just the Arguments: 100 of the Most Important Arguments in Western Philosophy*, edited by Michael Bruce and Steven Barbone, 156–8. Malden, MA: Wiley-Blackwell, 2011.

DePoe, John M. "Hold on Loosely, But Don't Let Go: Evaluating the Evidential Impact of Religious Disagreement." *Philosophia Christi* 20, no. 1 (2018): 253–64.

DePoe, John M. "Indirect Realism with a Human Face." *Ratio* 31, no. 1 (2018): 57–72.

DePoe, John M. "Positive Skeptical Theism and the Problem of Divine Deception." *International Journal for Philosophy of Religion* 82, no. 1 (2017): 89–99.

DePoe, John M. "The Epistemic Framework for Skeptical Theism." In *Skeptical Theism: New Essays*, edited by Trent Dougherty and Justin P. McBrayer, 32–44. Oxford: Oxford University Press, 2014.

DePoe, John M. "The Significance of Religious Disagreement." In *Taking Christian Moral Thought Seriously: The Legitimacy of Religious Beliefs in the Marketplace of Ideas*, edited by Jeremy Evans, 48–76. Nashville: Broadman & Holman, 2011.

DePoe, John M. "What's (Not) Wrong with Evidentialism." *The Global Journal for Classical Theology* 13, no. 2 (September 2016). Accessed August 1, 2017. http://www.globaljournalct.com/wp-content/uploads/2016/09/DePoe-Vol-13-No-2-Whats-Not-Wrong-with-Evidentialism.pdf.

DePoe, John M., and Timothy J. McGrew. "Natural Theology and the Uses of Argument." *Philosophia Christi* 15, no. 2 (2013): 299–310.

DeRose, Keith. "Contextualism and Knowledge Attributions." *Philosophy and Phenomenological Research* 52, no. 4 (1992): 913–29.

Descartes, René. *The Philosophical Writings of Descartes*. Translated by John Cottingham, Robert Stoothoff, and Dugald Murdoch, vol. 1. Cambridge: Cambridge University Press, 1985.

Dougherty, Trent. "Faith, Trust, and Testimony: An Evidentialist Account." In *Religious Faith and Intellectual Virtue*, edited by Laura Frances Callahan and Timothy O'Connor, 97–123. Oxford: Oxford University Press, 2014.

Dougherty, Trent. "Further Epistemological Considerations Concerning Skeptical Theism." *Faith and Philosophy* 28, no. 3 (2011): 332–40.

Dougherty, Trent. "The Common Sense Problem of Evil," n.d.

Dougherty, Trent, and Patrick Rysiew. "Experience First." In *Contemporary Debates in Epistemology*, 3rd ed., edited by Mattias Steup, John Turri, and Ernest Sosa, 17–21. London: Wiley-Blackwell, 2014.

Dougherty, Trent, and Jerry L. Walls, eds. *Two Dozen (or so) Arguments for God: The Plantinga Project*. Oxford: Oxford University Press, 2018.

Fales, Evan. *A Defense of the Given*. Lanham, MD: Rowman & Littlefield, 1996.

Feldman, Richard. "Reasonable Religious Disagreement." In *Philosophers without Gods: Meditations on Atheism and the Secular Life*, edited by Antony Louise, 194–214. Oxford: Oxford University Press, 2007.

Feser, Edward. *Five Proofs for the Existence of God*. San Francisco, CA: Ignatius Press, 2017.

Fitelson, Branden. "A Bayesian Account of Independent Evidence with Applications." *Philosophy of Science* 68, no. S3 (2001): S123–40.

Flew, Antony. "The Presumption of Atheism." *Canadian Journal of Philosophy* 2, no. 1 (1972): 29–46.

Fodor, Jerry A. *Psychosemantics: The Problem of Meaning in the Philosophy of Mind*. Cambridge, MA: MIT Press, 1987.

Frege, Gottlob. *The Foundations of Arithmetic*. Translated by J. L. Austin. Oxford: Basil Blackwell, 1950.

Fumerton, Richard A. "Epistemic Conservatism: Theft or Honest Toil." In *Oxford Studies in Epistemology*, edited by Tamar S. Gendler and John Hawthorne, 2: 64–87. Oxford: Oxford University Press, 2007.

Fumerton, Richard A. *Metaepistemology and Skepticism*. Lanham, MD: Rowman & Littlefield, 1995.

Fumerton, Richard A. "The Internalism/Externalism Controversy." *Philosophical Perspectives* 2 (1988): 443–59.

Fumerton, Richard A. "What and about What Is Internalism?" In *Internalism and Externalism in Semantics and Epistemology*, edited by Sanford C. Goldberg, 35–50. Oxford: Oxford University Press, 2007.

Fumerton, Richard A. "You Can't Trust a Philosopher." In *Disagreement*, edited by Richard Feldman and Ted A. Warfield, 91–110. Oxford: Oxford University Press, 2010.

Gage, Logan Paul. "Can Experience Fulfill the Many Roles of Evidence?" *Quaestiones Disputatae* 8, no. 2 (2018): 87–111.

Gage, Logan Paul. "Evidence and What We Make of It." *Southwest Philosophy Review* 30, no. 2 (2014): 89–99.

Gage, Logan Paul. "Objectivity and Subjectivity in Epistemology: A Defense of the Phenomenal Conception of Evidence." Ph.D. diss., Baylor University, 2014.

Gage, Logan Paul. "Phenomenal Conservatism and the Subject's Perspective Objection." *Acta Analytica* 31, no. 1 (2016): 43–58.

Geivett, R. Douglas. "David Hume and a Cumulative Case Argument." In *In Defense of Natural Theology: A Post-Humean Assessment*, edited by Douglas Groothuis and James F. Sennett, 297–329. Downers Grove, IL: InterVarsity, 2005.

Gendler, Tamar Szabó. "Alief and Belief." *The Journal of Philosophy* 105, no. 10 (2008): 634–63.

Gettier, Edmund L. "Is Justified True Belief Knowledge?" *Analysis* 23, no. 6 (1963): 121–3.

Goldberg, Sanford C. "Does Externalist Epistemology Rationalize Religious Commitment?" In *Religious Faith and Intellectual Virtue*, edited by Laura Frances Callahan and Timothy O'Connor, 279–98. Oxford: Oxford University Press, 2014.

Goldman, Alvin I. *Philosophy Meets the Cognitive and Social Sciences.* Cambridge, MA: MIT Press, 1992.

Goldman, Alvin I. "What Is Justified Belief?" In *Justification and Knowledge*, edited by G. S. Pappas, 1–23. Dordrecht: D. Reidel, 1979.

Goudriaan, Aza. *Reformed Orthodoxy and Philosophy, 1625-1750: Gisbertus Voetius, Petrus Van Mastricht, and Anthonius Driessen.* Leiden: Brill, 2006.

Hahn, Scott W. *Romans.* Grand Rapids, MI: Baker, 2017.

Hankey, Wayne J. "Aquinas, Plato, and Neoplatonism." In *The Oxford Handbook of Aquinas*, edited by Brian Davies and Eleonore Stump, 55–64. Oxford: Oxford University Press, 2012.

Harrison, Victoria S. "Human Holiness as Religious Shape Apologia." *International Journal for Philosophy of Religion* 46, no. 2 (1999): 63–82.

Hasan, Ali. *A Critical Introduction to the Epistemology of Perception.* New York: Bloomsbury, 2017.

Hasan, Ali. "Classical Foundationalism and Bergmann's Dilemma for Internalism." *Journal of Philosophical Research* 36 (2011): 391–410.

Hasan, Ali. "Internalist Foundationalism and the Sellarsian Dilemma." *Res Philosophica* 90, no. 2 (2013): 171–84.

Hasan, Ali. "Phenomenal Conservatism, Classical Foundationalism, and Internalist Justification." *Philosophical Studies* 162, no. 2 (2013): 119–41.

Henry, Douglas V. "Does Reasonable Nonbelief Exist?" *Faith and Philosophy* 18, no. 1 (2001): 75–92.

Henry, Douglas V. "Reasonable Doubts about Reasonable Nonbelief." *Faith and Philosophy* 25, no. 3 (2008): 276–89.

Herdt, Jennifer A. "Alasdair MacIntyre's 'Rationality of Traditions' and Tradition-Transcendental Standards of Justification." *The Journal of Religion* 78, no. 4 (1998): 524–46.

Hick, John. *Evil and the God of Love*, 2nd ed. New York: Harper & Row, 1978.

Hick, John. *The New Frontier of Religion and Science: Religious Experience, Neuroscience, and the Transcendent*. New York: Palgrave Macmillan, 2006.

Hodge, Charles. *Romans*. Wheaton, IL: Crossway, 1994.

Huemer, Michael. "Compassionate Phenomenal Conservatism." *Philosophy and Phenomenological Research* 74, no. 1 (2007): 30–55.

Huemer, Michael. *Skepticism and the Veil of Perception*. Lanham, MD: Rowman & Littlefield, 2001.

Jenkins, John I. *Knowledge and Faith in Thomas Aquinas*. Cambridge: Cambridge University Press, 1997.

Kant, Immanuel. "An Answer to the Question: What Is Enlightenment?" In *Perpetual Peace and Other Essays*, translated by Ted Humphrey, 41–8. Reprint ed. Indianapolis, IN: Hackett, 1983.

Kim, Joseph. *Reformed Epistemology and the Problem of Religious Diversity: Proper Function, Epistemic Disagreement, and Christian Exclusivism*. Cambridge: James Clarke, 2012.

King, Nathan L. "Disagreement: What's the Problem? Or a Good Peer Is Hard to Find." *Philosophy and Phenomenological Research* 85, no. 2 (2012): 249–72.

Klein, Peter D. "Human Knowledge and the Infinite Regress of Reasons." *Noûs* 33 (1999): 297–325.

Knight, Kelvin. *Aristotelian Philosophy: Ethics and Politics from Aristotle to MacIntyre*. Malden, MA: Polity, 2007.

Kyriacou, Christos. "Metaepistemology." Edited by James Fieser and Bradley Dowden. *Internet Encyclopedia of Philosophy*, n.d. http://www.iep.utm.edu/meta-epi/.

Law, Stephen. "The X-Claim Argument against Religious Belief." *Religious Studies* 54, no. 1 (2018): 15–35.

Lessa, William A. "Review of Mark Graubard's Astrology and Alchemy: Two Fossil Sciences." *American Anthropologist* 56, no. 6 (1954): 1162–3.

Lewis, C. S. "Is Theology Poetry?" In *The Weight of Glory*, edited by Walter Hooper, 116–40. Reprint ed. New York: Harper, 2001.

Lewis, C. S. "Man or Rabbit?" In *God in the Dock*, edited by Walter Hooper, 108–13. Reprint ed. Grand Rapids, MI: Eerdmans, 2002.

Lewis, C. S. *Mere Christianity*. Reprint ed. New York: Touchstone, 1999.

Lewis, C. S. "On Obstinacy in Belief." In *The World's Last Night: And Other Essays*, 11–30. Reprint ed. San Francisco, CA: HarperOne, 2017.

Lewis, C. S. "Religion: Reality or Substitute?" In *Christian Reflections*, 45–53. Reprint ed. Grand Rapids, MI: Eerdmans, 2014.

Lewis, C. S. *The Weight of Glory*. Reprint ed. New York: Macmillan, 1996.

Lewis, Clarence Irving. *Mind and the World-Order: Outline of a Theory of Knowledge*. Reprint ed. Mineola, NY: Dover, 1956.

Lisska, Anthony J. *Aquinas's Theory of Perception: An Analytic Reconstruction*. Oxford: Oxford University Press, 2016.

Locke, John. *An Essay Concerning Human Understanding*. Edited by Kenneth Winkler. Reprint ed. Indianapolis, IN: Hackett, 1996.

Lutz, Christopher Stephen. *Tradition in the Ethics of Alasdair MacIntyre: Relativism, Thomism, and Philosophy*. Lanham, MD: Lexington Books, 2004.

MacIntyre, Alasdair C. *After Virtue*. Notre Dame, IN: University of Notre Dame Press, 2013.

MacIntyre, Alasdair C. *Dependent Rational Animals: Why Human Beings Need the Virtues*. Chicago: Open Court, 1999.

MacIntyre, Alasdair C. "Epistemological Crises, Dramatic Narrative and the Philosophy of Science." In *The Tasks of Philosophy: Volume One*, edited by Alasdair MacIntyre, 3–23. Cambridge: Cambridge University Press, 2006.

MacIntyre, Alasdair C. "First Principles, Final Ends, and Contemporary Issues." In *The Tasks of Philosophy: Volume One*, edited by Alasdair MacIntyre, 143–78. Cambridge: Cambridge University Press, 2006.

MacIntyre, Alasdair C. *God, Philosophy, Universities: A Selective History of the Catholic Philosophical Tradition*. Lanham, MD: Rowman & Littlefield, 2009.

MacIntyre, Alasdair C. *Marxism and Christianity*. Notre Dame, IN: University of Notre Dame Press, 1968.

MacIntyre, Alasdair C. "Marxists and Christians." *The Twentieth Century* 170 (1961): 28–37.

MacIntyre, Alasdair C. "Moral Relativism, Truth and Justification." In *The Tasks of Philosophy: Volume One*, edited by Alasdair MacIntyre, 52–73. Cambridge: Cambridge University Press, 2006.

MacIntyre, Alasdair C. "Relativism, Power, and Philosophy." *Proceedings and Addresses of the American Philosophical Association* 59, no. 1 (1985): 5–22.

MacIntyre, Alasdair C. *Three Rival Versions of Moral Enquiry: Encyclopaedia, Genealogy, and Tradition*. Notre Dame, IN: University of Notre Dame Press, 1990.

MacIntyre, Alasdair C. *Whose Justice? Which Rationality?* London: Duckworth, 1988.

Maritain, Jacques. "The Range of Reason." Accessed December 21, 2018. https://maritain.nd.edu/jmc/etext/range01.htm.

Markie, Peter. "The Mystery of Direct Perceptual Justification." *Philosophical Studies* 126, no. 3 (2005): 347–73.

Marsden, George. "The Collapse of American Evangelical Academia." In *Faith and Rationality: Reason and Belief in God*, edited by Alvin Plantinga and Nicholas Wolterstorff, 219–64. Notre Dame, IN: University of Notre Dame Press, 1983.

McAllister, Blake. "Re-Evaluating Reid's Response to Skepticism." *Journal of Scottish Philosophy* 14, no. 3 (2016): 317–39.

McAllister, Blake. "Seemings as Sui Generis." *Synthese* 195, no. 7 (2018): 3079–96.

McAllister, Blake. "The Perspective of Faith: Its Nature and Epistemic Implications." *American Catholic Philosophical Quarterly* 92, no. 3 (2018): 515–33.

McAllister, Blake, and Trent Dougherty. "Reforming Reformed Epistemology: A New Take on the Sensus Divinitatis." *Religious Studies* (2018): 1–21.

McGrath, Matthew. "Phenomenal Conservatism and Cognitive Penetration: The 'Bad Basis' Counterexamples." In *Seemings and Justification: New Essays on Dogmatism and Phenomenal Conservatism*, edited by Christopher Tucker, 225–47. Oxford: Oxford University Press, 2013.

McGrew, Lydia. "Accounting for Dependence: Relative Consilience as a Correction Factor in Cumulative Case Arguments." *Australasian Journal of Philosophy* 95, no. 3 (2017): 560–72.

McGrew, Lydia. "Evidential Diversity and the Negation of H: A Probabilistic Account of the Value of Varied Evidence." *Ergo* 3, no. 10 (2016). Accessed December 24, 2018. http://hdl.handle.net/2027/spo.12405314.0003.010.

McGrew, Timothy J. "A Defense of Strong Foundationalism." In *The Theory of Knowledge: Classical and Contemporary Readings*, 3rd ed., edited by Louis Pojman, 194–206. Belmont, CA: Wadsworth, 2003.

McGrew, Timothy J. "Evidence." In *The Routledge Companion to Epistemology*, edited by Sven Bernecker and Duncan Pritchard, 58–67. New York: Routledge, 2011.

McGrew, Timothy J. "Has Plantinga Refuted the Historical Argument?" *Philosophia Christi* 6, no. 1 (2004): 7–26.

McGrew, Timothy J. *The Foundations of Knowledge*. Lanham, MD: Littlefield Adams, 1995.

McGrew, Timothy J., and Lydia McGrew. *Internalism and Epistemology: The Architecture of Reason*. New York: Routledge, 2007.

McNabb, Tyler Dalton. "Proper Functionalism and the Metalevel: A Friendly Response to Timothy and Lydia McGrew." *Quaestiones Disputatae* 8, no. 2 (2018): 155–64.

McNabb, Tyler Dalton. *Religious Epistemology*. Cambridge: Cambridge University Press, 2018.

McNabb, Tyler Dalton. "Warranted Religion: Answering Objections to Alvin Plantinga's Epistemology." *Religious Studies* 51, no. 4 (2015): 477–95.

McNabb, Tyler Dalton, and Erik Daniel Baldwin. "Divine Methodology: A Lawful Deflection of Kantian and Kantian-Esque Defeaters." *Open Theology* 3, no. 1 (2017): 293–304.

Michaelian, Kourken. *Mental Time Travel: Episodic Memory and Our Knowledge of the Personal Past*. Cambridge, MA: MIT Press, 2016.

Miller, Richard B. "The Reference of 'God.'" *Faith and Philosophy* 3, no. 1 (1986): 3–15.

Moo, Douglas J. *The Epistle to the Romans*. Grand Rapids, MI: Eerdmans, 1996.

Moon, Andrew. "How to Use Cognitive Faculties You Never Knew You Had." *Pacific Philosophical Quarterly* 99 (2018): 251–75.

Moon, Andrew. "Recent Work in Reformed Epistemology." *Philosophy Compass* 11, no. 12 (2016): 879–91.

Moser, Paul K. *Empirical Justification*. Dordrecht: D. Reidel, 1985.

Muller, Richard A. *Dictionary of Latin and Greek Theological Terms: Drawn Principally from Protestant Scholastic Theology*. Grand Rapids, MI: Baker, 1985.

Muller, Richard A. *Post-Reformation Reformed Dogmatics: Prolegomena to Theology*, 2nd ed., vol. 1. Grand Rapids, MI: Baker, 2003.

Murray, Michael, and Jeffrey Schloss, eds. *The Believing Primate: Scientific, Philosophical, and Theological Reflections on the Origin of Religion*. Oxford: Oxford University Press, 2009.

Newman, John Henry. *An Essay in Aid of a Grammar of Assent*. Reprint ed. Notre Dame, IN: University of Notre Dame Press, 1992.

Niederbacher, Bruno. "The Relation of Reason to Faith." In *The Oxford Handbook of Aquinas*, edited by Brian Davies and Eleonore Stump, 337–47. Oxford: Oxford University Press, 2011.

Nietzsche, Friedrich. *The Portable Nietzsche*. Edited by Walter Kaufmann. Translated by Walter Kaufmann. Reprint ed. New York: Penguin, 1976.

Oliphint, K. Scott. "Because It Is the Word of God." In *Did God Really Say?: Affirming the Truthfulness and Trustworthiness of Scripture*, edited by David B. Garner, 1–22. Phillipsburg, NJ: Presbyterian & Reformed, 2012.

Oliphint, K. Scott. *Covenantal Apologetics: Principles and Practice in Defense of Our Faith*. Wheaton, IL: Crossway, 2013.

Oliphint, K. Scott. "Gauch's 'Gotchas': Principia and the Problem of Public Presuppositions." *Philosophia Christi* 17, no. 2 (2015): 443–56.

Oliphint, K. Scott. "Review of Evangelical Exodus: Evangelical Seminarians and Their Paths to Rome." *Themelios* 41, no. 2 (2016): 360–3.

Oliphint, K. Scott. "The Irrationality of Unbelief." In *Revelation and Reason: New Essays in Reformed Apologetics*, edited by K. Scott Oliphint and Lane G. Tipton. Phillipsburg, NJ: Presbyterian & Reformed, 2007.

Oliphint, K. Scott. *Thomas Aquinas: Philosopher Theologian*. Phillipsburg, NJ: Presbyterian & Reformed, 2017.

Owen, John. *The Works of John Owen*. Edited by William H. Goold. London: T&T. Clark, 1862.

Pascal, Blaise. *Pensées*. Translated by A. J. Krailsheimer. Reprint ed. New York: Penguin, 1995.

Paxson, Thomas, and Keith Lehrer. "Knowledge: Undefeated Justified True Belief." *The Journal of Philosophy* 66, no. 8 (1969): 225–37.

Persinger, Michael A. "Are Our Brains Structured to Avoid Refutations of Belief in God? An Experimental Study." *Religion* 39, no. 1 (2009): 34–42.

Persinger, Michael A. "Religious and Mystical Experiences as Artifacts of Temporal Lobe Function: A General Hypothesis." *Perceptual and Motor Skills* 57, no. 3 (suppl.) (1983): 1255–62.

Peterson, Michael, William Hasker, Bruce Reichenbach, and David Basinger. *Reason and Religious Belief: An Introduction to the Philosophy of Religion*, 2nd ed. Oxford: Oxford University Press, 1998.

Pitt, David. "The Phenomenology of Cognition or What Is It Like to Think That P?" *Philosophy and Phenomenological Research* 69, no. 1 (2004): 1–36.

Plantinga, Alvin. "Pluralism: A Defense of Religious Exclusivism." In *The Rationality of Belief and the Plurality of Faith: Essays in Honor of William P. Alston*, edited by Thomas Senor, 172–92. Ithaca, NY: Cornell University Press, 1995.

Plantinga, Alvin. "Reason and Belief in God." In *Faith and Rationality: Reason and Belief in God*, edited by Alvin Plantinga and Nicholas Wolterstorff, 16–93. Notre Dame, IN: University of Notre Dame Press, 1983.

Plantinga, Alvin. "Replies to My Commentators." In *Plantinga's Warranted Christian Belief: Critical Essays with a Reply by Alvin Plantinga*, edited by Dieter Schönecker, 237–62. Berlin: De Gruyter, 2017.

Plantinga, Alvin. *Warrant and Proper Function*. Oxford: Oxford University Press, 1993.

Plantinga, Alvin. *Warrant: The Current Debate*. Oxford: Oxford University Press, 1993.

Plantinga, Alvin. *Warranted Christian Belief*. Oxford: Oxford University Press, 2000.

Plato. *Theaetetus*. Edited by Bernard Williams. Translated by M. J. Levett. Indianapolis, IN: Hackett, 1992.

Pollock, John L. "Defeasible Reasoning." *Cognitive Science* 11, no. 4 (1987): 481–518.

Pollock, John L., and Joseph Cruz. *Contemporary Theories of Knowledge*, 2nd ed. Lanham, MD: Rowman & Littlefield, 1999.

Poston, Ted. "The Argument from so Many Arguments." In *Two Dozen (or so) Arguments for God*, edited by Trent Dougherty and Jerry L. Walls. Oxford: Oxford University Press, 2018.

Pryor, James. "The Skeptic and the Dogmatist." *Noûs* 34, no. 4 (2000): 517–49.

Putnam, Hilary. "The Meaning of 'Meaning.'" In *Philosophical Papers: Mind, Language and Reality*, 215–71. Cambridge: Cambridge University Press, 1975.

Roberts, Robert C., and W. Jay Wood. *Intellectual Virtues: An Essay in Regulative Epistemology*. Oxford: Oxford University Press, 2007.

Rogers, Jason, and Jonathan Matheson. "Bergmann's Dilemma: Exit Strategies for Internalists." *Philosophical Studies* 152, no. 1 (2011): 55–80.

Rogers Jr, Eugene F. "The Narrative of Natural Law in Aquinas's Commentary on Romans 1." *Theological Studies* 59, no. 2 (1998): 254–76.

Rousselot, Pierre. *The Eyes of Faith*. New York: Fordham University Press, 1990.

Russell, Bertrand. "Knowledge by Acquaintance and Knowledge by Description." *Proceedings of the Aristotelian Society* 11 (1910): 108–28.

Russell, Bertrand. *Logic and Knowledge: Essays 1901–1950*. New York: Macmillan, 1956.

Russell, Bertrand. *Mysticism and Logic and Other Essays*. London: George Allen & Unwin, 1917.

Russell, Bertrand. *The Problems of Philosophy*. Edited by John Perry. Reprint ed. Oxford: Oxford University Press, 1997.

Schaff, Philip. *The Creeds of Christendom: With a History and Critical Notes*. 3 vols. New York: Harper, 1890.

Schellenberg, John L. *Divine Hiddenness and Human Reason*. Reprint ed. Ithaca, NY: Cornell University Press, 2006.

Schellenberg, John L. *The Hiddenness Argument: Philosophy's New Challenge to Belief in God*. Oxford: Oxford University Press, 2015.

Seife, Charles. *Zero: The Biography of a Dangerous Idea*. London: Penguin, 2000.

Shields, Christopher. "Aristotle." Edited by Edward N. Zalta. *The Stanford Encyclopedia of Philosophy*. Metaphysics Research Lab, Stanford University, 2016. Accessed December 25, 2018. https://plato.stanford.edu/archives/win2016/entries/aristotle/.

Shils, Edward. *Tradition*. Chicago: University of Chicago Press, 1981.

Shope, Robert. *The Analysis of Knowledge: A Decade of Research*. Princeton, NJ: Princeton University Press, 1983.

Sosa, Ernest. *A Virtue Epistemology: Apt Belief and Reflective Knowledge*. Oxford: Oxford University Press, 2009.

Stoker, Hendrik G. *Oorsprong En Rigting*. 2 vols. Kaapstad: Tafelberg-Uitgewers, 1970.

Stoker, Hendrik G. "Reconnoitering the Theory of Knowledge of Prof. Dr. Cornelius van Til." In *Jerusalem and Athens: Critical Discussions on the Theology and Apologetics of Cornelius van Til*, edited by E. R. Geehan. Phillipsburg, NJ: Presbyterian & Reformed, 1977.

Stubbens, Neil A. "Naming God: Moses Maimonides and Thomas Aquinas." *The Thomist: A Speculative Quarterly Review* 54, no. 2 (1990): 229–67.

Stump, Eleonore. "Aquinas on the Foundations of Knowledge." *Canadian Journal of Philosophy* 21, no. suppl. 1 (1991): 125–58.

Swinburne, Richard. *Epistemic Justification*. Oxford: Oxford University Press, 2001.

Swinburne, Richard. *Is There a God?*, 2nd ed. Oxford: Oxford University Press, 2010.

Swinburne, Richard. "Natural Theology, Its 'Dwindling Probabilities' and 'Lack of Rapport.'" *Faith and Philosophy* 21, no. 4 (2004): 533–46.

Swinburne, Richard. *Responsibility and Atonement*. Oxford: Oxford University Press, 1989.

Swinburne, Richard. *The Christian God*. Oxford: Clarendon Press, 1994.

Swinburne, Richard. *The Existence of God*, 2nd ed. Oxford: Oxford University Press, 2004.

Swinburne, Richard. *The Resurrection of God Incarnate*. Oxford: Oxford University Press, 2003.

Taber, Tyler, and Tyler Dalton McNabb. "Is the Problem of Divine Hiddenness a Problem for the Reformed Epistemologist?" *The Heythrop Journal* 59, no. 5 (2018): 783–93.

Tien, David W. "Warranted Neo-Confucian Belief: Religious Pluralism and the Affections in the Epistemologies of Wang Yangming (1472–1529) and Alvin Plantinga." *International Journal for Philosophy of Religion* 55, no. 1 (2004): 31–55.

Tolhurst, William. "Seemings." *American Philosophical Quarterly* 35, no. 3 (1998): 293–302.

Tooley, Michael. "Michael Huemer and the Principle of Phenomenal Conservatism." In *Seemings and Justification: New Essays on Dogmatism and Phenomenal Conservatism*, edited by Christopher Tucker, 306–27. Oxford: Oxford University Press, 2013.

Tucker, Chris. "Phenomenal Conservatism and Evidentialism in Religious Epistemology." In *Evidence and Religious Belief*, edited by Kelly James Clark and Raymond VanArragon, 52–73. Oxford: Oxford University Press, 2011.

Tucker, Chris. *Seemings and Justification: New Essays on Dogmatism and Phenomenal Conservatism*. Oxford: Oxford University Press, 2013.

Tucker, Chris. "Why Open-Minded People Should Endorse Dogmatism." *Philosophical Perspectives* 24, no. 1 (2010): 529–45.

Tucker, Chris. "The Refutation of Skepticism." In *Contemporary Debates in Epistemology*, 3rd ed., edited by Mattias Steup, Ernest Sosa, and John Turri, 108–19. Malden, MA: Wiley-Blackwell, 2014.

Vogel, Jonathan. "Cartesian Skepticism and Inference to the Best Explanation." *The Journal of Philosophy* 87, no. 11 (1990): 658–66.

Vos, Arvin. *Aquinas, Calvin, and Contemporary Protestant Thought: A Critique of Protestant Views on the Thought of Thomas Aquinas*. Exeter: The Paternoster Press, 1985.

Wainwright, William. "The Burden of Proof and the Presumption of Theism." In *Does God Exist?: The Craig-Flew Debate*, edited by Stan W. Wallace, 75–84. New York: Routledge, 2003.

White, Michael J. *Partisan or Neutral?: The Futility of Public Political Theory*. Lanham, MD: Rowman & Littlefield, 1997.

Williamson, Timothy. *Knowledge and Its Limits*. Oxford: Oxford University Press, 2000.

Wittgenstein, Ludwig. *On Certainty*. Edited by G. E. M. Anscombe and G. H. von Wright. Translated by Paul Denis and G. E. M. Anscombe. New York: Harper & Row, 1969.

Wojtyla, Karol. *Love and Responsibility*. Reprint ed. San Francisco, CA: Ignatius Press, 1993.

Wood, W. Jay. *Epistemology: Becoming Intellectually Virtuous*. Downers Grove, IL: InterVarsity, 1998.

Wykstra, Stephen J. "Not Done in a Corner: How To Be a Sensible Evidentialist About Jesus." *Philosophical Books* 43 (2002): 92–116.

Wykstra, Stephen J. "Toward a Sensible Evidentialism: On the Notion of 'Needing Evidence.'" In *Philosophy of Religion: Selected Readings*, 2nd ed., edited by William Wainwright and William L. Rowe, 426–37. New York: Harcourt Brace Jovanovich, 1989.

Zagzebski, Linda Trinkaus. *Virtues of the Mind: An Inquiry into the Nature of Virtue and the Ethical Foundations of Knowledge*. Cambridge: Cambridge University Press, 1996.

Contributors

Erik Baldwin (PhD, University of Notre Dame) teaches philosophy at Indiana University, Northwest. Baldwin specializes in Epistemology, Philosophy of Religion, and Comparative Philosophy. Baldwin has published papers in venues such as *Religious Studies* and *Philosophia Christi*. Baldwin is the coauthor of *Plantingian Religious Epistemology and World Religions: Prospects and Problems*.

John M. DePoe (PhD, University of Iowa) is the academic dean of the Schools of Logic and Rhetoric at Kingdom Preparatory Academy in Lubbock, Texas. DePoe's academic work has focused on topics in Epistemology, Philosophy of Religion, and Metaphysics, which can be found in academic journals such as *International Journal for Philosophy of Religion, Ratio, Philosophical Studies, Philosophia Christi, Acta Analytica*, and many others.

Logan Paul Gage (PhD, Baylor University) is an assistant professor of philosophy at Franciscan University. Gage specializes in Epistemology and Philosophy of Religion. Gage has published papers in venues such as *Acta Analytica* and *The Routledge Companion of Contemporary Philosophy of Religion*.

Blake McAllister (PhD, Baylor University) is an assistant professor of philosophy at Hillsdale College. McAllister specializes in Epistemology and Philosophy of Religion. McAllister has published papers in venues such as *Synthese* and *American Catholic Philosophical Quarterly*.

Tyler Dalton McNabb (PhD, University of Glasgow) is a post-doctoral fellow at the University of Macau. McNabb specializes in Epistemology, Philosophy of Religion, and Comparative Philosophy. McNabb has authored or coauthored a dozen articles that are published or are forthcoming. McNabb is also the author of *Religious Epistemology* and is the coauthor of *Plantingian Religious Epistemology and World Religions: Prospects and Problems*.

K. Scott Oliphint (PhD, Westminster Theological Seminary) is dean of faculty and professor of apologetics and systematic theology at Westminster Theological Seminary. Among Oliphint's specializations are Reformed Theology and Reformed Apologetics, especially the work of Cornelius Van Til. He is the author of many academic articles and books, including *Covenantal Apologetics*, *Should You Believe in God*, and *Christianity and the Role of Philosophy*.

Index